Mountain Biking the Washington, D.C./ Baltimore Area

Fourth Edition

An Atlas of Northern Virginia, Maryland, and D.C.'s
Greatest Off-Road Bicycle Rides

Scott Adams & Martín Fernández

FALCONGUIDES®

GUILFORD, CONNECTICUT
HELENA, MONTANA
AN IMPRINT OF THE GLOBE PEQUOT PRESS

FALCONGUIDES®

Photo credits: Scott Adams and Martín Fernández

ISBN: 978-0-7627-2657-8

Manufactured in the United States of America
Fourth Edition/Fourth Printing

Contents

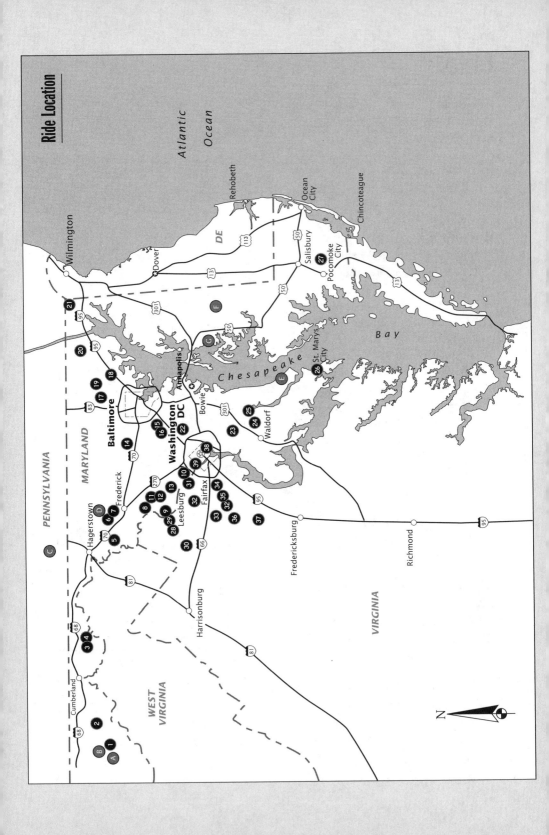

Acknowledgments

A special thanks to all the folks who have ever supported my efforts and desires to get to this point. It goes without saying that I would be hard-pressed to manage my ideas and dreams without all of the regular and unending encouragement, extra helping hands, and borrowed elbow grease from those around me and from those who believe in me. Thanks.

Scott Adams

Without my wife, Courtney, this book would not be possible. Her encouragement and support has helped me every step of the way. To my *viejos,* my brother and sisters. A special thanks to MORE and MAMBO for the efforts they make to ensure that we have places like these to enjoy our sport. To all the park managers who showed me the way, especially the guys at Greenridge for welcoming mountain bikers like no one else in the state of Maryland. To Spooky (aka Elvis).

Keep the rubber side down and see you on the trail!

Martín Fernández

Preface

TRAIL OBSTACLES

Rocks, Roots, Trees, and . . . Politics?

Mountain Biking the Washington, D.C./Baltimore Area will help you find new trails. Other books on bicycling (and a lot of trial and error) will help you develop the skills you need to ride those new trails. Still other books will show you how to fix your bike when you get a flat tire on those trails. But what do you do when your favorite trails get closed to bikes? Well, there's no book to remedy that, really. It all depends on you.

Well, not quite. You see—it depended on you. When trails close and bikes are banned, chances are the "problem" had already existed for a while. Maybe a few cyclists had been rolling carelessly past hikers on the trail, frightening them. Or maybe a few cyclists had been riding muddy trails, damaging them. Or maybe the "problem" was that a vocal opponent of mountain bikes had been bending the park management's ear for the past year, worrying them. And finally, because management hadn't heard from bikers, management just gave in.

You see, if some people have their way, mountain bikes will be restricted to pavement, private property, rail-trails, and ski resorts in the off-season. Such people often get their understanding of our pastime from sensational television ads or magazine depictions of fearless teenagers engaged in death-defying feats. Sometimes, though, these people form their opinions based on a dangerous experience or a negative encounter on a trail. Fear motivates people. Scare someone today, even by accident, and your trail gets closed tomorrow.

Keeping Trails Open

Trail etiquette is a big part of the answer—the preventive solution. Just ask the International Mountain Bicycling Association (IMBA). Sure, the official IMBA "rules of the trail" are important. But simple courtesy, basic caution, and a little empathy for other trail users are the real requirements. In the long haul, they are more important than your bike gear, than your bike clothes—more important even than your bike. After all, a mountain bike isn't very useful if there isn't any place to ride it.

The second simple step in keeping trails open is to join together with other cyclists. Join your local mountain bike club or association so your head gets counted and your voice gets heard. Besides, it's often a great way to meet other riders and learn about trails before they're published in a book or a magazine. A year's membership rarely costs more than $20, the cost of a bike tire. You'll find it's well worth it.

MORE

In Maryland, Virginia, and Washington, D.C., one of the principal mountain bike groups is MORE—the Mid-Atlantic Off-Road Enthusiasts. Around since 1992,

MORE is known for keeping trails open. For leading great rides. For building new trails and maintaining old ones. For raising money for parks. For educating riders. And, well—for giving mountain bikers a good name. Find out more about MORE by calling (703) 502–0359 or see their Web page at www.more-mtb.org. Or write them at MORE, P.O. Box 2662, Fairfax, VA 22031.

Better than Lincoln Logs

And if you think breaking a sweat in the woods on your bike is fun, then working on trails might be more fun than you think. Who needs Erector Sets, Lincoln Logs, or LEGOs when you can build or maintain a real trail? Constructing a new tread way—or fixing an old one—will leave you with a sense of satisfaction that you can't buy in a bike shop. Skeptical? Call MORE and try it once. It's that simple. And it's fun.

IMBA

Speaking of simple, how much did your bike cost? And your helmet? And the bike rack for the car? Add it up and think about it. Then consider writing out a check for the relatively paltry sum of $20 to the International Mountain Bicycling Association (IMBA). IMBA is the national voice for mountain bikers, and $20 gets you membership for a year—and helps support the association's effort to keep trails and land open to mountain bikers across the nation.

20-20-20

Twenty dollars to your local mountain bike group, twenty dollars to IMBA, and twenty hours a year as a trail volunteer. That's the recipe for access. That's the formula for keeping trails open and healthy. That's the ticket for preserving your fun. You've got the book and the bike. Time to do the rest.

This fine guide not only reveals some of the best shared-use trails around, but it also makes clear one crucial fact: Cyclists' continued access to trails depends upon their courtesy toward hikers and equestrians and their willingness to help maintain those trails. The information in this book, and that message, is the key to some great riding!

—Andy Carruthers

Andy Carruthers is one of the region's core mountain bike advocates, working diligently and successfully to keep local trails accessible to cyclists. Many thanks should go to him and all the volunteers who work to keep our trails open and healthy.

Introduction

You'll find that this guide contains just about everything you'll ever need to choose, plan for, enjoy, and survive a ride in Virginia, Maryland, and Washington, D.C. Stuffed with useful Washington, D.C./Baltimore-specific information, this book features thirty-nine mapped and cued rides and seven honorable mentions, as well as everything from advice on getting into shape to tips on mountain bike camping and getting the most out of cycling with your dog.

We've designed this FalconGuide to be highly visual, for quick reference and ease of use. This means that the most pertinent information rises quickly to the top, so you don't have to waste time poring throught bulky ride descriptions to get mileage cues or elevation stats. They're set aside for you. Yet a FalconGuide doesn't read like a laundry list. Take the time to dive into a ride description and you'll soon realize that this guide is not just a good source of information; it's a good read. In the end you get the best of both worlds: a quick reference guide and an engaging look at a region.

How to Use This Book

Mountain Biking Washington, D.C./Balitmore is divided into five sections, each representing one of the five major geographic regions in Maryland, Virginia, and D.C. Within each section are the featured rides found in the region. Each ride is then subsequently divided into a variety of components. The *Ride Specs* are fairly self-explanatory. Here you'll find the quick, nitty-gritty details of the ride: where the trailhead is located, the nearest town, ride length, approximate riding time, difficulty rating, type of trail terrain, elevation gain, if dogs are permitted, and what other trail users you may encounter. Our *Getting There* section gives you dependable directions from a nearby city, right down to where you'll want to park. The *Ride Description* is the meat of the chapter. Detailed and honest, it's our carefully researched impression of the trail. While it's impossible to cover everything, you can rest assured that we won't miss what's important. In *Miles and Directions,* we provide mileage cues to identify all turns and trail name changes, as well as points of interest. Between this and the route map, you simply can't get lost. *Ride Information* contains more useful information, including trail hot lines (for updates on trail conditions), park schedules and fees, and a list of maps available to the area. We'll also tell you where to stay, what to eat, and what else to see while you're riding in the area. The *Honorable Mentions* section details additional rides in each region that will inspire you to get out and explore.

▶ Any other important or useful information, such as local attractions, bike shops, and nearby accommodations, will also be listed here.

How to Use These Maps

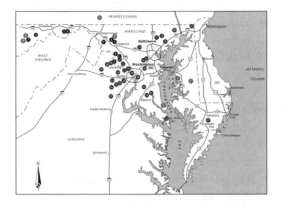

Regional Location Map

This map helps you find your way to the start of each ride from the nearest sizable town or city. Coupled with the detailed directions at the beginning of the cue, this map should visually lead you to where you need to be for each ride.

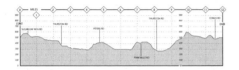

Profile Map

This helpful profile gives you a cross-sectional look at the ride's ups and downs. The elevation is labeled on the left, and the mileage is indicated on the top. Road and trail names are shown along the route, with towns and points of interest labeled in bold.

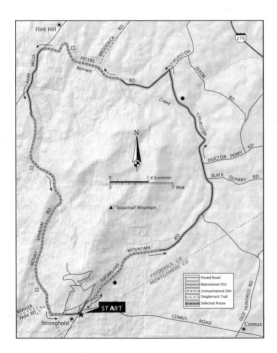

Route Map

This is your primary guide to each ride. It shows all of the accessible roads and trails, points of interest, water, towns, landmarks, and geographical features. It also distinguishes trails from roads and paved roads from unpaved roads. The selected route is highlighted, and directional arrows point the way. Shaded topographic relief in the background gives you an accurate representation of the terrain and landscape in the ride area.

The Maps

We don't want anyone, by any means, to feel restricted to just the roads and trails that are mapped here. We hope you will have an adventurous spirit and use this guide as a platform to dive into Washington's backcountry and discover new routes for yourself. One of the simplest ways to begin this is to just turn the map upside down and ride the course in reverse. The change in perspective is fantastic and the ride should feel quite different With this in mind, it will be like getting two distinctly different rides on each map.

For your own purposes, you may wish to copy the directions for the course onto a small sheet to help you while riding, or photocopy the map and cue sheet to take with you. These pages can be folded into a bike bag, stuffed into a jersey pocket, or used with a map holder (see www.cycoactive.com for more info). Just remember to slow or even stop when you want to read the map.

Map Legend

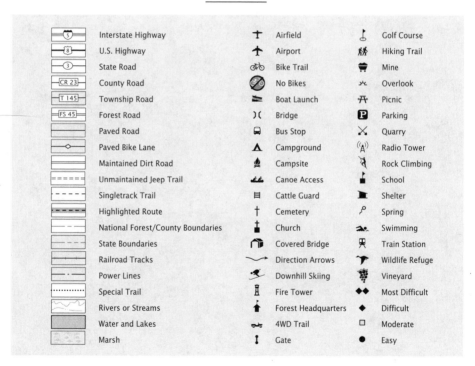

Symbol	Label	Symbol	Label	Symbol	Label
5	Interstate Highway	Airfield		Golf Course	
8	U.S. Highway	Airport		Hiking Trail	
3	State Road	Bike Trail		Mine	
CR 23	County Road	No Bikes		Overlook	
T 145	Township Road	Boat Launch		Picnic	
FS 45	Forest Road	Bridge		Parking	
	Paved Road	Bus Stop		Quarry	
	Paved Bike Lane	Campground		Radio Tower	
	Maintained Dirt Road	Campsite		Rock Climbing	
	Unmaintained Jeep Trail	Canoe Access		School	
	Singletrack Trail	Cattle Guard		Shelter	
	Highlighted Route	Cemetery		Spring	
	National Forest/County Boundaries	Church		Swimming	
	State Boundaries	Covered Bridge		Train Station	
	Railroad Tracks	Direction Arrows		Wildlife Refuge	
	Power Lines	Downhill Skiing		Vineyard	
	Special Trail	Fire Tower		Most Difficult	
	Rivers or Streams	Forest Headquarters		Difficult	
	Water and Lakes	4WD Trail		Moderate	
	Marsh	Gate		Easy	

Western Maryland

Maryland is perhaps one of the most diverse states in the country. Composed of five distinct geographic provinces, Maryland offers a tremendous variety of off-road cycling destinations. The Blue Ridge creates a distinct division in the state's topography. To the east of the Blue Ridge, the Maryland Piedmont area gives way to the prolific shores of the Chesapeake Bay. To the west of the Blue Ridge, the majestic Appalachians rise to give Maryland an extraordinary array of diversity. Within a couple of hours, one can be on the plains and shores of the Chesapeake and then in the hills of western Maryland.

The terrain in the western part of Maryland is well suited for mountain biking. Rocky, technical, and extremely changeable, the landscapes provide the perfect place to enjoy challenging East Coast Riding. There are climbs that are long enough to test every muscle in your body, but the rewarding descents that follow will make it all worthwhile.

Fat-tire enthusiasts will find that there just isn't enough time in a single season to ride the countless number of trails and dirt roads open to cycling in the counties of western Maryland, made up of the Blue Ridge, Great Valley, Valley and Ridge, and Appalachian Plateau provinces. In this guide, we have selected what we think are some of the best examples of what this wonderful region has to offer.

The popularity of mountain biking has prompted many natural resource officials to reevaluate the way that lands in western Maryland are managed. While there are areas where cycling is still prohibited, the majority of state parks and forests allow bikers access on their trails. Many parks are starting specific programs to attract mountain bikers to the region.

Green Ridge State Forest is a pioneer in this arena. Having been host to the Maryland Mountain Bike State Championship, the rangers at Green Ridge State Forest saw an opportunity to increase the amount of visitors that came to their jurisdiction. With the help of volunteers and the community, they built a superb 12-mile singletrack loop. The ride, featured in this guide, is one of several in Green Ridge and a small tatste of what other areas in western Maryland have to offer.

Deep Creek Lake offers a vast network of trails bound to satisfy the most ardent cyclist. Add to it, the well-maintained and -marked trails available in Wisp, and you have yourself a full week of riding. But if you prefer to mix activities, you can instead enjoy an array of water sports on Maryland's largest man-made body of water. Come winter, Deep Creek is transformed into a skier's paradise. The very same trails you bike during the summer are used by snowmobiles and cross-country skiers during the winter.

Green Ridge State Forest is also home to some of the best off-road-vehicle (ORV) trails in the area. In addition, there are more than 20 miles of snowmobile trails, numerous campsites, and opportunities for hunting, fishing, and other outdoor activities. Other parks and forests in the area offer the same and/or more opportunities. In short, if you love the outdoors you'll find that the mountain side of Maryland is a great place to visit.

1 Deep Creek Lake State Park

Situated in one of Maryland's most popular vacation spots, the trails at Deep Creek Lake State Park offer a challenging network of rides that is bound to satisfy even the most demanding mountain biker. Expect a well-marked trail system that will take you, among other places, up to the heights of Deep Creek Lake's lookout tower, where breathtaking views of western Maryland's mountainous terrain await. Climbing is not all you'll do, though. Upon reaching the summit and the lookout tower, you'll be treated to some outstanding western Maryland singletrack that takes you downhill all the way back to the car.

Start: Meadow Mountain Trail trailhead
Length: 12 miles
Approximate riding time: 1.5–3 hours (depending on ability)
Difficulty: Moderate to difficult due to extended climbs and rutted singletrack
Trail surface: Doubletrack, singletrack, and forest roads
Lay of the land: Wooded and hilly terrain surrounding Deep Creek Lake
Land status: State park
Nearest town: Thayerville, MD
Other trail users: Hikers, cross-country skiers, hunters, paddlers, and snowmobile riders
Trail contacts: Deep Creek Lake State Park, Swanton, MD, (301) 387–4111 www.deepcreeklake.org
Schedule: July to early October
Maps: USGS map: McHenry, MD

Getting There: From Cumberland, MD: Take Interstate 68 west to Exit 14 and U.S. Highway 219. Follow U.S. Highway 219 south through McHenry toward Thayerville. Before crossing the main bridge over Deep Creek Lake, turn left on Rock Ledge Road. Follow Rock Ledge Road for 2.5 miles, then turn right on State Park Road. Continue on State Park Road for 2.5 miles, then turn right on Waterfront Avenue. Take an immediate right, traveling parallel to State Park Road, and park at the furthermost end of the last parking lot. The trailhead is directly across State Park Road. *DeLorme: Maryland/Delaware Atlas & Gazetteer:* Page 65, C-6

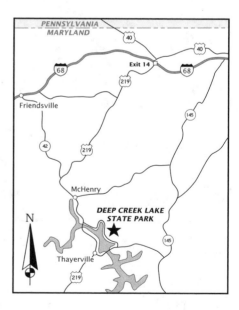

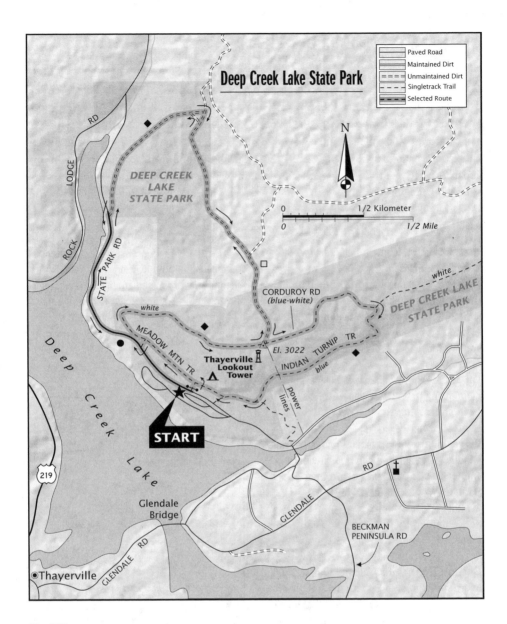

Deep Creek Lake State Park

Legend
- Paved Road
- Maintained Dirt
- Unmaintained Dirt
- Singletrack Trail
- Selected Route

DEEP CREEK
LAKE
STATE PARK

LODGE RD

ROCK

STATE PARK RD

0   1/2 Kilometer
0   1/2 Mile

white

CORDUROY RD
(blue-white)

white

DEEP CREEK LAKE
STATE PARK

MEADOW MTN TR

Thayerville
Lookout
Tower

El. 3022

INDIAN TURNIP TR

blue

power
lines

START

219

D e e p   C r e e k   L a k e

Glendale
Bridge

GLENDALE

RD

BECKMAN
PENINSULA RD

GLENDALE RD

Thayerville

The Ride

If you're interested in traveling to a place with more to offer than just mountain biking, Deep Creek Lake State Park, in the far western panhandle of Maryland's Garrett County, may be just the place.

Not only is Deep Creek Lake State Park one of Maryland's premier mountain biking destinations, it is also a favorite vacation spot for people of all interests throughout the Mid-Atlantic. Some of the park's more popular activities apart from mountain biking include hiking, cross-country skiing, boating, dining, and an array of other outdoor opportunities.

Deep Creek Lake, Maryland's largest inland body of water, was formed by damming the junction of Deep Creek and the Youghiogheny River in 1953. The park officially opened for public use in July 1959. Today, Deep Creek Lake State Park and Deep Creek Lake are two of Maryland's most popular destinations for outdoor recreation.

Famous for its mountains, Garrett County is a prime location for mountain biking in Maryland. There are over 100 miles of trails available for everyone ranging from beginners to the most experienced of riders. This ride is intended to be an introduction to Garrett County trail riding and includes some of the climbs and views associated with western Maryland's scenic mountain ranges.

▶ **The park officially opened for public use in July 1959. Today, Deep Creek Lake State Park and Deep Creek Lake are two of Maryland's most popular destinations for outdoor recreation.**

A short drive from the West Virginia border, Deep Creek Lake State Park is located just 10 miles northeast of Oakland, Maryland. As you enter the park from Rock Ledge Road and State Park Road, pay close attention to your left, keeping your eyes peeled for a sign reading MEADOW MOUNTAIN TRAIL: 50 YARDS. This is where your ride begins. Park in the parking lot to your right, on the other side of the trees directly across from this sign. If you enter the park from Glendale Road, turn left onto State Park Road, and left again onto Waterfront Avenue. An immediate right turn will lead you into the parking area.

So as not to spend the first mile and a half on paved surface, we start this ride opposite the parking lot at the trail marker and continue into the woods for approximately 50 yards before turning left on Meadow Mountain Trail. This ride primarily follows the white-blazed trail, though it will deviate a bit so that you may end up back at your starting point without too much trouble. Ride parallel to State Park Road for approximately three-quarters of a mile, then pedal the pavement for a quick stretch until you reach Fire Tower Road.

At mile marker 1.5, you reach the intersection with Fire Tower Road and State Park Road. Turn right on the dirt road and follow the gradual ascent up the mountain for the next 2.5 miles. When you reach the top, take a break and soak in the view

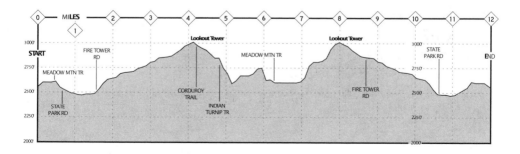

of Deep Creek Lake far below (the best viewing time comes when the trees are bare). At mile marker 3.9 (the top of the climb), turn left. This is Meadow Mountain Trail. Follow this trail downhill for approximately 1 mile. This section of singletrack is unique, with a surface not often experienced by cyclists. Because of the trail's swampy nature, park officials have layered a 150-yard section of trail with railroad ties. This section of the trail is known locally as Corduroy Road, and it makes for very interesting riding. When you see this, try and imagine the labor that went into laying so many railroad ties side by side.

Reach the intersection of Indian Turnip Trail (blue blazed) at mile marker 4.8 and turn right, continuing downhill along exciting singletrack. Meadow Mountain Trail continues straight at this point. For more information on where you'll end up if you travel straight, contact High Mountain Sports. They have a great trail guide of the entire area.

Our ride continues down a twisty, technical trail called Indian Turnip that takes you back to the base of the mountain. Be careful on this trail, as it is very narrow, with plenty of opportunities to unload your bike and yard sale into the trees!

At mile marker 6.0, turn right and continue along the trail beneath the power lines. A short distance later, turn left and head back along Meadow Mountain Trail. Should you continue straight beneath the power lines, you will end up back at the fire tower. This is not a recommended adventure, however, because of the steep and loose-surfaced ride to the top.

Continue straight, following the white blazes of Meadow Mountain Trail. The trail becomes more level and much wider, with a pleasant easiness about it. Following this trail to mile marker 6.2 takes you back to the point where your ride began. Should you choose to turn left back to your car and bail out here, you will miss the 2.5-mile descent that whisks you to the completion of this ride. Keep this in mind and consider your choices carefully. If you choose to finish the ride in its entirety, continue straight, following the white blazes. You will again head toward the fire tower, climbing up to the top of the mountain. At mile marker 8.1, reach the top of the climb and the fire tower, grab one last glimpse of this great view, then turn left and descend for 2.5 miles for unadulterated downhill adventure!

At the bottom of the descent, turn left on State Park Road and continue back to the parking lot where your car awaits.

Miles and Directions

0.0 **START** at the sign reading MEADOW MOUNTAIN TRAIL: 50 YARDS.

0.03 Turn left on Meadow Mountain Trail following the white blazes.

0.5 Come to a trail intersection. Continue straight.

0.53 Come to a trail intersection. Turn left and continue downhill toward State Park Road.

0.7 Turn right on State Park Road.

Meadow Mountain Trail has a level, wide stretch that is pleasant and easy.

1.5 Turn right on Fire Tower Road. Continue on this dirt road for 2.5 miles uphill to the lookout tower.

3.9 Reach Thayerville Lookout Tower. Turn left at the T, continuing to follow the white blazes (this portion of trail is blazed both white and blue). Following a short descent, you will reach Corduroy Road. Continue to the next intersection.

4.8 Turn right at this intersection on Indian Turnip Trail and follow the blue blazes. The white trail continues straight. The blue trail continues downhill through scenic, technical single-track.

5.2 Turn right, crossing over a wooden bridge. Continue following the blue blazes. The next section of the trail levels out and becomes more technical. No dabs allowed!

6.0 Come to an intersection. Turn right.

6.06 Turn right at this intersection and continue uphill, directly beneath the power lines.

6.1 Come to an intersection. Turn left on Meadow Mountain Trail. Continue following the white blazes.

6.2 Come to an intersection. This is where our ride began. Continue straight to complete the rest of this ride.

7.0 Come to an intersection. Continue straight following the white trail blazes. Remain on the white trail until you reach Thayerville Lookout Tower.

8.1 Turn left at this intersection and reach Thayerville Lookout Tower. It's a 2.5-mile descent back to State Park Road. Be careful!

10.6 Turn left on State Park Road. Head back to the park.

12.0 Arrive back where you started. Do it again!

Ride Information

Local Information
Garrett County Tourism (301) 387-4FUN
www.deepcreeklake.org
High Mountain Sports Oakland, MD
(301) 387-4199

Local Events and Attractions
Garrett County Chamber Office
(301) 387-6171
Contact the Deep Creek Lake Park office for various activities within the park
(301) 387-5563

Accommodations
Deep Creek Lake is one of Maryland's most popular vacation destinations. There are campsites, bed-and-breakfasts, inns, hotels, cottages, and more. Depending on the time of year you visit, reservations might be necessary. For a complete listing of accommodations online: www.garrettchamber.com/menu accommodations.htm

2 New Germany State Park

While the trails in New Germany State Park were originally built for hikers and cross-country skiers, they are no less popular with off-road cyclists who see the park as a great mountain biking destination. Located in western Maryland, this ride offers a mere glimpse at what is available in the 52,800-acre Savage River Forest. The park is located on what was once a very prosperous milling center for Garrett County. It now boasts 455 acres of scenic forest, including a 13-acre lake.

Start: Poplar Lick Run ORV Trail parking area (Big Run State Park)
Length: 15.8 miles
Approximate riding time: 3 hours
Difficulty: Technically moderate due to relatively flat but rocky and wet terrain. Physically moderate due to length.
Trail surface: Unimproved dirt roads, double-track, and singletrack
Lay of the land: Dense woodlands along a well-fed creek
Land status: State park
Nearest town: Grantsville, MD
Other trail users: Hikers, cross-country skiers, off-road vehicles, and campers.
Trail contacts: New Germany State Park, Grantsville, MD
(301) 895-5453
High Mountain Sports, McHenry, MD
(301) 387-4199
www.highmountainsports.com
Schedule: Open from dawn till dusk, year-round
Fees and permits: $2.00 day-use area $12.00 camping fees during the summer season
Maps: USGS maps: Bittinger, MD; Barton, MD; Grantsville, MD; Avilton, MD

Getting There: From Cumberland, MD: Take Interstate 68 west to Exit 24. Follow signs to New Germany/Savage River State Forest. Continue 4 miles past the New Germany State Park entrance on New Germany Road and turn left onto Big Run Road. Continue straight on Big Run Road for approximately 4 miles and turn left on Savage River Road. Follow Savage River Road for another 4 miles and turn left on Poplar Lick Run Off-Road-Vehicle Road. Park immediately to the left. The ride begins here. *DeLorme: Maryland/Delaware Atlas & Gazetteer:* Page 62, B-2

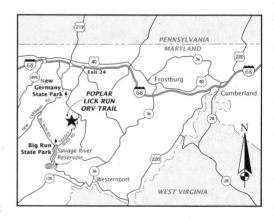

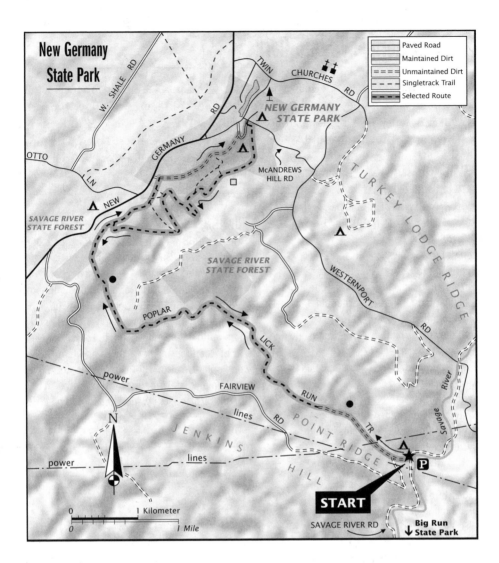

Paved Road
Maintained Dirt
Unmaintained Dirt
Singletrack Trail
Selected Route

NEW GERMANY STATE PARK

TWIN CHURCHES RD

W. SHALE RD

GERMANY RD

OTTO LN

McANDREWS HILL RD

NEW

SAVAGE RIVER STATE FOREST

TURKEY LODGE RIDGE

SAVAGE RIVER STATE FOREST

WESTERNPORT RD

POPLAR

LICK

power lines

FAIRVIEW RD

RUN

POINT RIDGE

TR

Savage River

JENKINS

power lines

HILL

N

0   1 Kilometer
0   1 Mile

START

SAVAGE RIVER RD

P

Big Run
↓ State Park

The Ride

New Germany State Park and Big Run State Park both lie within the 52,800-acre Savage River State Forest, the largest of Maryland's state forests. Our ride covers only a small portion of this vast wilderness area, and the possibilities for other equally great rides are numerous. Detailed maps and directions can be obtained from forest headquarters, as can information regarding sensitive and restricted areas. For additional information, maps, and rides in the Savage River State Forest, your best bet is to contact High Mountain Sports in Deep Creek.

Savage River State Forest is the birthplace of both the Savage and Casselman Rivers. Lying on opposite sides of the Eastern Divide, the two rivers flow in opposite directions; the Savage River running south into the Chesapeake Bay and eventually the Atlantic, and the Casselman River flowing north into the Youghiogheny, then the Mississippi, and ultimately the Gulf of Mexico.

Your ride begins on the Poplar Run ORV Trail in Big Run State Park and works its way to the mountain biking trails of New Germany State Park. A mixture of moderate climbing, singletrack and doubletrack, and dirt roads makes this a wonderfully varied ride. After parking, ride straight through the first of several creek crossings. It's recommended you make this ride during warm spring and summer days, because you will more than likely get very wet. Ride on this road for approximately 5 miles, the majority of which will be uphill. The grade, however, is not very significant, so don't be too worried. Stay on guard, though, because this area does allow motorized vehicles, and you may occasionally have to share the trails with a four-wheel-drive vehicle.

▶ You can also rent rowboats for a quick sail or simply hang out by the water and cool your feet.

When you reach mile marker 5.1, turn right and go through a gate. This marks the entrance to New Germany State Park. The next 4 miles are spent on a variety of exciting singletrack and doubletrack trails.

To proceed, enter the park's forest directly ahead of the gate and follow the blue blazes, making sure the creek is on your right. Approximately three-quarters of a mile later, bear left and follow the green blazes. At this point, you are at the center of New Germany State Park's trail system. As great as these trails are, they unfortunately cover only a small section of the park. Following any of the clearly marked trails will always keep you within 2 to 3 miles of New Germany's Parking Lot 5, the starting point for all of the trails within the park.

Turn left and cross over a small wooden bridge and begin following what is now a yellow-blazed trail. This is a fun section of singletrack that culminates in approximately three-quarters of a mile with a short, steep descent. At mile marker 6.5, turn left, continuing to follow the yellow blazes. The trail to the right is also blazed yellow. If you follow it, you will end up where you got on the yellow trail in the first place. If you enjoyed that last section, turn right here and do this small yellow-blazed loop again.

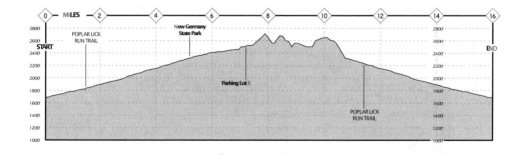

The Western Maryland countryside is spectacular.

Continue straight on the green trail until you reach the road and the lake. This thirteen-acre lake was formed many years ago when Poplar Lick Run was dammed for mill operations. Today, the lake is a popular swimming hole and picnic area. Feel free to take a break from riding and jump in for a swim. You can also rent rowboats for a quick paddle or simply hang out by the water and cool your feet. When you're ready to move on, turn right and head up the road. To your right is Parking Lot 5 and New Germany State Park's main trailhead.

Continue up the road, then bear right toward the amphitheater. A short distance later you will turn left, then left again onto a clearly marked red-blazed trail. Continue along the red-blazed trail for approximately three-quarters of a mile before turning left onto the light blue trail (notice the one-way sign on the red trail).

Continue on the light blue trail that eventually merges with the green trail and later the dark blue trail. At mile marker 9.75, you will have reached the top of the ascent. The ride is all downhill from here to your car. Turn right and get ready for a big-ring descent! Follow the blue blazes until you reach the gate. Turn left and follow Poplar Lick Run ORV Trail all the way down to your car. Five fun-filled downhill miles later, you're back to the beginning of this ride.

Miles and Directions

0.0 **START** from the Poplar Lick Run ORV parking area and head toward the creek. You must right away make the first of several creek crossings. Follow Poplar Lick Run ORV Trail, a gravel/dirt road, for approximately 5 miles.

5.1 After a 5-mile gradual ascent, turn right and pedal through the gate, continuing straight on the blue trail.

5.8 Bear left and continue on the green trail.

5.9 Immediately after crossing the bridge, turn left on the yellow trail. Follow the yellow blazes to the left.

6.5 After a short, steep downhill, turn left, continuing to follow the yellow blazes. The trail to the right is also blazed yellow. This branch of the trail will take you back toward the small bridge you crossed earlier.

6.6 Make a ninety-degree turn to the right and continue straight toward the green trail. Turn left at the green trail.

6.7 Continue straight on the green trail.

7.0 Bear left over the wooden bridge.

7.1 Turn right on the park road, then bear right at the Y intersection (by the phone booth), heading toward the amphitheater. Parking Lot 5 is to the right. **(Note:** This is where all trails in New Germany State Park begin. If you would like to ride trails not included in this ride, come back, study the trail map, and go for a few extra miles.)

7.3 Turn right at this road. The red trailhead is immediately to your left. Continue on the red trail for approximately half a mile, at which point the trail will level out and treat you to a short but fast downhill.

8.1 Turn left onto the light blue trail. Notice the "one way" sign on the red trail.

8.6 Continue straight on the blue trail.

9.0 Turn left following the green blazes.

9.6 Turn left following the blue blazes.

9.75 Turn right, continuing to follow the blue blazes. Don't go beyond the gate and the "No Jeep" sign unless you're confident of your backcountry skills. Information on this trail is available at New Germany State Park headquarters on New Germany Road.

9.78 Continue straight at this intersection, staying on the blue trail. Prepare yourself for a big-ring descent. It's all downhill from here! Yee haa! What a descent!

10.7 Turn left through the yellow gate, then left and downhill. You're back on Poplar Lick Run ORV Trail. Continue straight for the next 5.1 miles back toward Savage River Road.

15.8 Arrive back where you began this ride. **(Option:** Drive back to New Germany State Park and park in Parking Lot 5, where the entire park's trails start. Try some of the trails we didn't cover in this loop!)

Ride Information

Local Information

Garrett County Tourism
(301) 387-4FUN
www.deepcreeklake.org
High Mountain Sports
Oakland, MD
(301) 387-4199

Local Events and Attractions

Garrett County Chamber Office
(301) 387-6171

Accommodations

Thirty-seven inidividual campsites
Eleven furnished cabins
Modern bathhouses with hot showers
Walnut Ridge Bed & Breakfast,
Grantsville, MD—restored farmhouse
(circa 1864) (888) 419-2568

3 Green Ridge State Forest MTB Loop

The rangers at Green Ridge State Forest really go out of their way to cater to mountain bikers. In the last couple of years they have hosted the Maryland Mountain Bike State Championships and built a permanent 12-mile loop. To celebrate this new trail, they have held an annual event strictly devoted to this sport. By welcoming the mountain bike community, the rangers hope they will increase public awareness about this tremendous natural resource. So if you happen by one of the rangers, stop, say hello, and thank the ranger for his or her efforts in providing everybody with a safe and enjoyable off-road cycling environment.

Start: From the Mountain Bike Trail parking area

Length: 12-mile loop

Approximate riding time: 2–4 hours (depending on skill level)

Difficulty: Difficult due to elevation changes and rocky trails

Trail surface: Singletrack loop

Land status: State forest

Nearest town: Cumberland, MD

Other trail users: Hikers, campers, equestrians, and pets

Trail contacts: Green Ridge State Forest Headquarters, Flintstone, MD, (301) 478–3124

Schedule: Open from dawn till dusk, year-round

Fees and permits: Camping fees: $6.00 per night plus $1.00 per person in a group of six or more

Maps: USGS maps: Artemas, MD; Paw Paw, MD

Getting There: **From Hagerstown:** Take Interstate 70 West to Interstate 68 West, then take Exit 62 (about 19 miles east of Cumberland) and turn right at the stop sign. Make an immediate left onto State Highway 144 West and continue for approximately 1.3 miles. Turn left onto Old Williams Road. Follow Old Williams Road for 1 mile, then bear left onto Black Sulphur Road. Stay on Black Sulphur

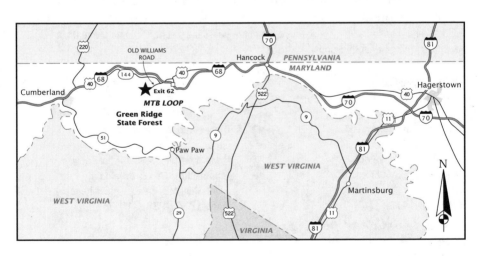

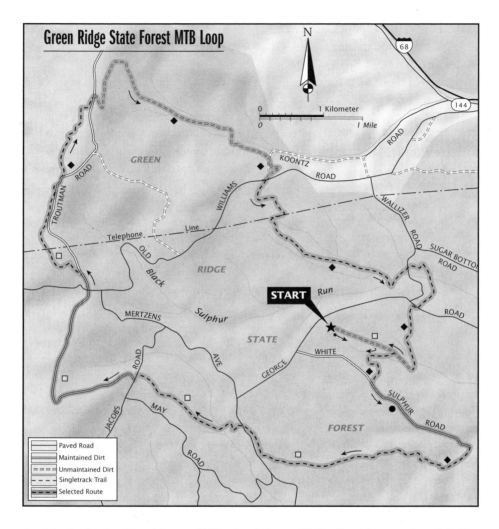

Road for 1 mile, then bear right onto Wallizer Road. Stay on Wallizer Road for approximately half a mile, then turn left into a large field. Park at the far end, in front of the large brown Mountain Bike Trail sign. The ride begins here. *DeLorme: Maryland/Delaware Atlas & Gazetteer:* Page 69, A-3 **Note:** Immediately upon reaching the stop sign after Exit 62, you will notice a small mountain bike sign mounted on the stop sign post. These markers have been placed at selected locations to guide you straight into the camping and parking area for the mountain bike trail.

The Ride

The rangers at Green Ridge State Forest have realized that mountain bikers are well worth catering to, even while many other land managers have not. In an effort to generate interest in the forest and the great outdoors, and to bring more visitors to this vast system of trails and roads, Green Ridge State Forest officials have built a permanent 12-mile mountain bike course. In addition to the ride already summarized in this book and the hundreds of miles of dirt roads readily available to cycling, most of the hiking trails and the nearby C&O Canal Towpath (bordering the south side of the forest) are also open to bikes.

Designed specifically for off-road bicycles, but not limited to them, the trail is a challenging loop that will test the abilities of all mountain bikers and hikers. Made almost entirely of singletrack, this trail is bound to become an East Coast favorite. For folks not used to the mountainous terrain around here, the rangers at Green Ridge have made four easy bailouts, located along the trail, offering tired legs more moderate rides back to the trailhead.

▶ **For folks not used to the mountainous terrain around here, the rangers at Green Ridge have made four easy bailouts, located along the trail, offering tired legs more moderate rides back to the trailhead.**

With the trail, the rangers and officials at Green Ridge State Forest hope to attract more visitors to the Maryland mountainside. Shortly after the trail's completion in the summer of 1998, and to celebrate its public opening, the rangers at Green Ridge held the first annual mountain bike weekend. It was a celebration of the many hours that went into building the trail system and a chance for riders from Maryland, Pennsylvania, and West Virginia to gather in a central location.

A small contingent of riders from around the Washington metropolitan area, Pittsburgh, and Harrisburg attended the celebration. In all, more than fifty cyclists were treated to a weekend packed full of events that included scheduled and impromptu rides, a local bluegrass band, and a festive campfire. Games of "Frizbike" developed in the camping area, and a campfire cooking competition took place. The second annual festival, in 1999, was just as successful, prompting Green Ridge officials to repeat the event in the new millennium, creating a tradition for cyclists throughout the Mid-Atlantic to enjoy year after year.

One of the characteristic features of Green Ridge State Forest is its vast network of dirt roads. There are more than 200 miles of forest service roads on which to ride. The new mountain bike loop takes advantage of several of these roads by providing riders with "easy outs" throughout the course, making this trail system unique as well as accessible to all skill levels. Although it's a difficult ride, novice and intermediate riders can sample smaller sections of the trail without having to commit to the entire loop.

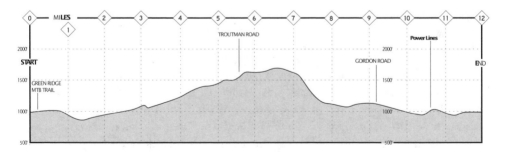

A series of short, steep climbs and difficult switchbacks mark the beginning of the trail. Then a deceiving descent appears within the first mile of the ride, just a way to get you to the very bottom so that you can pedal back up to the top. After the initial descent, the climbing seems endless. Nearly at the halfway point, however, things change. The trail takes a downward turn and becomes slightly more difficult. Although easier on the thighs, the trail now begins to take a toll on your arms and your mind. Total concentration is required on the second half of the ride because of the fast and technical design. Suspension was invented for this kind of trail. Fast doubletrack and singletrack descents will test every muscle in your body, and your skills will all be called upon to keep you upright—absolutely a rider's paradise. After completing the loop, you'll want to do it all over again.

THE MARYLAND SKINNY

Maryland is comprised of twenty-three counties and one independent city (Baltimore) and has a population of just over five million people, all of whom live within its 9,775 square miles of land.

Miles and Directions

0.0   **START** at the trailhead immediately to the right of the large brown sign. Enter here and continue on the doubletrack. Notice the small brown 11.5 mile marker. Throughout the ride, you will see these small brown mountain bike signs and "E-Z out" signs. The rangers have done a terrific job of marking these trails. Each intersection is clearly marked with a directional sign. Getting lost on this course is not an option.

0.31   Turn right at this intersection. The trail is clearly marked with an arrow and "Entrance" sign.

0.6   Continue following the trail to the right.

0.7   Turn left at this intersection.

0.9   Continue straight past this intersection and the buildings on the right. You will now go down a fast doubletrack descent.

1.7   Make a right into the singletrack. Get in an easy gear and prepare to climb.

2.4   Turn right at this intersection.

2.8   Follow the trail to the right.

3.2   Continue straight through this intersection.

3.3   See an E-Z out sign. Continue straight across the road to complete the ride.

4.1   Continue on the trail across the road. You are given another E-Z out option.

4.2   Turn left at this intersection. More climbing!

4.7   Turn left at this intersection.

5.4   Continue straight at this intersection.

5.5   Another E-Z out. Continue straight and up onto Troutman Road. Approximately 50 yards ahead, you will see the trail marker on the left. Turn left onto the twisting singletrack. Continue following the mountain bike signs.

5.6   Bear left at this intersection.

7.2 Come out of the singletrack and turn right onto the doubletrack. Cross the road. The trail picks up directly across the road and is clearly marked. It's mostly downhill from here.

7.6 Continue bearing right at this intersection.

8.6 After the downhill, turn left onto the clearly marked trail. It's immediately after the second bridge.

8.9 Come out of the woods and continue up and straight on the dirt road.

9.1 Turn right at this intersection. The trail is clearly marked. If you reach a road intersection, you've gone too far.

9.2 Turn right onto Gordon Road, then immediately turn left onto the doubletrack. The intersection is clearly marked.

9.5 Turn right at this intersection. The trail continues down and under the power lines.

9.7 Turn left at this intersection. Get ready for a fast downhill.

10.6 Continue straight through and under the power lines. As you reach the road, the trail continues directly on the other side. Just a little more climbing and you'll reach your car.

11.1 Turn right and continue toward the road. Make an immediate left onto the clearly marked trail. One mile to go.

11.6 Turn right at this intersection and continue toward the parking area.

12.0 Arrive back at your car.

Ride Information

Local Events and Attractions

Annual Mountain Bike Festival
For details contact the Green Ridge State Forest at (301) 478-3124

Accommodations

Green Ridge State Forest, Flintstone, MD, (301) 478-3124
There are more than ninety-two primitive and eight group campsites; $6.00 per night plus $1.00 per person in a group of six or more.

Visit www.mdmountainside.com for information on lodging in around Cumberland.
The Inn at Walnut Bottom, Cumberland, MD, (800) 286-9718
Mt Aerie B&B, Cumberland, MD, (301) 724-5397

In Addition

The Geographic Regions of Maryland

There are five natural regions in the state of Maryland, rising from sea level in the east along the Chesapeake Bay to more than 3,000 feet in the western Allegheny Mountains.

The **Coastal Plain** covers the eastern half of the state from the Delmarva Peninsula through southern Maryland. This tidewater area is low and flat and is cut by lots of streams. At the center of Maryland's coastal plain is the Chesapeake Bay, which separates southern Maryland on the west and the peninsula on the east.

The **Piedmont Plateau** lies just west of Maryland's Coastal Plain. These two regions are separated by a fall line of rivers. The fall line indicates a drop in land level, often marked by waterfalls. This line extends from the head of the Chesapeake Bay southwest through Baltimore and Washington, D.C. The Piedmont Plateau is about 40 miles wide and rolls upland toward the western mountains. Included in Maryland's Piedmont Plateau is the Frederick Valley, which is drained by the Monocacy River.

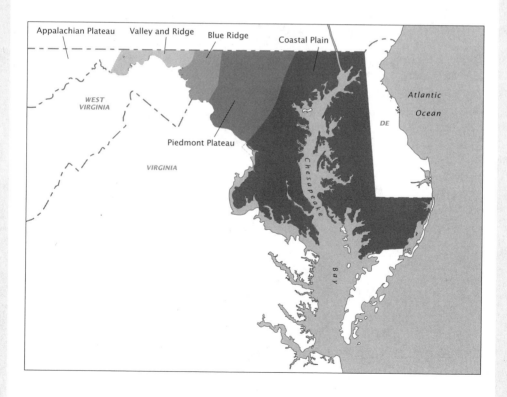

The **Blue Ridge** extends across Maryland from north to south, along the Frederick-Washington county line. The Blue Ridge is a range of the Appalachian Mountain chain and extends from southern Pennsylvania to northern Georgia. In Maryland, the eastern end of the Blue Ridge Mountains is Catoctin Mountain, a section of the Blue Ridge extending from the Pennsylvania border south to Virginia. Camp David, the presidential retreat, is located in this part of Maryland.

The **Valley and Ridge** region of Maryland occupies part of the narrow neck of western Maryland. Its outstanding feature is Hagerstown, just north of Frederick. Hagerstown is a manufacturing center located in the fertile Cumberland Valley.

The **Appalachian Plateau** covers Maryland's extreme western panhandle. Running northeast-southeast, the Appalachian Plateau is made up of a series of parallel mountain ranges and thick-forested valleys, all within the Allegheny Mountains. Backbone Mountain, Maryland's highest peak, rises to 3,360 feet in this area.

Maryland is one of the country's smaller states, measuring only 10,577 square miles—this compared to Virginia's 40,817 square miles or Texas's 267,338 square miles. Despite its size, Maryland enjoys an abundance of natural resources, with fertile soil, valuable mineral deposits, and a thriving seafood industry. Nearly 50 percent of the land is forested, with pine and oak dominating the coastal region, while mixed hardwoods fill in the rest of the state.

4 Green Ridge State Forest Race Route

Green Ridge State Forest stretches across the mountains of western Maryland with over 100 miles of dirt roads and trails readily available for some exciting off-road riding. This particular ride takes you along the 15.6-mile racecourse for the Maryland Mountain Bike State Championships. Its design is not for the faint of heart or casual rider either. Rather, it's the perfect ride for the advanced cyclist looking for challenging climbs, tricky switchbacks, and fast forest-road descents that will put your every skill to the test.

Start: Green Ridge State Forest headquarters
Length: 15.6 miles
Approximate riding time: 3–4 hours
Difficulty: Moderate to difficult due to rugged, tricky singletrack, challenging climbs, and fast descents
Trail surface: Forest roads, doubletrack, and singletrack
Lay of the land: Hilly, wooded setting
Land status: State forest
Nearest town: Hancock, MD
Other trail users: Hikers, campers, anglers, canoeists, hunters, horseback riders, and snowmobile riders
Trail contacts: Green Ridge State Forest headquarters, Flintstone, MD (301) 478-3124

Schedule: Open from dawn till dusk, year-round
Fees and permits: See Accommodations
Maps: USGS maps: Artemas, MD; Paw Paw, MD

Getting There: From Hagerstown, MD: Take Interstate 70 west to Interstate 68 west toward Hancock. Approximately 14 miles west of Hancock, exit onto M. V. Smith Road (Exit 64). Follow the signs to Green Ridge State Forest headquarters. Your ride will begin there. *DeLorme: Maryland/Delaware Atlas & Gazetteer:* Pages 68-69, B-3

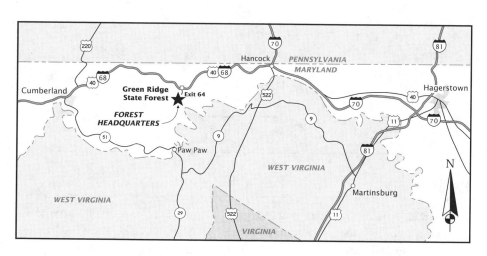

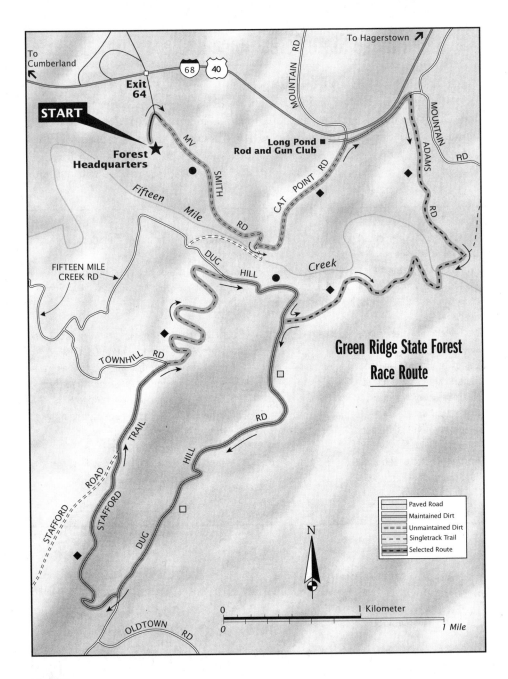

To Cumberland

To Hagerstown

Exit 64

68 40

MOUNTAIN RD

START

Forest Headquarters

MV

SMITH RD

Long Pond Rod and Gun Club

CAT POINT RD

MOUNTAIN

ADAMS RD

RD

Fifteen

Mile

DUG

HILL

Creek

FIFTEEN MILE CREEK RD

Green Ridge State Forest
Race Route

TOWNHILL RD

RD

STAFFORD

ROAD

TRAIL

HILL

STAFFORD

DUG

	Paved Road
	Maintained Dirt
	Unmaintained Dirt
	Singletrack Trail
	Selected Route

N

OLDTOWN RD

0   1 Kilometer

0   1 Mile

The Ride

Green Ridge State Forest, in east Allegany County, is a vast 40,000–acre forest stretching across the rugged mountains of western Maryland. The forest boasts more than one hundred remote camping sites, over 22 miles of trails, and more than 200 miles of forest roads on which to ride, making it an ideal getaway for avid cyclists and campers alike. Home also to the Maryland National Mountain Bike Championship, Green Ridge State Forest is fast becoming a destination for Washington, D.C., and Baltimore riders. Our ride takes you up and down many of the forest roads and singletrack trails that make up the Expert and Sport courses of the race. This will give non-competing cyclists a little taste of what the racers have to endure come race day.

▶ **Look to your right as you ride up Stafford Trail. You may be able to witness some great views of the Potomac River meandering off in the distance through the forest below. In the fall, you will be treated to a spectacular array of colors comparable only to those found in New England.**

The ride begins at the forest headquarters. Take a moment to walk to the overlook opposite the parking lot on the other side of the building. Take a peek at the terrain over which you will be riding. Make sure to bring plenty of water and be prepared for a roller-coaster ride through the forest.

To begin, ride away from the forest headquarters and turn right on M.V. Smith Road, the first part of which is a fast descent. Soon after the pavement ends, you will be greeted by a wide dirt road and a sign welcoming you into the forest.

After a small creek crossing at the bottom of the descent, turn left heading uphill on Catpoint Road. If you reach Fifteen Mile Creek, you've gone too far. As you reach the top of this climb, you may begin to hear sounds of I–68 straight ahead. Before crossing beneath I–68, turn right on Mountain Road, which changes to dirt rather quickly. Follow the steel cable railing on the right. As soon as the cable railing ends just before Mountain Road curves to the right, turn right into the woods on a singletrack trail called Adams Road. Pay close attention because this trailhead is well hidden. For the next mile and a half, you will be cruising downhill through the forest along some great Maryland singletrack.

At mile marker 3.6, turn right, traveling parallel to the creek off to your left. You will soon be crossing this creek, and your feet are certain to get wet. Once across the creek, the trail is marked with white diamonds. At mile marker 4.6, reach an opening in the forest, continue following the white blazes down a short descent, and end up at the intersection of Adams Road and Dug Hill Road. Turn left here and continue uphill for the next 2 miles toward the intersection of Dug Hill Road and Stafford Trail.

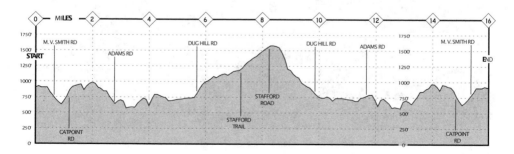

Green Ridge State Forest is home to the Maryland National Mountain Bike Championship.

Turn right on Stafford Trail and continue uphill for 1 more mile—all this climbing will soon pay off. Look to your right as you ride up Stafford Trail. You may be able to witness some great views of the Potomac River meandering off in the distance through the forest below. In the fall, you will be treated to a spectacular array of colors comparable only to those found in New England.

At mile marker 8.3, you will reach Stafford Road and the end of the climb. Turn right and continue down this road. Immediately after making this turn, there is an overlook off to your right. Stop and take a break here and gather your wits. The following downhill section will require that all your senses be tuned and in check. Continue on your way, paying close attention to the right for the trail. As soon as Stafford Road curves sharply to the left, you need to turn right into the woods on the singletrack trail. If you're lucky, the trail will be marked by a leftover race marker, but don't count on it. If you miss this turn and reach campsite 48E, you've gone too far.

What follows on this trail is some serious downhill singletrack, with a series of switchbacks designed to test your entire range of bike handling skills. Be careful and don't get in over your head—figuratively or literally! After approximately 1 mile of this section, you'll reach the end of the descent and connect with Dug Hill Road. Continue straight down along the road for about a half mile, until you reach the intersection with Adams Road. If you'd like, continue straight at this intersection and do it all over again. Or, like most sane people, turn left and return along Adams Road, crossing the creek, and then back up Mountain Road to Catpoint Road and M.V. Smith Road.

All in all, this loop is about 16 miles of climbs and descents. By studying maps provided by the state forest, you could ride a far longer course. But unless your backcountry skills are extraordinary and you plan to spend the night in the forest, stick to this ride for now. Come back another day to tackle the rest of Green Ridge State Forest's more than 200 miles of dirt roads and trails.

POINTS OF INTEREST

East of Green Ridge State Forest is one of the northeastern United States's greatest rock exposures. It's called Sideling Hill. If you've got the time, a short visit to this massive road-cut rock exposure could prove an excellent lesson in geology.

Green Ridge State Forest is a remote area that is especially popular among hunters. Take every precaution to ensure that your visit is enjoyable and safe. Call the forest headquarters for hunting season schedules and information: (301) 478-3124.

If you're thirsty for a cold brew after the ride, visit Bill's Place in Little Orleans, off Orleans Road (Exit 62 off I-68). They'd be glad to fix you up with some delicious beverages. Bill's Place is also accessible from the C&O Canal. So if you're on your way to Cumberland along the canal, stop in for a bite to eat.

Sideling Hill is one of the United States's greatest rock exposures.

Miles and Directions

0.0 START from the forest headquarters parking lot and head toward M. V. Smith Road.

0.1 Turn right on M. V. Smith Road.

0.9 Turn left immediately after a small creek crossing on Catpoint Road. Start climbing!

1.3 How do your legs feel?

1.6 Turn right at this intersection on Mountain Road. I-68 will be to your left.

2.0 Approximately 10 yards after the steel cable railing on your right ends, turn right on a singletrack trail into the woods called Adams Road. Keep your eyes peeled for this trailhead. It's easy to miss. If you've gotten as far as where Mountain Road curves to the right away from I-68, you've missed it. Immediately after you enter the singletrack, turn right and follow the trail downhill, paralleling Mountain Road.

3.6 Turn right at this intersection. Downhills like the last one make climbing a bit easier to endure!

3.8 The trail continues across the creek. Look for the white diamond blazes marking the trail.

4.35 The trail turns sharply left, away from the creek. Get ready for a short steep climb.

4.6 Come out into a large clearing in the forest. The trail continues straight ahead. Look for the tree with a white diamond blaze.

5.5 Reach the intersection of Adams Road and Dug Hill Road. Turn left and continue up Dug Hill Road.

7.2 Approximately one-tenth of a mile after campsite 49E, turn right on Stafford Trail. This intersection should be clearly marked. Still climbing!

8.3 Reach the intersection of Stafford Trail and Stafford Road. Our ride takes us to the right, continuing along Stafford Trail. The longer version of the Maryland State Mountain Bike Championship continues to the left. More information on this ride can be obtained from park headquarters.

8.6 Immediately to your right is an overlook from which you can see Big Ridge and the Potomac River. Continue straight.

8.8 Pay attention! Stafford Road turns sharply left. Turn right at this point into the woods along a singletrack trail. A series of steep singletrack switchbacks leads you down the mountain. Be careful, pay attention, and pick a good line. If you pass the entrance to campsite 48E, you missed this turn.

9.8 Continue straight (bear right) at this intersection with Dug Hill Road.

10.3 Reach the intersection of Dug Hill Road and Adams Road again. It's time to backtrack the first 5.5 miles of your ride.

12.0 Cross the creek again and get wet. Continue straight on the other side.

12.2 Turn left at this intersection. It's time to head straight back up this hill to the top.

13.5 Turn left and continue up Mountain Road for three-tenths of a mile.

13.8 Turn left on Catpoint Road, continuing downhill toward M. V. Smith Road. The next three-quarters of a mile will treat you to the final downhill of the ride.

14.5 Turn right at this intersection and get ready for the final uphill of the ride.

15.4 Turn left at this intersection and continue straight to your car.

15.6 Reach the car.

Ride Information

Local Information
(301) 463-6347

Local Events and Attractions
Annual Mountain Bike Festival—contact the forest for details

Maryland National Mountain Bike Championship—contact the forest for details

Sideling Hill—one of the best rock outcrops in the northeastern United States. See www.geol.umd.edu/HUTTON/sideling.html.

Accommodations
There are more than ninety-two primitive and eight group campsites ($6.00 per night, plus $1.00 per person over six people).
Red Lamp Post B&B, Cumberland, MD (301) 797-3262

5 Greenbrier State Park

Greenbrier State Park provides many recreational opportunities. Mountain biking is just one of them. Home to a number of mountain bike races, Greenbrier has become a favorite destination for many Washington, D.C., riders. The challenging trails are great for the intermediate rider who's not quite ready for the arduous trails further west in Allegany and Garrett Counties. After your ride, take advantage of the beautiful man-made freshwater lake and go for a swim, or simply sit back and lounge on the beach.

Start: Beach/lake parking lot
Length: 5.2 miles
Approximate riding time: 1.5–3 hours
Difficulty: Moderate to difficult
Trail surface: Singletrack, doubletrack, and forest roads
Lay of the land: Rocky terrain in mountainous, wooded area
Land status: State park
Nearest town: Hagerstown, MD
Other trail users: Hikers, campers, cross-country skiers, anglers, canoeists, and hunters
Trail contacts: South Mountain Recreation Area, Boonsboro, MD, (301) 791-4767
Schedule: Open year-round
Camping quiet hours are from 11:00 P.M. to 7:00 A.M.
Fees and permits: $2.00 a person
Maps: USGS maps: Funkstown, MD; Myersville, MD; Greenbrier State Park trail map

Getting There: From Washington: Take Interstate 270 north to U.S. Highway 40 west. Follow U.S. Highway 40 west for approximately 11 miles. The Greenbrier State Park entrance is on your left. Continue straight, parking at the lake parking lot. *DeLorme: Maryland/Delaware Atlas & Gazetteer:* Page 71, C-6

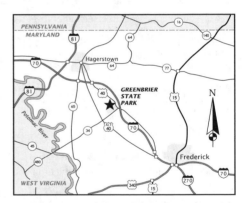

The Ride

Greenbrier State Park, 10 miles east of Hagerstown along U.S. Highway 40, is rich in both history and great places to ride.

Nestled in the scenic Appalachian Mountains, one of the world's oldest mountain ranges, Greenbrier was once a popular area for fur trapping, trading, exploration, and farming. Early in its history, farmers settled into the fertile river valleys. Today, the surrounding roads still follow many of the same paths used by those early industrious pioneers. As you ride along the park's many scenic trails, pay close attention to your surroundings—evidence of foundations from old farmhouses, once-thriving iron furnaces, and old log cabins still exist. The singular and distinctive flat circular

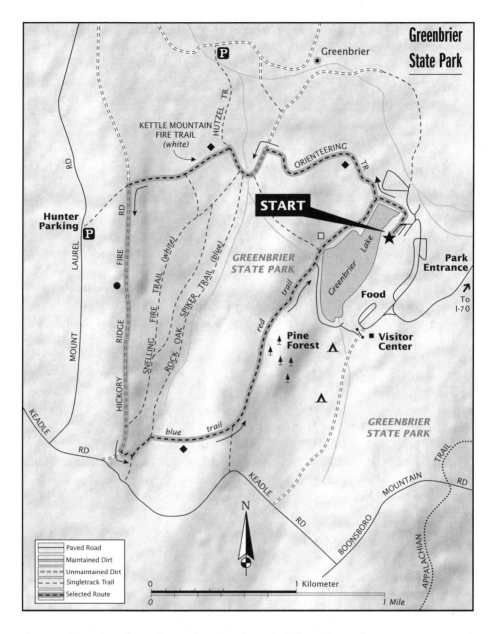

Greenbrier State Park

KETTLE MOUNTAIN FIRE TRAIL (white)

HUTZEL TR

ORIENTEERING TR

START

Hunter Parking P

LAUREL RD

MOUNT

FIRE RD

HICKORY RIDGE

SNELLING — FIRE — TRAIL — (white)

ROCK OAK SPIKER TRAIL (blue)

GREENBRIER STATE PARK

red trail

Greenbrier Lake

Park Entrance

To I-70

Food

Pine Forest

■ **Visitor Center**

blue trail

KEADLE RD

GREENBRIER STATE PARK

KEADLE RD

BOONSBORO MOUNTAIN RD

APPALACHIAN TRAIL

N

	Paved Road
	Maintained Dirt
	Unmaintained Dirt
	Singletrack Trail
	Selected Route

0 _____ 1 Kilometer

0 _____ 1 Mile

shapes of hearths where charcoal was made to fuel the old iron furnaces are scattered throughout the area as well.

Because of its unique history, 1,200 acres of woodlands, forty-two-acre man-made lake, and miles of mountainous trails, Greenbrier State Park has become one of Maryland's most popular public recreational areas and has most recently begun hosting races for the Maryland Mountain Bike Point Series.

Greenbrier State Park is also fairly close to some other great off-road riding areas, including Green Ridge State Forest (see chapters 3 and 4), home of the Maryland State Mountain Bike Championship. This vast 40,000-acre forest is filled with trails and unimproved dirt roads great for riding. And if you're traveling west already, continue a bit farther to Deep Creek Lake State Park (see chapter 1). Southeast a bit from Greenbrier State Park is Gambrill State Park (see chapters 6 and 7), boasting, unquestionably, some of the East Coast's greatest singletrack, with over 18 miles of trails, including a section of the famed Catoctin Mountain Trail.

▶ **Your ride here at Greenbrier begins at the parking lot directly above the lake. Start by pedaling to the other side of the lake along the grassy area on the northern edge.**

Your ride here at Greenbrier begins at the parking lot directly above the lake. Start by pedaling to the other side of the lake along the grassy area on the northern edge. When you reach the sign marked ORIENTEERING TRAIL, the real ride begins. There are approximately 12 miles of trails in Greenbrier State Park. This ride covers only about 5.5 miles, leaving quite a bit left over for you to discover yourself.

Start out on the white trail, crossing over the first of a handful of hills in the first three-quarters of a mile. Enjoy this descent because the next part of the ride will mostly be up a steady climb to the ridge. At mile marker 0.8, turn left on a coarse gravel road. You will be on this road for just three-quarters of a mile before turning right onto more singletrack, continuing to follow the white blazes. At this right turn, be sure to ride away from the Rock Oak Fire Trail. Cross a small creek and continue along the white-blazed trail. The white blazes connect three of the park's main trails: the Hickory Ridge Trail, the Snelling Fire Trail, and the Mountain Fire Trail. You are currently on the Mountain Fire Trail heading to the Hickory Ridge Trail.

At mile marker 2.0, you will have reached the end of your climb. Prepare for a series of technical off-camber sections of East Coast singletrack at its best. This section is fun and challenging and will surely test your balance and stamina. Just remember that momentum is your friend. Pedaling too slowly along this trail may allow the singletrack to have its way with you.

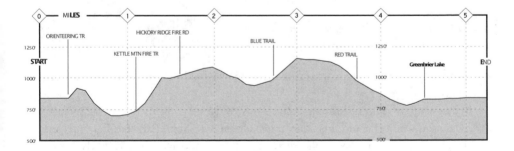

Greenbrier's trails are very popular with riders from the Washington, D.C., area.

After a series of short ascents and one great downhill that empties you into a wonderful rock garden, you will intersect with the white and blue trails. Turn left and continue on the blue trail. This turn will lead you uphill for 1 mile to the top of the ridge. The ascent is gradual and slow but is rewarded with a fast, loose-terrain descent that will bring you back to the lake. This is a very popular trail because of its proximity to the lake.

At mile marker 4.8, reach the lake. Continue riding with the lake on your right. If you choose, you can head left and pick up the fire road that initially took you to the white trail. If you look hard, you may see the trailhead to your left at the bottom of the hill. At this point, your car should be clearly visible at the other side of the lake.

If you're up to it, go for another loop. If not, head on back to the beaches at the other side of the lake and relax under the sun.

Miles and Directions

0.0 **START** at the parking lot and head to the other side of the lake from the boat launch. Once you cross to the opposite side of the lake, enter the woods at the trailhead marked ORIENTEERING TRAIL.

0.3 Bear right (straight) at this intersection and continue downhill.

0.8 Turn left at the gravel road.

1.1 Turn right off the gravel road onto the singletrack trail and continue right. Follow the white blazes, riding away from the trail marked ROCK OAK FIRE TRAIL.

1.2 Continue straight (right) immediately after crossing the creek. Turn left at this intersection and follow the white blazes up the mountain.

1.7 Bear right and continue uphill. You have just come out of the Kettle Mountain Fire Trail.

1.9 Bear left and follow the Hickory Ridge Fire Trail sign.

2.0 Turn right at this trail intersection and get ready for a series of off-camber technical sections. This is a challenging section of trail that will test your balance and stamina.

2.9 Turn right at this trail section, then immediately left, heading back in the direction from which you just came.

3.1 Turn right at this intersection and get ready for a short, fast descent that drops you into a small rock garden, then immediately sends you back up a rocky technical ascent.

3.3 Turn right at this trail intersection.

3.4 Turn left at this trail intersection, following the blue blazes, and get ready for a 1-mile gradual climb.

4.0 Continue straight, heading downhill toward the lake for approximately 1 mile. This is a fast descent, so pay attention and be ready to slow down quickly. This section of trail is closest to the lake and is used by a lot of hikers.

4.8 Reach an opening with the lake to your right. At this point, you can see the parking lot on the other side of the lake. Continue straight, riding parallel to the lake.

5.0 Bear left on the fire road, away from the lake.

5.1 If you choose to ride the loop again, turn left. After a short downhill, this trail will put you at mile marker 0.3. Otherwise, bear right and continue toward the Orienteering Trail trailhead.

5.2 Reach the Orienteering Trail trailhead. Travel to the other side of the lake on the grass toward the boat launch. You may also continue straight along the fire road. This trail also takes you to the boat launch.

Ride Information

Local Information

Washington County's regional information Web site http://pilot.wash.lib.md.us
Washington County Visitors Bureau, Hagerstown, MD, (301) 791-3246

Local Events and Attractions

Antietam National Battlefield, Sharpsburg, MD—bloodiest battle of the Civil War (301) 432-5124, www.nps.gov/anti
Crystal Grottoes Caverns—limestone caverns with stalactite and stalagmite formations. Guided tours on illuminated walkways (301) 432-6336
www.quikpage.com/C/cgrottoes

Accommodations

Wingrove Manor Inn, Hagerstown, MD (301) 797-7769
Lewrene Farm Bed & Breakfast, Hagerstown, MD, (301) 582-1735

6 Gambrill State Park: Yellow Trail

Maintained by MORE (Mid-Atlantic Off-Road Enthusiasts), the Yellow Trail in Gambrill State Park is a challenging and demanding ride. Gambrill is one of the most popular mountain biking destinations in the state of Maryland, attracting riders from as far south as Richmond, Virginia. The Yellow Trail, at 6.5 miles, is the longest loop in the Gambrill trail system and the perfect trail for up-and-coming mountain bikers looking to test their mettle on some difficult singletrack.

Start: High Knob Scenic Area parking lot
Length: 6.3 miles
Approximate riding time: 1–1.5 hours
Difficulty: Difficult due to strenuous climbs and rocky singletrack terrain
Trail surface: Rocky singletrack
Lay of the land: Mostly in dense woods over mountainous terrain
Land status: State park
Nearest town: Frederick, MD
Other trail users: Hikers, campers, cross-country skiers, and dogs

Trail contacts: Gambrill State Park (301) 271-7574
South Mountain Recreation Area, Boonsboro, MD, (301) 791-4767
MORE www.more-mtb.org
Schedule: Open daily from dawn till dusk, year-round
Fees and permits: Fees for picnic shelters, tearoom, and campsites (call the park for current prices)
Maps: USGS maps: Myersville, MD; Catoctin Furnace, MD; Middletown, MD; Frederick, MD; Gambrill State Park trail map

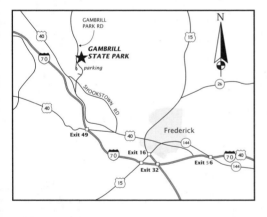

Getting There: From Frederick, MD: Take U.S. Highway 40 (Baltimore National Pike) west and turn right on Shookstown Road. Follow Shookstown Road to Gambrill Park Road and turn right. Enter the park, pass the parking lot on your right, and continue to the T intersection. Go left to the High Knob Scenic Area and park in the first lot on your left, directly across from the swings. *DeLorme: Maryland/Delaware Atlas & Gazetteer:* Page 72, D-2

The Ride

Six miles northwest of Frederick, Maryland, on Catoctin Mountain, is Gambrill State Park—a jewel for mountain bikers. Named for the late James H. Gambrill Jr. of Frederick, the park had its beginnings when spirited conservationists bought the land on the mountain and donated it to the city of Frederick. In September 1934, the park was presented to the state, and since then it has been a recreational favorite.

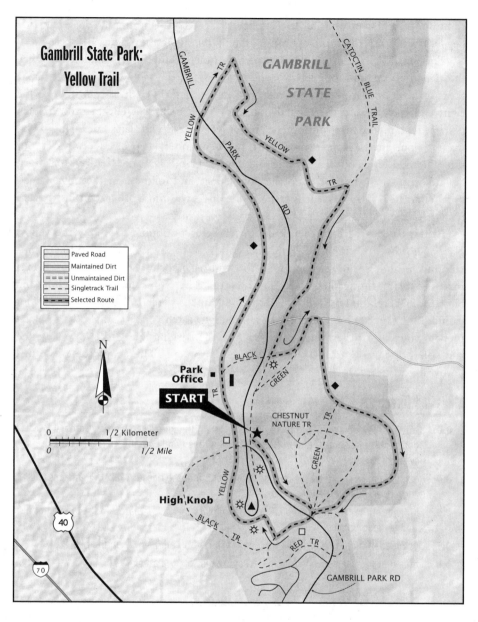

Gambrill State Park: Yellow Trail

GAMBRILL STATE PARK

CATOCTIN – BLUE TRAIL

GAMBRILL TR

YELLOW

PARK

YELLOW TR

RD

Paved Road
Maintained Dirt
Unmaintained Dirt
Singletrack Trail
Selected Route

N

BLACK

GREEN

Park Office

START

CHESTNUT NATURE TR

GREEN TR

0   1/2 Kilometer
0   1/2 Mile

YELLOW

High Knob

BLACK — TR

RED TR

40

70

GAMBRILL PARK RD

Your ride starts with a fast descent paralleling Gambrill Park Road. By the time you reach the main trail parking lot, you will have had a fair sampling of what's to come. From the parking lot, cross the street and head back into the woods toward the first grueling climb. Once at the top, take the chance to enjoy some of the breathtaking views of Middletown Valley, southwest of the mountain. Soon after the overlooks, hook up with the Black Trail. Had enough? You can bail out here by turning right and heading up the hill to Gambrill Park Road—the point where the ride began. If you wish to go on, continue straight, following the Yellow/Black Trail.

The terrain changes slightly as you catch quick glimpses of Middletown Valley through the trees on your left. Continue following the yellow/black blazes up a short technical hill to a divide. You'll want to veer left. The Black Trail splits to the right and back toward the High Knob area. After a short ascent, begin a gradual descent that, in a matter of moments, becomes covered with large menacing rocks, making your advance much more difficult. Remember, keep momentum on your side. The trail levels out for a while and ends at Gambrill Park Road with a short, fast descent. Cross the road onto the doubletrack and follow it to the power lines. Turn right here. This descent is fast and furious—you must pay attention to every nuance of the trail. A mistake here can cost you dearly.

At the base, turn right, then immediately left, continuing to follow the yellow blazes. Shortly thereafter, the Yellow Trail continues to the right back up the mountain and meanders through the forest. You will reach a short descent along a forest road and turn right heading back into the forest. The trail is now blazed yellow and blue. From here, the trail follows a long, off-camber descent that will test all your riding skills. Once at the bottom, take a minute to catch your breath. Loosen up and prepare yourself for the tough climb back to the parking lot. At the lot, take a left and continue up toward the High Knob recreation area. This should be a ride that you will not soon forget.

Miles and Directions

0.0 **START** at the parking lot and head downhill toward the intersection. Cross Gambrill Park Road at this intersection and turn right. The trail runs parallel to the road beneath the power lines.

0.4 Reach the main trailhead parking lot at the bottom of the descent. Take a right, crossing the road, and follow the yellow blazes.

0.6 Turn right at the trail intersection. Continue to follow the yellow blazes and get ready for a grinding steep uphill.

0.7 Continue left on the Yellow Trail at the storm shack. You are halfway up the hill.

0.8 Turn left at the intersection. Continue following the yellow blazes.

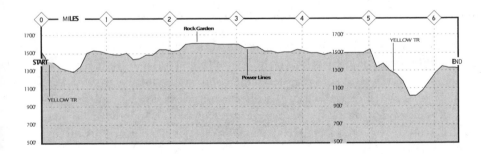

0.9	Take a minute to soak in the view from the overlook. On a clear day looking south, you can see Crampton's Gap, a Civil War landmark.
1.3	Reach the intersection of the Yellow and Black Trails. Continue straight. If you turn right, you will reach your starting point.
1.5	Make a sharp right. To your left are the Frederick Valley and a monumental view.
1.7	Continue straight, following the Yellow Trail up the ascent. Get ready for the Rock Garden, a truly technical section.
2.9	Finish the Rock Garden. Did you dab? Continue following the yellow blazes.
3.1	Cross the road and follow the doubletrack into the woods.
3.3	Turn right at the power lines and head down the hill. Be careful. This is a fast and tricky descent.
3.5	Turn right at the end of the descent.
3.6	Continue following the Yellow Trail up the hill. Good luck.
4.0	Reach the gravel road and cross it. Continue straight on the Yellow Trail. At the double-track, bear left and continue downhill on the Yellow Trail.
4.2	Turn right into the woods. The trail is now blazed yellow and blue.
4.5	Turn left, heading downhill, bearing to the right. This will turn into an off-camber descent. Pay attention. This is a great descent.
4.8	Cross through this intersection and continue straight.
5.2	What a descent! Turn right. It's time to pay your dues and head straight up the hill along the Yellow Trail, continuing straight through the next two intersections.
5.8	Back at the parking lot. Turn right and continue on the Yellow Trail up the first descent. If you'd like, choose another loop from the trail map.
6.3	Back at the intersection. Turn left toward High Knob and your car. What a ride!

Ride Information

Local Information

Tourism Council of Frederick County, Frederick, MD, (301) 663-8687

Local Events and Attractions

See Frederick County's online visitors' guide for links about local events and attractions: www.visitfrederick.org

Accommodations

There are thirty-four campsites in the Rock Run area. Fees range from $7.00 to $21.00.

Beaver Creek House, Hagerstown, MD (301) 797-4764 or (888) 942-9966

7 Gambrill State Park: Blue Trail

Are you ready for a beating? This trail is probably one of the primary reasons full suspension was invented. Like its neighbor the Yellow Trail, this is one of the toughest and most sought-out rides in Maryland. Advanced riders and serious mountain bikers flock to this and the other trails in Gambrill for their sheer difficulty. Cleaning one of the several rock gardens throughout this trail will definitely make you feel like you've accomplished something great. It's long, technically difficult, and brutal. Bring your suspension. Leave weakness at home.

Start: Trailhead parking lot; Gambrill State Park

Length: 10.5 miles

Approximate riding time: 2.5–3 hours

Difficulty: Very difficult due to extended, steep climbs, rocky terrain, and long miles

Trail surface: Rugged, rocky singletrack; paved and dirt roads

Lay of the land: Dense woodlands over mountainous terrain

Land status: State park

Nearest town: Hagerstown or Frederick, MD

Other trail users: Hikers, campers, horseback riders, and dogs

Trail contacts: Gambrill State Park (301) 271-7574
South Mountain Recreation Area, Boonsboro, MD, (301) 791-4767
MORE, www.more-mtb.org

Schedule: Open daily from dawn till dusk, year-round

Fees and permits: Fees for picnic shelters, tearoom, and campsites (call the park for current prices)

Maps: USGS maps: Myersville, MD; Catoctin Furnace, MD; Middletown, MD; Frederick, MD; Gambrill State Park trail map

Getting There: From Frederick, MD: Take U.S. Highway 40 (Baltimore National Pike) west and turn right on Shookstown Road. Follow Shookstown Road to Gambrill Park Road and turn right. Go 0.5 miles up Gambrill Park Road and park in the small parking lot on the right side of the road, just before the hill gets very steep. *DeLorme: Maryland/Delaware Atlas & Gazetteer:* Page 72, D-2

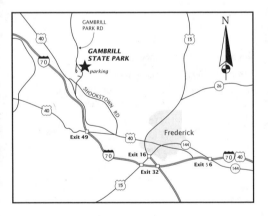

The Ride

The terrain is steep, the rocks are hard, and the trail is mostly unforgiving. This is perhaps one of Maryland's toughest trails open to mountain bike riding. The Catoctin Trail leads you deep into Gambrill and Frederick State Forest, over relentless

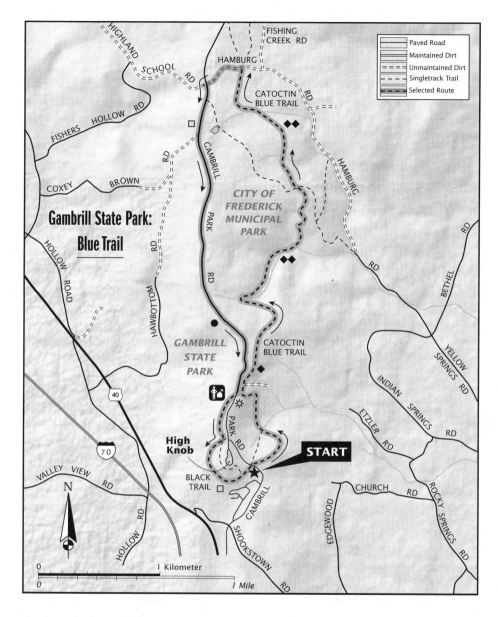

singletrack that will have your body aching for pavement—that is, unless you've loaded the suspension onto your bike. For those skeptics of bicycle suspension, here's your chance to test its mettle.

On the lighter side, tall stands of chestnut oak, hickory, and black birch canopy the Catoctin Mountain, shielding out hints of a more hectic world beyond its wooded boundaries. Only the occasional sound of bicycle chains slapping against chain stays will interrupt the refreshing sounds of cascading streams, calling birds, and feeding deer.

CAMP DAVID We hear all the time that the president of the United States has lifted off from the White House and gone on retreat to Camp David. But did you know that Camp David is located just a few miles north of Gambrill State Park in Catoctin Mountain Park? This 134-acre presidential retreat was established in 1942 by Franklin Roosevelt, who named the area Shangri-La. In 1953, President Eisenhower renamed the hideaway Camp David, after his grandson. The most famous summit held at Camp David took place in September 1978 between Egypt's President Anwar Sadat and Israel's Prime Minister Menachem Begin. President Carter hosted the historic meeting that produced The Camp David Accords, which provided a framework for peace in the Middle East.

The Catoctin Trail starts where all trails begin in Gambrill—from the parking lot on the east side of Gambrill Park Road. In its entirety, the Catoctin Trail travels north nearly 18 miles through Gambrill State Park, Frederick Watershed, Cunningham Falls State Park, and Catoctin Mountain National Park. Unfortunately, mountain bike access is cut short just north of Frederick Watershed. Follow the dark blue blazes up and down Catoctin's steep, jagged slopes all the way to Hamburg Road.

The name Catoctin is believed to have come from a tribe of Native Americans called Kittoctons, who lived at the foothills of the mountains along the Potomac. European settlers first arrived in 1732 from Philadelphia, attracted by Lord Baltimore's offer of 200 acres of rent-free land for three years. The land would then cost only one cent per acre per year. Early settlers used the land for logging and supplied charcoal to local iron furnaces. Catoctin's resources, though, were eventually stripped and depleted from extensive clear-cutting. Then, in 1935, the federal government purchased more than 10,000 acres of this land to be made into a recreational area. The National Park Service and Maryland Park Service manage the land today, permitting Catoctin to redevelop back into the hardwood forest of pre-European settlement.

This trail is not recommended to the novice off-road cyclist and will be extremely challenging even to those who are well-versed in rugged terrain.

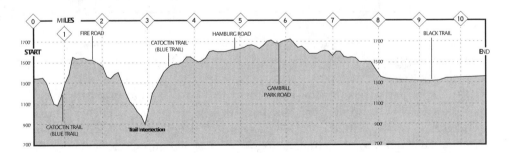

Miles and Directions

0.0 **START** at the trailhead parking lot, where all the trails begin. Follow the Blue Trail into the forest, heading north. This quickly becomes a steep, rocky, fast descent, straight down the mountain.

0.6 Come to a trail intersection. Turn right, following the Blue Trail (indicated by the blue blazes on the trees).

0.7 Bear left up the mountain, continuing on the Blue/Yellow Trail.

1.4 Reach the summit of this brutally steep climb. The Blue/Yellow Trail splits. Turn left off the present trail, then immediately right, continuing on the Blue Trail. The Yellow Trail goes left at this point and heads back toward High Knob.

1.6 Turn right on the dirt road (you will turn off this road very soon).

1.65 Turn left off the dirt road, back into the woods, continuing on the Blue Trail. (**Note:** Keep your eyes peeled to the left for the blue blazes on the trees. This trailhead is difficult to spot.) Begin a very long, steep, rocky descent down the mountain.

2.8 Reach the bottom of the long, rocky descent. It's beautiful down here! Turn left, crossing the stream, and continue on the Blue Trail. Start climbing again up this mountainside. This climb is even more brutal!

3.6 Reach the summit. Finally! How does the back feel?

5.5 Turn left on Hamburg Road (dirt road).

5.9 Turn right on Gambrill Park Road (paved).

9.3 Turn right off Gambrill Park Road on the Black Trail. This turnoff is just before the first stone overlook to the left. (You should see the black arrow pointing the way.)

9.4 Turn left on the Yellow/Black Trail.

9.6 Bear left, continuing down. Overlook on the right.

9.8 Turn right at the turn near the main road, continuing to follow the Black Trail.

10.5 Cross Gambrill Park Road and arrive at the trailhead parking lot. You deserve a serious drink after that ride.

Ride Information

Local Information

Tourism Council of Frederick County, Frederick, MD, (301) 663–8687

Local Events and Attractions

See Frederick County's online visitors' guide for links about local events and attractions: www.visitfrederick.org

Accommodations

There are thirty-four campsites in the Rock Run area. Fees range from $7.00 to $21.00.

Beaver Creek House, Hagerstown, MD, (301) 797–4764 or (888) 942–9966

Sword Fireplace Country, Hagerstown, MD (301) 582–4702

Sundays Bed & Breakfast, Hagerstown, MD (301) 797– 4331 or (800) 221–4828

8 Sugarloaf's Scenic Circuit

Privately owned, the trails in Sugarloaf Mountain used to be a popular mountain biking destination. In the past few years, however, overused trails prompted the managers of the Sugarloaf Trail system to close the area to bikes during the weekend. Today, portions of the Saddleback Trail remain open to mountain biking but only during specific times. The Sugarloaf Scenic Circuit is an alternative to the otherwise excellent but off-limits trails up on the mountain. This circuit of dirt, gravel, and paved roads surrounding the mountain will allow cyclists to experience all the beauty and serenity this Maryland countryside has to offer. For information about the Saddleback Trail and when it is open to mountain bikes, contact the Stronghold Corporation directly.

Start: Sugarloaf Park entrance in Stronghold
Length: 12 miles
Approximate riding time: 1.5–2 hours
Difficulty: Moderately challenging length, with rolling hills along dirt, gravel, and paved roads
Trail surface: Paved and unpaved roads
Lay of the land: Rolling scenic countryside
Land status: Public roadways circumnavigating private land trust
Nearest town: Frederick, MD
Other trail users: Horseback riders and automobiles
Trail contacts: Stronghold Corporation (301) 869–7846; Sugarloaf Mountain Staff (301) 874–2024

Schedule: Sugarloaf Mountain Park and Stronghold Corporation are open daily from early morning to sunset, year-round.
Fees and permits: None
Maps: USGS maps: Buckeystown, MD; Urbana, MD
ADC Maps: Frederick road map

Getting There: From the Capital Beltway (Interstate 495): Take Interstate 270 north approximately 21 miles to the Hyattstown exit (Exit 22). Circle under I–270, heading southwest on State Highway 109 (Old Hundred Road). Follow Old Hundred Road 3 miles to the town of Comus, then turn right on Comus Road. You will see Sugarloaf Mountain from here. Follow Comus Road straight into Stronghold to the entrance of the mountain. There is parking, but it is extremely tight. So get here early.
From the Baltimore Beltway (Interstate 695): Take I–70 west approximately 38 miles to Frederick. From Frederick, follow I–270 south 9.5 miles to the Hyattstown exit (Exit 22). Get on Highway 109 (Old Hundred Road) and continue as above. *DeLorme: Maryland/Delaware Atlas & Gazetteer:* Page 55, C-6

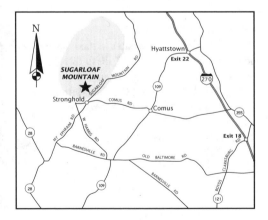

Sugarloaf Mountain can be seen in the background.

The Ride

Named after the sugar loaf by early pioneers because of its shape, Sugarloaf Mountain stands at an elevation of 1,282 feet, more than 800 feet above the Monocacy Valley. The mountain dominates the landscape for miles in all directions and has attracted its share of attention throughout history. The earliest known map of Sugarloaf was sketched by a Swiss explorer in 1707, when the American colonies were still part of Great Britain. General Edward Braddock marched past the mountain in 1755 during the French and Indian War. Later in American history, during the Civil War, the mountain was a matter of contention between the North and South, as its summit and overlooks provided ideal observation of the valleys below.

During the very early part of the twentieth century, the mountain's main peak and surrounding land was purchased by Gordon Strong, who in 1946 organized Stronghold, Incorporated, a nonprofit organization designed for "enjoyment and education in an appreciation of natural beauty." Strong's original plan was for a vacation retreat. He built the Strong Mansion atop the mountain and a number of homes at the foot of the mountain in what is now Stronghold. Since Strong's death in 1954,

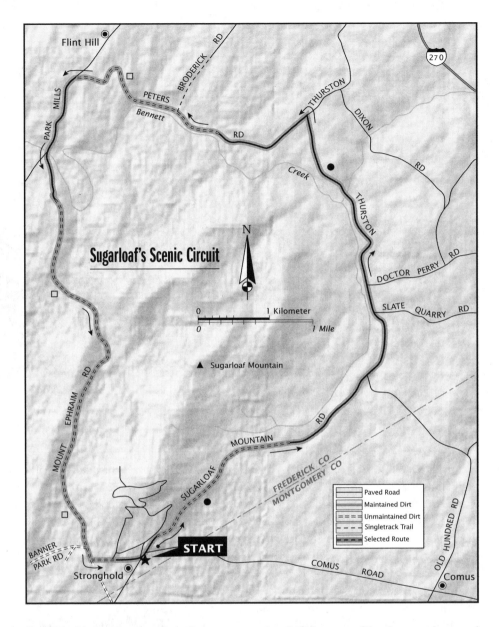

Flint Hill

270

BRODERICK RD

PETERS
Bennett
PARK MILLS
RD

THURSTON

DIXON
RD

Creek

THURSTON

DOCTOR PERRY RD

N

SLATE QUARRY RD

Sugarloaf's Scenic Circuit

0   1 Kilometer
0   1 Mile

▲ Sugarloaf Mountain

RD

MOUNTAIN

MOUNT EPHRAIM RD

SUGARLOAF

FREDERICK CO
MONTGOMERY CO

| Paved Road |
| Maintained Dirt |
| Unmaintained Dirt |
| Singletrack Trail |
| Selected Route |

BANNER PARK RD

START

OLD HUNDRED RD

Stronghold

COMUS ROAD

Comus

Stronghold, Inc. has continued to manage the 3,250 acres of land on and around Sugarloaf Mountain as a place of natural beauty and wildlife, with a commitment to maintaining its natural state.

This loop travels on both paved and unpaved roads. Sugarloaf Mountain is always looming above you as you pedal past magnificent horse farms and along the rush-

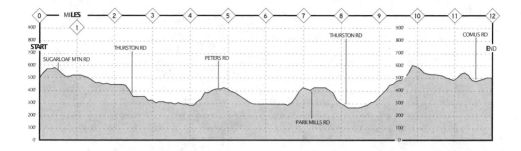

ing waters of Bennett Creek. This ride is not recommended for a regular road bike, since many roads are gravel and dirt. As you climb back over the mountain toward Stronghold on Mount Ephraim Road, all remnants of pavement disappear, and you are transported deep into a mountain forest.

Geologically speaking, Sugarloaf Mountain is what's called a monadnock. This is a hill or mountain that remains standing high above the surface after much of the surrounding land has eroded away. It took nearly 14 million years for Sugarloaf to look the way it does today.

This is a great ride for cyclists wanting the adventure and unique scenery often associated with riding off the beaten path but not interested in the severe challenges of singletrack trails twisting up and down the mountain slopes.

CASUALTY BY POPULAR DEMAND
In 1993, under the staff supervision of the Stronghold Corporation, groups of off-road cyclists, hikers, and Boy Scouts worked together to create a trail system that combined both forest roads and challenging singletrack. The result was a fantastic course ideal for mountain biking, hiking, and horseback riding. Unfortunately, the trail's popularity was far more than its narrow, twisting pathways could bear, as hundreds of cyclists each weekend saddled up and crowded its course. Land managers were forced to reassess the trail's design and concluded that, with parking spilling into nearby towns and the trail's capacity way overextended, limited access was the only answer. Currently, the Saddleback Trail (yellow blazed) is open to cyclists from June through October, Monday through Friday. It is not open to bikes on the weekends at any time of the year. While this may appear unfair and inconvenient to some, remember that Sugarloaf Mountain is a privately owned resource. Thankfully, the Stronghold Corporation is generous enough to allow the Saddleback Trail to remain open to cyclists at certain times.

Scenic back roads like this beat the Beltway any day.

Miles and Directions

0.0 **START** from the park entrance at the base of the mountain in Stronghold. Facing east, turn left on Sugarloaf Mountain Road. This road starts out paved, then turns to gravel after a quarter mile.

2.5 Turn left on Thurston Road (paved).

4.8 Turn hard left on Peters Road (becomes unpaved).

7.0 Turn left on Park Mills Road (paved).

7.7 Turn left on Mount Ephraim Road (unpaved).

11.5 Turn left on Comus Road (unpaved).

11.9 Arrive back at Stronghold. What a gorgeous ride!

Ride Information

Local Information
Tourism Council of Frederick County, Frederick, MD, (301) 663-8687

Local Events and Attractions
See Frederick County's online visitors' guide for links about local events and attractions: www.visitfrederick.org

Accommodations
Rocker Inn, Poolesville, MD (301) 973-3543

9 River Ride

This easygoing loop along the Potomac River connects two places that, at one time, signified an age when the ferry was the most convenient means across the river. The ride begins at Whites Ferry and travels south along flat dirt roads to Edwards Ferry, which quit operations in 1936. You'll head back to Whites Ferry along the C&O Canal, preserved now as a national historic park.

Start: Whites Ferry
Length: 10 miles
Approximate riding time: 1–1.5 hours
Difficulty: Easy; flat pedaling with no technical challenges
Trail type: Hard dirt (towpath); unpaved roads
Lay of the land: Hardwood scenery along the banks of the Potomac River
Land status: National historic park and public roadways
Nearest town: Poolseville, MD
Other trail users: Hikers, horseback riders, and automobiles
Trail contacts: C&O Canal headquarters (301) 739–4200
Schedule: Open year-round
Fees and permits: $3.00 per vehicle for ferry ($5.00 round-trip) or $.50 per bicycle
Maps: USGS maps: Waterford, VA, MD; Poolesville, VA, MD; Leesburg, VA, MD; Sterling, VA, MD
ADC maps: Montgomery County, MD

Getting There: Maryland—from the Capital Beltway (Interstate 495): Take Interstate 270 north and go 10.5 miles to State Highway 117 West. Turn left at the second stoplight on State Highway 124 (Quince Orchard Road). Go 2.8 miles on Quince Orchard Road, and then make a right at the stoplight on State Highway 28 (Darnestown Road). Bear left after 6 miles on State Highway 107 (Fisher Avenue, then Whites Ferry Road). Continue for 11.3 miles to Whites Ferry on the Potomac and park in the parking lot on the right. *DeLorme: Maryland/Delaware Atlas & Gazetteer:* Page 55, D-4
Northern Virginia—from the Capital Beltway (I-495): Take Exit 10, U.S. Highway 7 (Leesburg Pike), all the way west to Leesburg (22 miles). Just before Leesburg, take U.S. Highway 15 (James Monroe Highway) north. Go approximately 3.5 miles on U.S. Highway 15, then make a right turn on Whites Ferry Road. This will take you down to the ferry. You must pay the $3.00 toll and cross the river to park and begin the ride. *DeLorme: Maryland/Delaware Atlas & Gazetteer:* Page 55, D-4

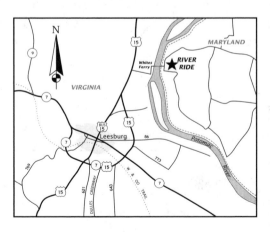

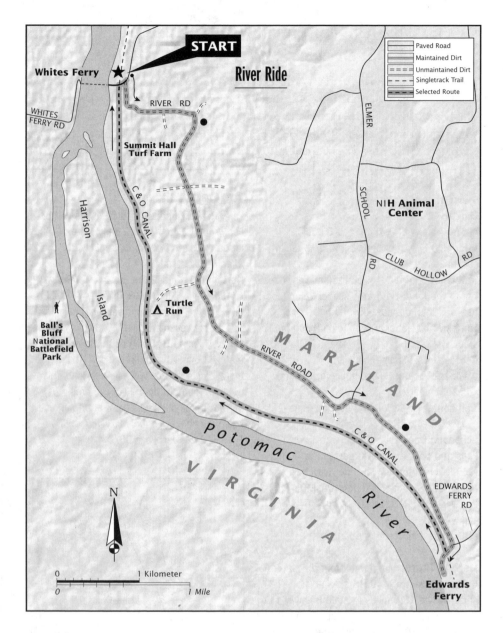

START

Whites Ferry

River Ride

RIVER RD

Summit Hall
Turf Farm

C & O CANAL

Harrison

Island

Ball's
Bluff
National
Battlefield
Park

Turtle
Run

WHITES
FERRY RD

ELMER

SCHOOL

NIH Animal
Center

CLUB HOLLOW RD

RD

RIVER ROAD

M A R Y L A N D

C & O CANAL

Potomac

VIRGINIA

River

EDWARDS
FERRY
RD

N

Edwards
Ferry

| Paved Road |
| Maintained Dirt |
| Unmaintained Dirt |
| Singletrack Trail |
| Selected Route |

0   1 Kilometer
0   1 Mile

The Ride

At one point, back in the 1700s, there were at least seven ferries carrying Loudoun County residents across the Potomac. Records of the county court show that by the end of the eighteenth century, not long after the signing of the Declaration of Independence, five ferries crossed the Potomac to connect the Maryland and Virginia shores. One of them was Edwards. Whites Ferry, formerly known as Conrad's Ferry, began operations in 1836, carrying horse-drawn wagons, merchants, and supplies from shore to shore. Later in the nineteenth century, Whites and Edwards Ferries served quite different purposes, however, and the results were often disastrous.

During the Civil War, both Union and Confederate troops used the ferries to carry troops back and forth across the Potomac. In one instance, on the night of October 20, 1861, Union troops under General Stone's command at Edwards Ferry and Whites Ferry reported a Confederate camp near Leesburg. In an attempt to intimidate the Confederates to leave the area, General Stone set in motion events that ultimately resulted in the Battle of Ball's Bluff (see chapter 29), costing the Union a severe and gruesome loss. Alternately, Confederate General Jubal A. Early, for whom the present ferryboat at Whites Ferry is named, used both Edwards Ferry and Whites Ferry in retreat after his daring attack on Washington in July 1864.

Today, Whites Ferry is the last of the ferries to carry customers across the Potomac, operating seven days a week from 6:00 A.M. to 11:00 P.M. In fact, it's the only place between Point of Rocks, Maryland, and the Capital Beltway to cross the river—a stretch of 40 miles.

As you ride back along the C&O Canal Towpath, be sure to notice Harrison Island on your left. During the Civil War, the island served as a temporary hospital to care for the Union's wounded soldiers after their dramatic loss at the battle on Ball's Bluff. One of the wounded taken to Harrison Island was a recent Harvard graduate and a future Supreme Court justice, First Lieutenant Oliver Wendell Holmes Jr. He was shot through the leg and the small of the back but was diagnosed on the island as "doing well."

This ride, rich in history, is meant for the lighter side of mountain biking, as it travels along flat dirt roads and the C&O Canal Towpath. You won't have to worry much about traffic and should enjoy pedaling past an enormous replica of what many home owners work a lifetime to achieve—a perfect lawn. The Summit Hall Turf Farm, along River Road, grows a magnificent 380-acre "lawn," carpeted in thick green zoysia, bluegrass, bent grass, and mixtures of blue and rye grass. The sod is then harvested and sent to area golf courses, local landscapers, and some very fortunate home owners.

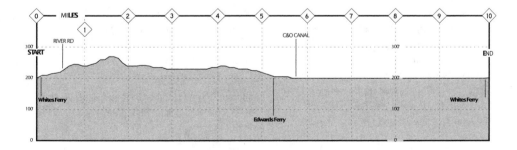

Ferryboats have been crossing the Potomac since the 1700s.

Miles and Directions

0.0 **START** at the Whites Ferry parking lot on the Maryland side of the Potomac River. Approximately 50 feet north of the parking lot, turn right off Whites Ferry Road on River Road (unpaved). This runs parallel to the C&O Canal Towpath to the right.

3.7 At the three-way intersection, continue right on River Road.

5.2 Turn right on Edwards Ferry Road. Cross over the C&O Canal and arrive at Edwards Ferry. Return along the C&O Towpath back to Whites Ferry.

10.0 Arrive at the Whites Ferry parking lot.

Ride Information

Local Information

Whites Ferry, Dickerson, MD, (301) 349-5200
www.vdest.com/dc/WhitesFerry
Summit Hall Turf Farm (301) 948-2900
Maryland County's Web site, with information
about local events and attractions:
www.cvbmontco.com
Montgomery County Visitors Bureau, Germantown, MD, (301) 428-9702
Loudoun Tourism Council (800) 752-6118

Local Events and Attractions

Leesburg Calendar of Events
www.leesburgonline.com
Waterford Homes Tour and Crafts Exhibit in
October, (540) 882-3085
www.waterfordva.org

Accommodations

Loudoun County Guild of Bed-and-Breakfasts
(800) 752-6118, www.vabb.com
Rocker Inn, Poolesville, MD, (301) 973-3543

Honorable Mentions

Western Maryland

Compiled here is an index of great rides in western Maryland that didn't make the A list this time around but deserve recognition. Check them out and let us know what you think. You may decide that one or more of these rides deserves higher status in future editions, or perhaps you may have a ride of your own that merits some attention.

A Swallow Falls State Park

Located in the far western panhandle of Maryland, 9 miles northwest of Oakland in Garrett State Forest. Although the park occupies only 257 acres of Garrett State Forest's 7,400 acres of land, visitors are treated to a 63-foot waterfall, spectacular scenery, nature trails, and the rapids of the Youghiogheny River. Cyclists will enjoy Swallow Falls's 11-mile round-trip trail system that connects the park's two sections, formed from old logging roads and rail lines. Mountain bikers and cross-country skiers enjoy the diverse terrain, from hard-packed doubletrack to rocky singletrack. Swallow Falls State Park has fishing, boating, unrestricted camping, winter sports, and a historic area. *DeLorme: Maryland/Delaware Atlas & Gazetteer:* Page 65, D-5

B Wisp Ski Area

Operating as a four-season resort for nearly forty years, Wisp hasn't always been as hospitable to vacationers and recreationalists as it is today. Fifty years ago, Wisp was a towering and treeless mound of earth known only as Marsh Mountain. The only activity it saw was a herd of cattle grazing its slopes. Today, Helmuth Heise, his wife, Evelyn, and several Garrett County businessmen can sit back and reflect on their successful efforts in transforming this area into a four-season vacation land. It continues to be one of the only continuously family-owned and -operated ski resorts in the country. Mountain bikers can hop on one of the chairlifts, go to the top, and ride down logging roads, ski trails, and rugged singletrack. There is a lift fee and a nominal admission fee. Stop by nearby High Mountain Sports to get a two-for-one coupon. *DeLorme: Maryland/Delaware Atlas & Gazetteer:* Page 65, C-5

C Whitetail Ski Resort

Whitetail is in Pennsylvania and therefore must have snuck its way into this book as a Washington/Baltimore area mountain bike hot spot. It's no secret, however, that when the weather turns warm and the snow melts away, Whitetail is transformed into one of the region's greatest mountain bike resorts. Fully equipped with a fleet of top-end mountain bike rentals, ski lifts to the top of Two Top Mountain, and singletrack trails all the way down and around, Whitetail has cultivated itself into a local hub for metropolitans looking for lots of legal and well-maintained singletrack. For those interested in a long weekend of mountain biking coupled with pampered lounging in the lodge, this is the most dedicated mountain bike resort in town. Whitetail Resort is located in Mercersburg, Pennsylvania, north of Hagerstown, Maryland, off Interstate 70. For more information, call (717) 328–9400. *DeLorme: Pennsylvania Atlas & Gazetteer:* Page 90, B-1

D Frederick Watershed

Just north of Frederick, Maryland, adjacent to Gambrill State Park, Frederick Watershed is a fantastic mountain bike playground. There are miles of unpaved forest roads winding all over Catoctin Mountain. All of them are perfectly suitable for off-road bikes. The terrain is very steep and rugged, but if you're heading toward Gambrill or the Catoctin Blue Trail anyway, take a small detour and check out the Frederick Watershed. *DeLorme: Maryland/Delaware Atlas & Gazetteer:* Page 72, C-2

Maryland Piedmont Region

Maryland Piedmont is the area framed by the foothills of the Blue Ridge Mountains and the Chesapeake Bay. By definition, a piedmont is an area formed or lying at the foot of a mountain or mountain range. Its proximity to the Chesapeake Bay and agricultural richness has made the Piedmont one of the most populated areas in Maryland. Encompassing the counties of Montgomery, Howard, and Baltimore, the Maryland Piedmont area has seen a tremendous amount of development in the last few years.

The development of the region has directly affected the areas where mountain bikers practice their sport. The increased demand placed by all trail users forced many park managers to close trails to cyclists. These closures were usually based on the erroneous idea that bicycles caused severe trail damage and erosion. Education, advocacy, and involvement by the cycling community has, in many places, changed that feeling, and today cycling is again allowed in many of the parks in the area.

To ensure that access to trails in these areas continues, Maryland fat-tire enthusiasts continue to be involved in advocacy, trail maintenance, and user education. Groups such as the Mid-Atlantic Off Road Enthusiasts (MORE) and the Maryland Association of Mountain Bike Operators (MAMBO) continue to gain access to previously closed trails and continue to build new sanctioned singletrack.

Cabin John Regional Park and Black Hill Regional Park were closed to bikes until 1997. MORE advocacy members challenged Montgomery County officials to open their trails to the mountain bike community. After demonstrating that cyclists were a responsible and valuable trail user group, MORE was able to convince the Montgomery County officials to open the parks on a trial basis for one year. The trial was a success, and the program is currently in place in other Montgomery County parks, including Little Bennett Regional Park. Today, cyclists in Maryland can enjoy creek-side trails at Cabin John and singletrack networks through the fields of Black Hill.

Another example of successful advocacy and user involvement exists in the network of trails at Schaeffer Farms. Located within county-leased farmlands in Gaithersburg, Schaeffer Farms is a network of superb trails built by mountain bikers, for mountain bikers. Park officials saw the need to create new trails for an increasingly large group of trail users. Although initially slated to be a mountain-bike-only trail network, Schaeffer Farms is enjoyed by hikers and equestrians alike.

The terrain and land in the piedmont plains of Maryland lends itself to some of the best mountain biking in the area. Although not mountainous, the Piedmont offers a tremendous mixture of plains and stream valleys that make mountain biking one of the region's most practiced activities. In addition, the trails in the area are also very popular equestrian and hiking destinations. The tremendous growth in the region has placed an immense demand on the trails in the Piedmont. However, active participation and education by the cycling community and its users has ensured that fat-tire enthusiasts continue to have access and enjoy the Piedmont trails.

10 Cabin John Regional Park

Located in Montgomery County, Maryland, Cabin John Regional Park is a great destination for any local mountain biker who can't get away to more remote locations. It's also great for the visitor looking for a quick ride close to the urban landscape. Recently opened to mountain biking, Cabin John offers a wide variety of rolling trails that descend and run parallel to Cabin John Creek. Its proximity to the Beltway; Rockville, Maryland; and the conveniences of Montgomery Mall make it the ideal getaway.

Start: From the parking lot adjacent to the Field 4–Westlake Drive entrance
Length: 10.9-mile out and back
Approximate riding time: 1.5–2.5 hours (depending on ability)
Difficulty: Easy to moderate
Trail surface: Singletrack, paved roads
Lay of the land: Rolling trails
Land status: State park
Nearest town: Bethesda, MD
Other trail users: Hikers, equestrians, and pets (on leashes)
Trail contacts: Cabin John Park manager's office, (301) 299-0024
Schedule: Varies. Call park manager's office directly for information
Fees and permits: None
Maps: USGS map: Rockville

Getting There: From Washington, D.C.: Take the Beltway (Interstate 495) to the Interstate 270 North split. Exit on Old Georgetown Road and head west. Turn right onto Democracy Boulevard. Immediately after Montgomery Mall, turn right onto West Lake Drive. Turn left after the second light, into Cabin John Regional Park. Turn right immediately after turning into the park. Follow the road to the last lot on the left; you should be able to see the trailhead sign as you park your car.
DeLorme: Maryland/Delaware Atlas & Gazetteer: Page 46, B-2

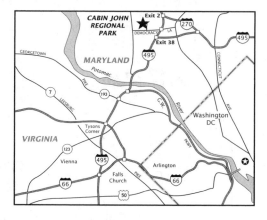

The Ride

Say the name Captain John several times. Continue saying the name long enough, and you'll begin to notice that *captain* slurs into *cabin*. At least that's what local folklore suggests. Rumor has it that the area was named after the famed British explorer Captain John Smith. Over time, however, the word *captain* simply evolved into *cabin*. As you read this guide, you'll notice Captain John Smith making several appearances. He was, by all standards, an accomplished man whose adventures and explorations helped shape the colonies.

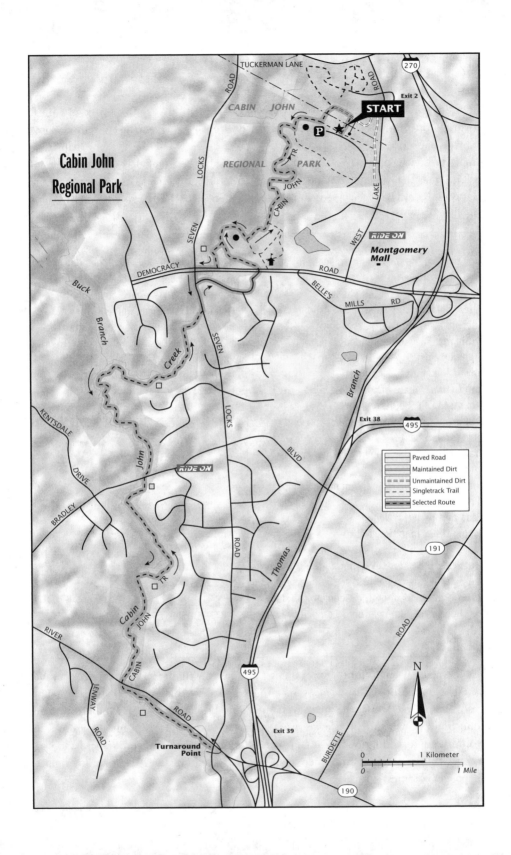

Cabin John
Regional Park

CABIN JOHN

REGIONAL PARK

TUCKERMAN LANE

START

Exit 2

270

ROAD

ROAD

TR

JOHN

CABIN

LOCKS

SEVEN

P

WEST LAKE

RIDE ON

Montgomery Mall

Buck

Branch

Creek

DEMOCRACY

ROAD

BELLE'S

MILLS RD

SEVEN

Branch

LOCKS

BLVD

Exit 38

495

John

KENTSDALE

DRIVE

RIDE ON

BRADLEY

Thomas

ROAD

191

Cabin

JOHN

TR

CABIN

RIVER

JENWAY ROAD

ROAD

495

Exit 39

BURDETTE ROAD

Turnaround Point

190

N

| Paved Road |
| Maintained Dirt |
| Unmaintained Dirt |
| Singletrack Trail |
| Selected Route |

0   1 Kilometer

0   1 Mile

After settling in Jamestown, Virginia, in the winter of 1607, Captain John Smith survived an ambush by native Algonkian Indians. He was captured and taken as prisoner to the chief of the tribal confederacy, Chief Powhatan. Impressed by Smith's confidence and determination, Powhatan interviewed his captive about his colonies and travels. The chief allowed Smith to participate in a ritual or trial. It was a test to determine his worth and courage. Painfully unaware of his fate, Smith endured and passed all the challenges placed upon him. With the help of Pocahontas, Powhatan's eleven-year-old daughter, Smith survived and was made a subordinate chief of the tribe. After four weeks of captivity, Smith left the tribe in friendship. He returned to the settlement of Jamestown, with the assistance of Native American guides he had befriended.

► **Until recently, mountain biking in many of Montgomery County's regional parks was prohibited.**

As a result of unrest, lack of supplies, and dissent within the colony, Smith left Jamestown to explore and map the Chesapeake Bay region. Because of his mapping endeavors within the region, the colonists were able to more easily expand their settlements.

To examine another historical moment within the area, we must enter the eighteenth century. It's 1776, and the colonists have declared their independence from England. Newly elected officials are taking office throughout the colonies and are quickly implementing unprecedented changes. In Maryland, of lesser import, but not to be diminished, Montgomery County is formed.

On August 31, 1776, Dr. Thomas Sprigg Wootton introduced a bill to divide Frederick County into three distinct areas: Frederick County, Washington County, and Montgomery County. The bill was passed on September 6, 1776, thus creating the first three counties to be established by elected officials in the United States of America.

In keeping with the popular sentiment of the time, the traditional naming convention for new counties was discarded. Instead of naming the newly established counties after Old World figures, two popular Americans of the time were selected, George Washington and Richard Montgomery.

It is in this area that Cabin John sits. Originally an agricultural community, Montgomery County has seen tremendous growth and is quickly becoming an important contributor to Maryland's economy. The federal government remains the largest

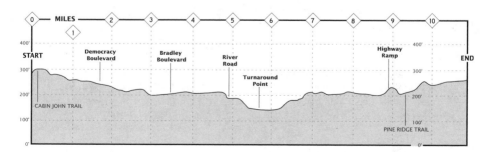

The trail runs parallel to Cabin John Creek.

employer in the city of Rockville, but the I–270 corridor has become a hotbed for high-technology firms. In fact, the agricultural lands that once defined this area have drastically dwindled in size because of the emerging growth of businesses and population. New urban developments pop up every day at an alarming rate, and that's exactly why this regional park is so important. Unlike neighboring counties to the north and west, Montgomery County's proximity to Washington, D.C., has made it one of the richest counties in the nation.

Until recently, mountain biking in many of Montgomery County's regional parks was prohibited. But thanks to the hard work of several volunteer members from MORE, the Mid-Atlantic Off-Road Enthusiasts, the county's lands are welcoming this sport.

Miles and Directions

0.0 START at the trailhead, marked by the trail map. Immediately after entering the trail, turn left. The trail is blazed blue. Follow Cabin John Trail markers to the power lines and turn left onto the gravel road. After a short descent on the power line trail, turn left at the marker for the Cabin John Trail. In less than a tenth of a mile, turn right and continue following the blue blazes.

0.38 Continue right at this intersection. Follow the arrow toward the Goose Neck Loop Trail. The trail is now blazed blue/yellow.

0.55 Turn right at this intersection. You are now on the Hawk Ridge Loop. Continue following the blue blazes.

0.95 After a brief singletrack descent, turn left and cross the small bridge. Continue following the trail parallel to the creek.

1.13 Bear sharply to the right at this intersection. Go over the small wooden bridge and continue following the blue blazes.

1.26 You have reached another Cabin John Trail sign. Turn right and continue toward the open field.

1.40 Turn right at this intersection. There is a brown marker with an orange arrow.

1.69 Continue to the right toward Democracy Boulevard. You return on the left branch.

1.79 You are now on Democracy Boulevard. Turn right, cross, and then turn left onto Seven Locks Road.

2.10 After riding a short distance on Seven Locks Road, the Cabin John Trail marker is on the right. Hop over the railing and continue on the trail to the right. The trail continues to be blazed blue and runs parallel to the creek.

3.45 Cross Bradley Boulevard. The trail continues on the other side.

4.80 Cross River Road. The trail continues directly on the other side and to the left. It's clearly marked by blue blazes. If you choose, this can be a shuttle point.

5.43 Turn around and backtrack.

8.76 You are back at Seven Locks. Cross it and turn left.

8.91 Shortly before you reach Democracy Boulevard, turn right onto the paved ramp heading uphill.

9.15 Turn left onto the paved driveway and continue uphill.

9.25 Turn left onto the singletrack. Two large white rocks mark the trail.

9.34 You are back on Democracy Boulevard. The park entrance is directly across the street. Cross Democracy Boulevard and turn left into the parking lot and ride to the far end and to a trail marker.

9.48 At the far end of the parking lot, enter the Pine Ridge Trail. An orange arrow marks the trail. Get ready for a great downhill.

9.65 Turn right and continue to backtrack to your car.

10.9 You are back at your car.

Ride Information

Local Information

City of Rockville, MD
www.ci.rockville.md.us/

Local Events and Attractions

City of Rockville, MD, events calendar:
www.ci.rockville.md.us/calendar/caleven.htm

Accommodations

Chevy Chase B&B, Chevy Chase, MD
(301) 656-5867

11 Black Hill Regional Park

Thanks to the efforts of local mountain bike advocates, the mountain bike community can now enjoy this previously off-limits area. Located in Montgomery County, Black Hill has a great network of singletrack that is bound to put a smile on an off-road cyclist's face. Without serious changes in elevation but with plenty of twists and turns, these trails will delight the casual rider as well as the more advanced mountain bike enthusiast time and time again.

Start: Little Seneca Lake, parking lot 5
Length: 9 miles
Approximate riding time: 1.5–2 hours
Difficulty: Easy to moderate
Trail surface: Mostly singletrack, rolling dirt trails, and some flat fields
Lay of the land: Typical Maryland piedmont and farmland surrounded by a fast-growing metropolis
Land status: Regional state park
Nearest town: Germantown, MD
Other trail users: Hikers and horseback riders

Trail contacts: Black Hill Regional Park Office, Boyds, MD, (301) 972–9396
MORE, www.more-mtb.org
Schedule: March through October, 6:00 A.M. to sunset; November through February, 7:00 A.M. to sunset; Park closed: Thanksgiving, Christmas, and New Year's Day
Fees and permits: None
Maps: USGS map: Germantown, MD

Getting There:
From the Capital Beltway (Interstate 495): Take Interstate 270 north and exit on State Highway 118 East. After approximately one-half mile on State Highway 118, turn left on State Highway 355 North. Follow State Highway 355 and turn left on West Old Baltimore Road. Follow this road for 1.5 miles to the park entrance and turn left on Lake Ridge Drive. Follow Lake Ridge Drive to parking lot 5, close to the rest rooms (far end) overlooking Little Seneca Lake. *DeLorme: Maryland/Delaware Atlas & Gazetteer:* Page 56, D-1
Public Transportation: Take the METRO Red Line to Shady Grove. Transfer to Ride-On bus 55 (Dorsey Mill) to the intersection of Highway 355 and Ridge Road. From the bus stop, head north on Highway 355 and turn left on West Old Baltimore Road. Cross over I–270 and pick up the ride at mile 3.3 at the Field Crest Spur trailhead on the left.

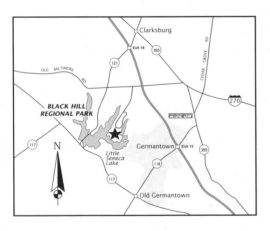

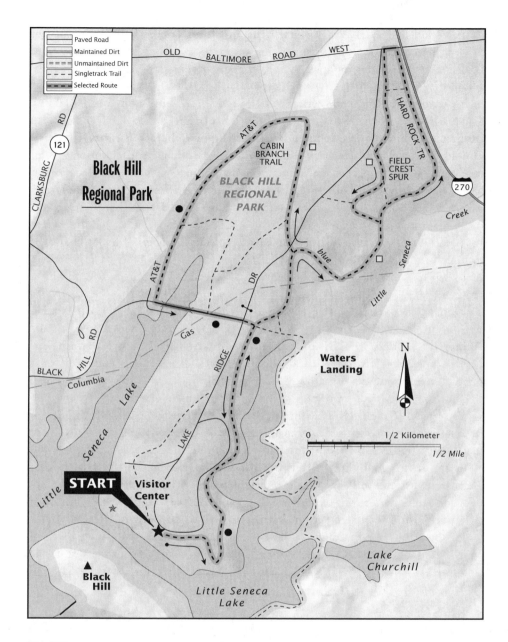

Map Legend

- Paved Road
- Maintained Dirt
- Unmaintained Dirt
- Singletrack Trail
- Selected Route

Black Hill Regional Park

OLD BALTIMORE ROAD WEST

121

CLARKSBURG RD

AT&T

CABIN BRANCH TRAIL

BLACK HILL REGIONAL PARK

HARD ROCK TR

FIELD CREST SPUR

270

Creek

AT&T

DR

blue

Seneca

Little

RIDGE

Gas

Little Seneca Lake

BLACK HILL RD

Columbia

Waters Landing

N

0 — 1/2 Kilometer
0 — 1/2 Mile

START

Visitor Center

Lake Churchill

Black Hill

Little Seneca Lake

The Ride

Montgomery County, the most populated county in Maryland, was established by state convention in 1776 and functioned under the county commission system until 1948. At that time, voters adopted a charter giving the county home rule with a council manager form of government. Named for Revolutionary War general Richard Montgomery, the county is as diverse as its parks and people.

Black Hill Regional Park, a popular area for all sorts of recreation, is situated in the northern part of Montgomery County, near Gaithersburg and Germantown. Black Hill is home to mountain biking, hiking, horseback riding, boating, fishing, and more.

Upon entering the park, visitors are treated to an outstanding view of Little Seneca Lake. The lake was built through the partnership of the Maryland National Park and Planning Commission and the Washington Suburban Sanitary Commission. Its design marked it as a dual-purpose lake, providing both recreation and an emergency water supply for the Washington metropolitan area. After a ride, consider having a picnic on the shores overlooking the lake or perhaps renting a boat ($4.75 per hour for a rowboat or canoe; $2.00 per person for pontoon boat rides).

In the summertime, expect the lake to be full of sailboats, canoes, and fishermen. In the fall, if you're here at the right time (early to mid-October), you may be treated to some of the area's most impressive fall colors. When you're ready to leave, take a short trip to Germantown and Olde Town Gaithersburg, two of Maryland's most prosperous little cities.

Unlike many areas of Maryland, the Germantown/Gaithersburg area doesn't show much evidence of early Indian settlements. However, its proximity to the Potomac and Monocacy Rivers, as well as Seneca Creek, made this area a very popular location for Native American living. It is believed that after the annual spring floods, Indians from the Piscataway, Susquehannock, and Seneca tribes traveled here to hunt roaming herds of bison and other large animals trapped by the swollen waters. Many of the trails by which the Native Americans traveled to reach this hunting ground later became the same routes and roadways that we use today, including Clopper Road and State Highways 28, 118, and 355.

In the early to mid-1800s, several German immigrants, most of whom were from German settlements in Pennsylvania, moved down to this area of Maryland and settled along the intersections of Clopper Road and the Darnestown/Neelsville Road (Highway 118). This settlement quickly became known as Germantown.

At about the same time, just south of Germantown, many of the younger sons of Maryland's Chesapeake Bay settlers began establishing themselves in the vast, fertile land of Montgomery County. One of the earliest settlements in this area—dating to

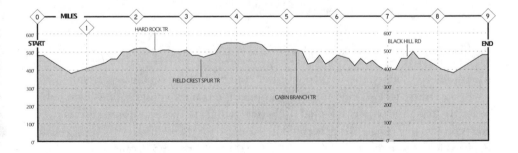

1802—was known as Forest Oak, named for the landmark tree still standing near the railroad crossing on Frederick Avenue. Today this area is called Gaithersburg. In 1802, a young settler named Benjamin Gaither built his house on this fertile land, unknowingly giving his name to the town.

With the arrival of the railroad and the invention of the automobile, businesses in Germantown and Gaithersburg began to prosper. Farmers planted and harvested more crops, easily transporting them to other markets throughout the area. Farmers no longer had to make several trips to town. With a newly built steam mill, they could make a single trip to mill their grains, purchase supplies, and market their products all by railroad. The railroad also brought people in from Washington. Soon it became fashionable to escape to the country, and many large estates were built.

Today, Germantown and Gaithersburg are prosperous and growing communities with combined populations reaching nearly one million. In the last couple of decades, both Gaithersburg and Germantown have seen a major boom in development. Its proximity to Washington, D.C., and Frederick, Maryland, has made this part of Montgomery County an attractive business location as well as a residential getaway. As you travel to Black Hill Regional Park, you can't help but witness the amount of new development along I–270's "Technology Corridor." You will be pleasantly surprised to find Black Hill Regional Park (among others) an oasis in the middle of this massive development. Although the lake did not exist when the first settlers came to the area, the beauty, abundance of wildlife, and thick forests in the park give you a glimpse and a sampling of this area's historic past.

Miles and Directions

0.0   **START** at parking lot 5. Ride away from the lake toward the rest rooms, following the hiker/biker sign to the paved trail.

0.28 Turn right on the paved trail at the Parcourse Fitness Circuit sign.

0.62 Turn right on the unpaved trail immediately after the ring station of the Parcourse Fitness section.

1.0   Continue straight at this small trail intersection. At this point you should be traveling parallel to Lake Ridge Drive.

1.5   Reach the intersection with the forest service road. Continue straight. If you turn right, you will head toward the Waters Landing Housing Community.

1.6   Turn left at this intersection and head uphill.

1.7   Cross the underground gas lines and continue straight.

1.9   At this trail intersection, bear right. This trail is blazed with blue diamonds and white letters. Make a wide U turn and head uphill. You are now riding in the opposite direction, parallel to the previous trail.

2.3   Cross the forest service road and continue straight on the Hard Rock Trail. Reach a field immediately after this intersection. Continue straight.

2.5   Turn right into the woods at the Hard Rock Trail pylon.

2.7 You can hear traffic on I-270. Bear right at this intersection and continue toward I-270. A fun, twisty, singletrack descent awaits.

2.9 Cross the creek and continue paralleling I-270.

3.3 Reach the intersection of I-270 and West Old Baltimore Road. Turn left on West Old Baltimore Road and head up the hill for approximately one-tenth of a mile. Look for the Field Crest Spur trailhead on your left.

3.6 Bear right and follow the doubletrack to the right.

3.7 Turn left and head back toward Hard Rock Trail.

3.8 Turn right on the singletrack into the woods.

4.3 Turn right at this intersection. If you wish, turn left and do the 1.5-mile loop (starting from marker 2.7) all over again.

4.5 Reach the field again. Continue straight through the grass.

4.6 Turn left at the Hill Crest pylon and continue riding through the grass.

4.7 Turn left into the woods (not the grass trail) along the doubletrack. This trail is blazed blue with white letters.

4.8 Turn right and head up the trail that you were on earlier in the ride.

5.2 Turn right and cross Lake Ridge Drive. Follow the trailhead marked "Cabin Branch Trail" on the other side of the road. Get ready for a great descent. Continue straight on this trail.

5.9 Turn left on the AT&T right-of-way (marked with orange pylons).

6.7 Continue straight, heading up the AT&T right-of-way. In the summertime, this trail is flanked on both sides with colorful wildflowers.

6.9 View of Little Seneca Lake.

7.1 Turn left on Black Hill Road.

7.4 Cross Lake Ridge Drive, then head straight through the yellow gate into the woods along the forest service road.

7.5 Turn right at this intersection. You should now be back on the trail you first started on.

8.5 Turn left on the paved trail.

8.8 Turn left at the paved trail intersection.

9.0 Reach the parking lot.

Ride Information

Local Information

Montgomery County Tourism
www.cvbmontco.com
Montgomery County Visitors Bureau
Germantown, MD, (301) 428-9702

Local Events and Attractions

The Official Montgomery County Web site:
www.co.mo.md.us

Accommodations

Rocker Inn, Poolesville, MD, (301) 973-7543
There are several hotels and motels along I-270 and in Gaithersburg.

12 Schaeffer Farms

These trails are a perfect example of mountain bike advocacy at work. A group of dedicated mountain bikers approached Maryland's Department of Natural Resources in hopes of gaining access to some nearby trails previously off-limits to bikes. The DNR went one step further and offered to build a new system of trails altogether in the Schaeffer Farms area. Today there are more than 12 miles of accessible singletrack through Schaeffer Farms' rolling fields and forests.

Start: The staging area
Length: 3.7 miles
Approximate riding time: .5–1 hour
Difficulty: Easy to moderate
Trail surface: Singletrack
Lay of the land: Rolling singletrack through farm fields and forest

Land status: State park
Nearest town: Germantown, MD
Other trail users: Equestrians and hikers
Trail contacts: MORE: (703) 502-0359
more@cycling.org or www.more-mtb.org
Schedule: Open daily, from dawn till dusk, year-round
Fees and permits: None
Maps: USGS map: Germantown, MD
ADC map: Montgomery County, MD

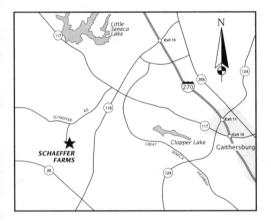

Getting There: From the Capital Beltway (Interstate 495): Take Interstate 270 north to State Highway 117 West (Clopper Road). Go approximately 4.5 miles along Clopper Road. Just past the eighth light at State Highway 118 (Darnestown-Germantown Road), turn left on Schaeffer Road. Follow Schaeffer Road for 2 miles, then turn left at Black Burn Farm. Follow the "Trail Parking" sign to the trailhead. *DeLorme: Maryland/Delaware Atlas & Gazetteer:* Page 56, D-1

The Ride

Once again, the efforts of a few individuals pay off for everyone. MORE members Dave McGill and Dave Skull achieved what few have been able to do in Montgomery County, Maryland, since mountain biking became popular—blaze and build new legal mountain bike trails. Thanks to their efforts and those of many other active mountain bikers, a steady series of new trails have been built in and adjacent to Seneca Creek State Park.

Schaeffer Farms, near Germantown (northern Montgomery County), is within the boundaries of Seneca Creek State Park (see Ride 13). This area is part of a stream

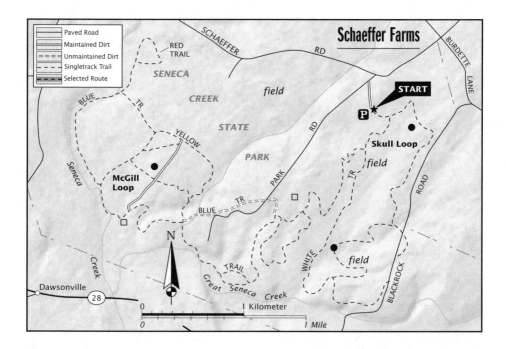

valley that extends approximately 12 miles along Seneca Creek. These new trails are located primarily on a portion of land leased by the county to local farmers, who use it to grow corn and a variety of other vegetables.

For some time, an adjacent tract of nearly 2,000 acres lay undeveloped and overgrown. Today, the 4-mile white-blazed trail (unofficially the Skull Loop) and the longer yellow-blazed trail (unofficially the McGill Loop) are complete. Extensions to both these trails, including the 2-mile Blue Trail, the nearly 1-mile Red Trail, and other trails, are still under construction. When all is said and done, Schaeffer Farms will have more than 15 miles of new singletrack for cyclists to enjoy. MORE's trail construction and maintenance efforts in this park and within Fountainhead Regional Park (see Ride 37) earned them IMBA's 1996 Model Program Award.

Park officials initially wanted the trails to be exclusive to mountain bikes but were persuaded by trail organizers to keep the area open to everyone, making it a multiuse trail system. Equestrians, hikers, and mountain bikers alike are welcome and find it perfect for whatever their activity is.

Your ride begins adjacent to the Black Burn Farm in the trail staging area. The trail is clearly marked with a brown pylon and an IMBA trail etiquette sign. Continue straight on some tight singletrack, then bear left at the first intersection. The right fork will give you access to the other loops in the park. Continue through the next section, twisting up and down; it's a roller-coaster-like trail filled with surprises. It becomes obvious once you're on this trail that it was built by mountain bikers for mountain bikers.

The corn can get pretty high on the McGill Loop.

After a series of small creek crossings, you will begin the first of a handful of short climbs. A quarter of a mile later, turn left into the woods onto the singletrack. Follow the white blazes for approximately 1 mile. At mile marker 2.3, cross the fire road and enter into the woods and through the grove of pines.

Shortly after, turn right and ride adjacent to the cornfield. If you manage to hit the trail at the right time of year, when the corn is high and the vegetation is thick, it may appear that you're in a corn stalk tunnel. Don't give in to temptation. Leave the corn alone. There is plenty of sweet corn at the local vegetable stands.

Continue down through a series of switchbacks (be careful, yours truly biffed at the bottom of the last switchback right into the creek). After crossing the creek, turn left and continue following the white blazes. The last half mile is on a flat twisty section of singletrack full of fun log jumps and bunny hops. Exactly 3.7 miles later, you're back where you parked. Now turn around and do the whole ride in the opposite direction. You know what they say: "It's a whole new trail in the opposite direction." This trail has all the makings of a classic mountain bike route. Its curves and whoop-de-doos make it a lot of fun. What it lacks in length is easily made up in challenging terrain. If you're interested in helping to build new trails like this one, contact your local mountain bike club and get involved.

▶ Your ride begins adjacent to the Black Burn Farm in the trail staging area. The trail is clearly marked with a brown pylon and an IMBA trail etiquette sign. Continue straight on some tight singletrack, then bear left at the first intersection.

Miles and Directions

Skull Loop: White blazes—3.7 miles of pure singletrack. The trail is very well marked and maintained.

McGill Loop: Yellow blazes—8.7 miles through the woods and fields of Schaeffer Farms. This loop is much like the Skull Loop, but longer.

Blue Loop: Blue blazes—This loop is accessible via the McGill Loop. Expect to find more singletrack through the woods and fields. The best time to ride this loop is when the corn is high. Experience field riding at its best.

Ride Information

Local Information

Maryland County's Web site, with information about local events and attractions: www.cvbmontco.com
Montgomery County Visitors Bureau Germantown, MD, (301) 428-9702

Local Events and Attractions

Montgomery County's official Web site with local information: www.co.mo.md.us

Accommodations

Gaithersburg Hospitality Bed & Breakfast Gaithersburg, MD, (301) 977-7377
Rocker Inn, Poolesville, MD, (301) 973–3543

In Addition

Maryland Census Statistics

If you're interested in Maryland, facts and figures from the 2000 U.S. Census provide a little insight into what each of the state's largest towns and cities are all about.

- Baltimore (pop. 651,154). Seaport on Patapsco River; historic and industrial city; automobile assembly; metals; chemicals; printing; clothing; shipping, insurance, and financial center; Fort McHenry; Washington Monument; Johns Hopkins University.
- Rockville (pop. 47,388). Residential city; biomedical technology; computer science; telecommunications; grave of F. Scott Fitzgerald; Strathmore Hall Arts Center; Montgomery College.
- Frederick (pop. 52,767). Industrial city in farm area; electronics and communications; biological products; air-conditioning equipment; clothing; cancer research; Barbara Fritchie House and Museum; Hood College.
- Gaithersburg (pop. 39,542). Suburb of Washington, D.C.; center for research and development; biomedical technology; computer science; telecommunications; Seneca Creek State Recreational Area nearby.
- Bowie (pop. 37,589). Residential and cultural area; International Renaissance Center; University of Maryland Science and Technology Center; Bowie State College.
- Hagerstown (pop. 36,687). Industrial and transportation hub of western Maryland; engines and transmissions; industrial machinery; printing; travel trailers; apparel; credit-card processing; Jonathan Hager House; Hagerstown Junior College.
- Annapolis (pop. 35,838). State capital on Severn River; communications; electronic engineering services; insurance; seafood processing; boat building; Maryland State House; United States Naval Academy; St. John's College.
- Cumberland (pop. 21,518). Industrial center of western Maryland; fine printing papers; blankets; clothing; boats; plastic containers; testing and production of guided missile equipment; Chesapeake and Ohio Canal National Historic Park; History House; George Washington's headquarters.
- College Park (pop. 21,927). Suburb of Washington, D.C.; communications equipment; engineering, architectural, and surveying services; main campus of the University of Maryland.
- Greenbelt (pop. 21,096). Suburb of Washington, D.C.
- Large unincorporated communities, suburbs of Baltimore and Washington, D.C., include: Silver Spring (pop. 76,046); Dundalk (pop. 65,800); Bethesda (pop. 62,936); Columbia (pop. 75,883); Towson (pop. 49,445); Wheaton-Glenmont (pop. 53,720); Aspen Hill (pop. 45,494); Essex (pop. 40,872); and Glen Burnie (pop. 37,305).

13 Seneca Creek State Park

Seneca Creek State Park is located in northern Montgomery County. The trails in this park are challenging and well maintained and are certain to satisfy the most demanding mountain biker. Beautiful vistas of the lake and historical points of interest along the trails will keep you both interested and educated as you pedal along.

Start: Clopper Lake boat center

Length: 5 miles

Approximate riding time: .5–1 hour

Difficulty: Easy to moderate due to relatively flat terrain with rooty and tight singletrack

Trail surface: Singletrack

Lay of the land: Wooded terrain and open fields surrounding Clopper Lake

Land status: State park

Nearest city: Gaithersburg, MD

Other trail users: Hikers, horseback riders, and anglers

Trail contacts: Maryland Forest, Park, and Wildlife Service, (301) 924–2127; Seneca Creek State Park, (301) 924–2127 www.dnr.state.md.us/publiclands/central/seneca.html

Schedule: Open every day April through September, 8:00 A.M. to dusk; October through March, 10:00 A.M. to dusk

Fees and permits: Weekdays are free; $1.00 per person—May through September on weekends

Maps: USGS maps: Germantown, MD; Gaithersburg, MD

ADC map: Montgomery County road map; Seneca Creek State Park trail map

Getting There: From the Capital Beltway (Interstate 495): Take Interstate 270 north toward Frederick. Just after passing through Gaithersburg on I-270, take the exit for State

Highway 124 (Orchard Road) to Darnesville. Follow Route 124 west one-half mile, then turn right on State Highway 117 (Clopper Road). Go 1.5 miles on Clopper Road to the entrance to Seneca Creek State Park on the left. Follow the entrance road into the park. You may park at any of the lots available, including the visitor center lot, the first stop on the right. You may also park at the boat center. Driving a car through the main gate may cost you an entrance fee of a couple of dollars.

DeLorme: Maryland/Delaware Atlas & Gazetteer: Page 56, D-2

Public Transportation: Take the METRO Red Line to Shady Grove Station. Transfer to Ride-On bus 61 to the Seneca Creek State Park entrance on Clopper Road. Follow the entrance road to the boat center.

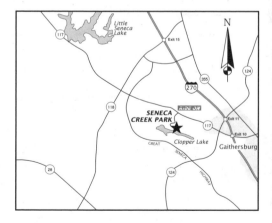

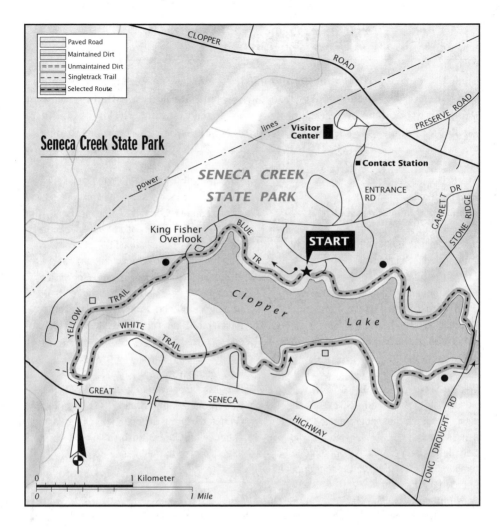

Seneca Creek State Park

Legend:
- Paved Road
- Maintained Dirt
- Unmaintained Dirt
- Singletrack Trail
- Selected Route

SENECA CREEK STATE PARK

Visitor Center

Contact Station

ENTRANCE RD

King Fisher Overlook

BLUE TR

START

Clopper Lake

YELLOW TRAIL

WHITE TRAIL

GREAT SENECA HIGHWAY

LONG DROUGHT RD

GARRETT DR

STONE RIDGE

PRESERVE ROAD

CLOPPER ROAD

power lines

N

0   1 Kilometer
0   1 Mile

The Ride

Here's a short but challenging ride around Seneca Creek State Park's Clopper Lake, taking you along tricky singletrack trails, through undeveloped natural areas, across open fields, along the lake's shores, and past evidence of times long past.

You'll begin the ride following the Lake Shore Trail, which crosses old fields and skirts the lake's shoreline. In the spring and summer, these fields are filled with colorful wildflowers that give way in the fall to thick, golden sage grass. Just before the dam, you'll be treated to a spectacular view of the lake from King Fisher Overlook. The trail quickly descends across the park road and follows Long Draught Branch, winding up, down, and around beneath a dense canopy of gray birch before crossing the wooded boardwalk to Mink Hollow Trail. Seneca Creek's longest developed trail, Mink Hollow, travels through pine groves and habitats of local wildlife, including white-tailed deer. Be careful once you begin the challenging ride along the undeveloped trail edging the lake. This trail can be tricky and challenging, as exposed roots, steep inclines, occasional flooding, and some quick descents may trip you up if you're not focused.

> ▶ While Seneca Creek Park extends nearly 13 miles from Gaithersburg south to the Potomac, only this northern section around Clopper Lake is developed for recreation.

While Seneca Creek Park extends nearly 13 miles from Gaithersburg south to the Potomac, only this northern section around Clopper Lake is developed for recreation. The lake itself is relatively new, created by damming Long Draught Branch. However, the name Clopper has a rich history in this area, dating back to the early 1800s when Francis C. Clopper, a successful tobacco merchant from Philadelphia, purchased more than 540 acres and an existing mill on Seneca Creek. The mill's most prosperous years were between 1830 and 1880, during which time Francis Clopper farmed the land and raised his family. The land remained in the hands of four generations of Clopper's descendants until 1955, when the state purchased it and added the land to Seneca Creek State Park.

Throughout the park there is evidence of this past: abandoned farms and old meadows now covered by new growth, traces of many of Clopper's old mills, and many of Clopper's old farm lanes. Mill ruins can still be seen from the intersection of Clopper Road and Waring Station Road, just west of the park entrance, and traces of the Clopper home are evident near the visitor center.

Be aware, as always, that many other outdoor enthusiasts share these same trails. Always yield the right-of-way to any other trail users, and ride cautiously, as the trails have many hidden turns and difficult negotiations.

Miles and Directions

0.0 START at Clopper Lake's boat center (soda machines available). Ride west to the end of the circular drive and go straight into the grass on the other side. Follow Lake Shore Trail (blue) signs.

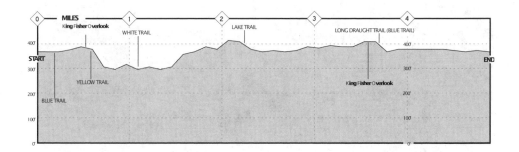

You and your riding companion will have plenty of fun at Seneca Creek.

0.3 Lake Shore Trail (blue) drops you into an open field. On the other side of this field, you will notice the blue trailhead marker. Cross the field and continue on Lake Shore Trail. To the left is the dam.

0.5 Lake Shore Trail (blue) brings you right up to King Fisher Overlook. You can catch a nice view of the lake from here. Follow the remainder of the blue-blazed trail into the woods, at the back of the circular drive. Go down the little hill through the woods and immediately cross the road.

0.55 Long Draught Trail (yellow) begins catty-corner to where the Blue Trail ends.

1.1 Turn left on Mink Hollow Trail (white).

1.2 Bear left, continuing on Mink Hollow Trail (white) over a narrow boardwalk, crossing the creek.

1.8 Cross the park road. Continue straight on the White Trail.

2.2 Mink Hollow Trail (white) comes to the lake. Turn right, following the trail around the lake.

3.4 This trail zips up on Long Draught Road. Cross Long Draught Road on the asphalt path. Once you're across the bridge, turn left through the guard rail and back on the trail around the lake.

3.7 This trail drops you down on a flat gravel path. Turn right. A left takes you to a dead end at the lake. Stay on this gravel path only about 20 feet. Then turn left across the creek to hook up with the path that continues to follow the perimeter of the lake.

4.3 Turn left, crossing over a little wooden bridge at the end of the alcove. Continue following the trail.

4.7 Arrive at the boat center and grab a soda from the soda machine. What a ride!

Ride Information

Local Information

Montgomery County's Web site, with local information: www.cvbmontco.com
Montgomery County Visitors Bureau
Germantown, MD, (301) 428–9702

Local Events and Attractions

Montgomery County's official Web site:
www.co.mo.md.us

Accommodations

Gaithersburg Hospitality Bed & Breakfast
Gaithersburg, MD, (301) 977–7377

14 Patapsco Valley State Park: McKeldin Area

Located in the southeastern corner of Carroll County at the confluence of the Patapsco River's north and south branches, the McKeldin area of Patapsco Valley State Park is best known for its rolling, wooded terrain, smooth singletrack, log piles, river crossings, and several hours' worth of great riding. While this area can become rather crowded with hikers and equestrians, especially on weekends, there are plenty of trails on which to ride, especially if you explore the trails across the river.

Start: Switchback Trail trailhead
Length: 6.8 miles of multiuse trails
Approximate riding time: 1-2 hours
Difficulty: Easy to moderate
Trail surface: Smooth singletrack and double-track
Lay of the land: Rolling, wooded terrain in the Patapsco River Valley
Land status: State park
Nearest town: Ellicott City, MD

Other trail users: Hikers and equestrians
Trail contacts: Patapsco Valley State Park headquarters, (410) 461-5005
Twenty-four-hour emergency number (410) 461-0050, TDD (301) 974-3683
Schedule: Open from 9:00 A.M. to sunset
Fees and permits: $2.00 on weekends and holidays
Maps: USGS map: Sykesville, MD
ADC maps: Carroll County, Baltimore County road maps; Patapsco Valley State Park trail map

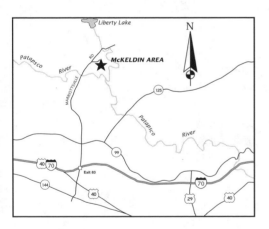

Getting There: From the Baltimore Beltway (Interstate 695): Take Interstate 70 west. Follow I-70 west for 8.5 miles to Exit 83 (Marriottsville Road North). Follow Marriottsville Road North for 4 miles, passing through Marriottsville. The McKeldin area entrance road is on the right. Turn right on the entrance road and follow it uphill to the parking area. *DeLorme: Maryland/Delaware Atlas & Gazetteer:* Page 57, A-5

The Ride

The McKeldin area of Patapsco Valley State Park is a perfect place for beginning to intermediate riders looking to hone their skills on hilly singletrack or to pedal peacefully along the scenic Patapsco River. Advanced riders will also enjoy the nearly 7 miles of singletrack within the park and will be thrilled to explore dozens of trails on the other side of the river.

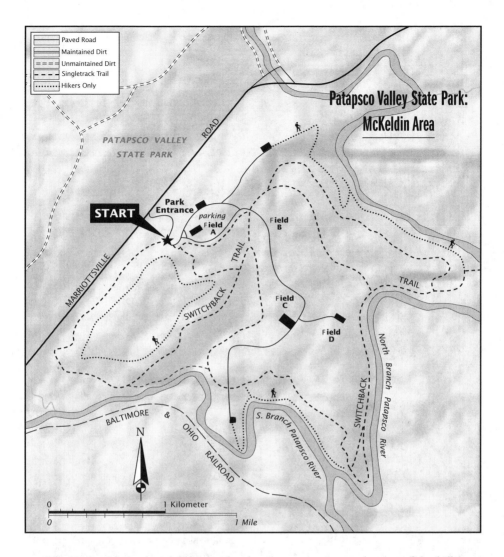

Paved Road
Maintained Dirt
Unmaintained Dirt
Singletrack Trail
Hikers Only

PATAPSCO VALLEY STATE PARK

ROAD

START

Park Entrance

parking
Field A

Field B

MARRIOTTSVILLE

SWITCHBACK TRAIL

Field C

Field D

TRAIL

SWITCHBACK

North Branch Patapsco River

BALTIMORE & OHIO RAILROAD

S. Branch Patapsco River

N

0   1 Kilometer
0   1 Mile

    The main ride in the park begins by the contact station at the top of the hill near the entrance to the park. It is a well-maintained, packed dirt and gravel trail called the Switchback Trail. Along the way, serene forested surroundings isolate you from the daily grind and hectic world of the Washington–Baltimore area, transporting you deep into a peaceful wilderness. Once you reach the picturesque south branch of the Patapsco River, this riverside trail turns into fun and challenging singletrack, rugged yet well maintained. The northernmost part of Switchback Trail becomes a hikers-only trail, but cyclists can continue a loop back toward the contact station where they parked by following the Plantation Trail. The Plantation Trail is steep, running along one of the McKeldin area's highest ridges.

The Switchback Trail takes you along the picturesque south branch of the Patasco River.

MARYLAND'S RIVERS

Formed by the junction of the north and south branches west of Baltimore, the Patapsco River flows southeast for 65 miles to the Chesapeake Bay.

Maryland's longest river is the Potomac, flowing east along the state's southern border. The primary eastward-flowing rivers north of the Potomac are the Patuxent, Severn, Patapsco, and Susquehanna. Each of these rivers, and most of those on the Eastern Shore, enter the Chesapeake Bay.

The Potomac River has its origins in northeast West Virginia, flowing nearly 285 miles along the Virginia–Maryland border into the Chesapeake Bay. It is navigable for large ships as far as Washington, D.C.

Patapsco State Park's McKeldin area is situated at the junction of Carroll County, Howard County, and Baltimore County, on the edge of Maryland's Coastal Plain and its Piedmont Plateau. The Piedmont is a rolling upland, about 40 miles in width, and includes the Frederick Valley, which is drained by the Monocacy River.

The McKeldin area is a unique stop in Patapsco Valley State Park. It's nudged into the southeast corner of Carroll County, where the north and the south branches of the Patapsco River converge. Scenic Liberty Lake, one of Baltimore's primary water supplies, fills the valley just north of McKeldin. Damming in the north branch created Liberty Lake, less than 1 mile from Switchback Trail. During late fall and winter, cyclists can enjoy a picturesque view of the lake at Liberty Dam Overlook, located at the northern end of Switchback Trail.

Switchback Trail is open to hikers, bikers, and equestrians alike and is quite popular throughout the year. Fortunately, the trail's design is well suited for all those wishing to enjoy its delightful scenery and can accommodate them well. However, please be very cautious when riding along the same trails as horseback riders. Remember also to smile and be courteous to all the hikers who are also there to enjoy the spoils of nature that the McKeldin area has to offer.

Miles and Directions

There's really not much to the directions for this ride, since cyclists can ride on any one of three multiuse trails in the park. The Switchback Trail (4 miles) is the primary trail through the park for cyclists, equestrians, and hikers, but it is closed to bikes at the northernmost section. So that cyclists don't have to turn around and go back the way they came, the park has opened the Plantation Trail (1.4 miles) to bikes. Cyclists can loop back on this trail through the northern part of the park and head back to where they parked. The Plantation Trail is pretty steep, so bring some climbing legs with you. One other trail open to cyclists is Tall Poplar Trail (1.4 miles). This trail is accessed from Shelter 576, across the road from the basketball courts. Tall Poplar Trail has some moderately steep sections and connects to the Switchback so that riding singletrack can go uninterrupted.

For explorers looking for more trails than can be found within the park's boundaries, start from the parking lot adjacent to the railroad tracks along Marriottsville Road and turn left onto Marriottsville Road. You'll cross two bridges and should notice the trailhead on the right. Miles and miles of trails wait for eager trail junkies, with river crossings, log piles, hills, a rock quarry, and a day's worth of singletrack.

Ride Information

Accommodations

Oak & Apple Bed & Breakfast of Distinction
Oakland, MD, (301) 334-9265
Deer Park Inn, Oakland, MD, (301) 334-2308
Red Run Inn, Oakland, MD, (301) 387-6606

15 Patapsco Valley State Park: Glen Artney/Avalon/ Orange Grove/Hilton Areas

One of the most popular off-road bicycling destinations in the region, the Avalon area offers the experienced rider some of the best singletrack in town. Often severe and unforgiving, the Avalon area is not for the faint of heart. With over 20 miles of trails on both sides of the Patapsco River, this is a place that will keep you coming back for more.

Start: Glen Artney area
Length: 20+ miles of singlestrack
Approximate riding time: 3–5 hours
Difficulty: Difficult, due to tight, muddy single-track over steep climbs, fast descents, and rugged terrain
Trail surface: Mostly rugged, hilly singletrack with some pavement
Lay of the land: Wooded and hilly terrain in a deep river valley
Land status: State park
Nearest Towns: Ellicott City, Columbia, and Elkridge, MD
Other trail users: Hikers and equestrians
Trail contacts: Patapsco Valley State Park headquarters (410) 461–5005
Twenty-four-hour emergency number (410) 461–0050
Schedule: Open from 10:00 A.M. to sunset, Thursday through Sunday
Fees and permits: $2.00 per car
Maps: USGS map: Sykesville, MD
ADC maps: Carroll County, Baltimore County road maps Patapsco Valley State Park trail map, available at the ranger station for $3.00

Getting There: From Washington: Take Interstate 95 north to Exit 47, then Route 195 east (toward BWI airport). Take the first exit onto Route 1 (Exit 3–Washington Boulevard) and turn right, heading south. Take the first right and immediately take the first left into Patapsco Valley State Park. Follow this road to the T intersection and turn right toward the Glen Artney area. Make your first left and park at the far parking lot by the fishing pond.
DeLorme: Maryland/Delaware Atlas & Gazetteer: Page 58, C-1

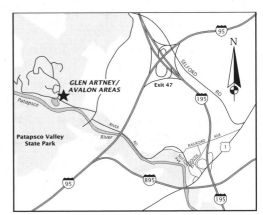

The Ride

In Celtic mythology, the word Avalon refers to an island paradise. The Avalon area of Patapsco Valley State Park might also be thought of as a sort of singletrack paradise in the middle of two huge metropolitan areas. Known simply as the Avalon area by most cyclists, this small corner of the Patapsco State Park is quite possibly one of

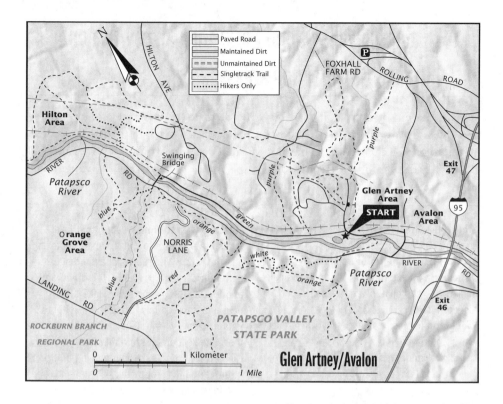

Washington, D.C./Baltimore's most popular mountain biking playgrounds. Avalon's terrain is oftentimes severe and nearly always challenging, but for serious off-roaders, these conditions represent nothing less than prime mountain biking real estate.

The riding begins at the Glen Artney parking lot near the Patapsco River. If you want to experience some great downhills, you'll have to climb up from this starting point, since it's at the bottom of the river valley. The best descents are in the Avalon area, accessible by following the purple blazes up Vineyard Trail. After a short climb, the trail quickly takes you barreling downhill along twisting singletrack toward the river. At one point further along this trail, you'll pass through a virtually pure beech forest, which in late autumn resembles a tunnel of thick gold. Enjoy Grist Mill Trail (green) while you can, because this flat paved path, which takes you over Patapsco's famous swinging bridge, is but a brief respite before the challenges of the Orange Grove and Hilton areas.

Like the beginning of the ride on the other side of the river, the terrain through the Orange Grove area becomes quite severe. Much of the Blue Trail is steep and rocky, which is why it's considered a prime location for off-road races throughout the season. After negotiating the near vertical descent back to the river, the ride returns, for the most part, along the same route. Before you head home, however, take the time to see the cascades just up the river from the swinging bridge.

After you cross the swinging bridge over the Patapsco River, take the time to see the cascades just up the river.

It's worth noting that there are countless routes within Patapsco Valley State Park. Given this area's proximity to Baltimore, it's easy to understand why this ideal section of parkland is so popular with off-road cyclists. The area's popularity does, however, raise some concerns regarding overuse and trail damage. Hundreds of cyclists, hikers, and equestrians may crowd this trail system on any given weekend, making trail maintenance a very serious issue, not to mention a serious challenge. To maintain access to this priceless off-road habitat, make sure you get involved with local clubs, organizations, park officials, and other trail users to help preserve the trails and the integrity of the area.

Miles and Directions

With more than 20 miles of singletrack and a seemingly endless network of trails winding up and down the river valley, this section of Patapsco Valley State Park is a do-it-yourselfer's paradise. Start from the Glen Artney area's parking lot (some still start from Landing Road, but the park long ago closed this area for safety reasons) and get a good look at the map of the trail system before you start. There's a very handy and fairly detailed map available for $3.00 at the ranger station. We highly recommend you get one before disappearing on such an extensive trail network. Plenty of people have gotten lost in this forest and have had to feel their way out in the dark. The trails are well marked with colored diamonds. With a good park map indictating all the newest trails in the area, you probably won't get lost.

Some trails that are now closed to bikes are the Buzzards Rock Trail in the Hilton area; the Saw Mill Branch Trail in the Hilton area (between the power lines and the river and between the youth group camping area and the river); the Valley View Trail in the Avalon area; and the Cascade Falls Trail leading to the falls from the parking area in the Cascade area. Each of these trails has been closed to bikes and equestrians for safety reasons and to curb erosion. Please pay attention to additional trail closures, don't ride after or during a rain, and join a trail maintenance crew to help preserve available trails for many years to come.

For even more miles of riding, consider pedaling through the Orange Grove area and crossing Landing Road. Rockburn Branch Regional Park has an additional 5 miles of singletrack, just across the road (see Ride 16).

Ride Information

Local Information

Columbia Association
www.columbiaassociation.com
Howard County Tourism Council
www.howardcountymdtour.com
Howard County, MD
www.howardcounty.com

Local Events and Attractions

For a complete and updated calendar of events for Howard County, MD, go to www.howardcountymdtour.com/pages/calendar/calendar.htm

Accommodations

The Wayside Inn Bed & Breakfast
Ellicott City, MD, (410) 461-4636
Hayland Farm, Ellicott City, MD
(410) 531-5593
There are several hotels and motels in Columbia and Ellicott City, MD

16 Rockburn Branch Regional Park

The Rockburn Branch Park area is an excellent place to introduce people to mountain biking. Its rolling trails give the novice to intermediate cyclist a chance to focus on developing skills rather than trying to make it up the next climb. Don't let this situation fool you, though. Rockburn is also a great place for the advanced cyclist to enjoy Howard County's great outdoors. And its proximity to Patapsco Valley State Park makes it a great addition to any ride. If you want to pack on the miles, you should definitely combine Rockburn's picturesque loop with the trails of the Avalon area.

Start: From parking lot adjacent to baseball field 8

Length: 5.3-mile loop

Approximate riding time: .5–1 hour (depending on skill level)

Difficulty: Easy, with mostly doubletrack trails and very few elevation changes

Trail surface: Mostly doubletrack, some singletrack, and one small section of asphalt

Lay of the land: Loop, with option to connect to Patapsco Valley State Park–Avalon area

Land status: Howard County Regional Park

Nearest town: Columbia, MD

Other trail users: Hikers, equestrians, and pets (Note: If you plan to hook up with Patapsco Valley State Park's Avalon area, leave the pooch at home. Patapsco is a dog-free zone.)

Trail contacts: Howard County Department of Recreation and Parks, (410) 313–4700 TTY (410) 313–4665 Rockburn Branch Park Manager, (410) 313–4955

Schedule: 7:00 A.M. to dusk (or as posted)

Fees and permits: None

Maps: USGS maps: Savage, MD; Relay, MD

Getting There:

From Washington, D.C.: Take the Capital Beltway (Interstate 495) to Interstate 95 north. Take

Exit 43B for Ellicott City and State Highway 100 West. Follow Highway 100 to the first exit, Exit 4, and Meadowridge Road. Turn right onto Meadowridge Road, heading north. Turn right at the first light onto Montgomery Road. Turn left at the first light (on Montgomery Road) to continue on Montgomery Road. Follow the road for approximately 0.5 miles and turn left immediately before Rockburn Branch Elementary School. There is a sign marking both the elementary school and the park. Follow this road to the entrance of the park and continue until it dead-ends at a parking lot, adjacent to baseball diamond 8. The trailhead is directly at the end of the road. *DeLorme: Maryland/Delaware Atlas & Gazetteer:* Page 57, C-6

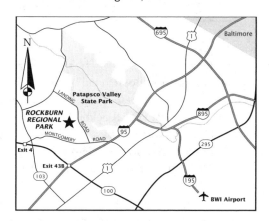

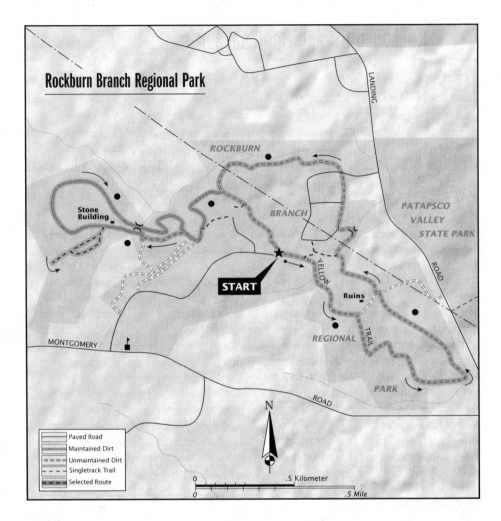

Rockburn Branch Regional Park

The Ride

One of the most popular riding destinations in the Washington, D.C./Baltimore area is Patapsco Valley State Park. But not many people know that adjacent to Patapsco Valley State Park is Rockburn Branch Regional Park, part of Howard County's 7,000-acre scenic park system. This vibrant parcel of parkland is managed by Howard County and has over 6 miles of dirt trails on which to ride.

Although not nearly as technical or hilly as the trails in Patapsco, Rockburn Branch offers a series of loops that will delight any mountain bike lover. The park, located in northern Howard County, is not only a trail playground but is also a popular destination for many sports enthusiasts. There are more than eight softball and baseball fields, numerous basketball courts, several soccer and football fields, four tennis courts, and several children's play areas. In addition, during the spring and summer months, the park has a snack and concession stand offering freshly cooked burgers and hot dogs. Rockburn is also a popular picnic destination for those less interested in adrenaline and more in pleasing the palate.

The well-marked trail system is home to several mountain bike races and is one of the preferred locations of the Bike and Run series, where partners alternately run and bike varied distances in a healthy competitive atmosphere. In addition, the park is home to many different species of birds. Local residents include green herons, Canada geese, wood ducks, black and turkey vultures, various types of woodpeckers, flycatchers, crows, and creepers. If you're lucky, you may get a glimpse of the bald eagle, which is known to migrate to the area from August to November. You may also spot Howard County's official bird, the American goldfinch, designated as such in 1978 by request of the county executive and the Howard County chapter of the Maryland Ornithological Society.

To match their biodiversity, Howard County and the Rockburn Branch Park area are also rich in history. The area was once the hunting and farming grounds for various Native American tribes. By the 1600s, Captain John Smith had

HOWARD COUNTY FIRSTS! Howard County boasts several memorable firsts:

In 1831, The Baltimore & Ohio Railroad came to Howard County. Its first 13 miles connected Baltimore to Ellicott's Mills. It is there that the country's first railroad terminal was built.

The first curved stone-arch bridge in the United States was built over the Patapsco River near Elkridge. Despite critics and skeptics who believed it would not support a train, the bridge has remained in service for more than 150 years.

In 1768, Benjamin Banneker, a notable son of freed slave and self-taught man of science, built the first clock made entirely in the United States. He disassembled and diagrammed a watch given to him by a friend, and then he carved all of the pieces out of wood. It took him two years to finish the clock, which kept accurate time throughout his life.

sailed up the Patapsco River, and Adam Shippley, the first known settler of the county, had arrived. At that time, a Native American settlement existed along the

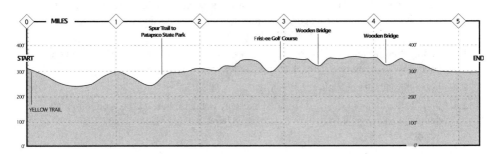

banks of the river in what is today Elkridge. Shippley's home, granted to him by Lord Baltimore, was located along the banks of the Patapsco. It is here that the roots of the county's rich agricultural heritage began.

In the 1700s, the family of Charles Carroll, one of the original signers of the Declaration of Independence, acquired over 10,000 acres of forests and farming grounds. They built an elaborate masonry home west of Ellicott City and called it Doughoregan. Today, heirs to the Carroll family still occupy the home, yet only about 3,000 acres of the original estate remain.

In 1772, John, Andrew, and Joseph Ellicott, Quakers from Bucks County, Pennsylvania, chose the picturesque wilderness area upriver of Elk Ridge to establish a flour mill. With the help of Charles Carroll, the Ellicotts revolutionized farming in the area. Wheat was chosen over tobacco, and fertilizer was first used to revitalize the county's soil. Soon, wheat, oats, and rye crops filled the rolling hills. Evidence of this rich agricultural heritage is proudly displayed in the county's flag, which incorporates a golden sheaf of wheat.

Rockburn is minutes away from the heart of Columbia, Maryland, one of this country's youngest planned communities. Designed to encourage interaction among its citizens, the thirty-two-year-old city of Columbia has 2,900 acres of open space, over 78 miles of pathways for walking, biking, and jogging, and a vast network of plazas and public areas. The streets and neighborhoods are named after historical figures as well as historic locations from Maryland's past. Its layout partially follows the original land grants made by five of the six members of the Calvert family, founders and proprietors of the royal colony of Maryland.

Miles and Directions

0.0 **START** from the parking lot adjacent to baseball field 8. Immediately after entering the trailhead, turn right. The trail is blazed yellow.

0.5 Reach a small open field with some old house ruins. Follow the trail to the right.

1.1 Turn right at this intersection. Following the trail to the left will loop you back toward the ruins.

1.6 Continue straight through this intersection. A left will take you back to the open field and ruins. A right will take you out to the power lines and the trailhead on Landing Road, directly across from Patapsco Valley State Park (described in Chapter 15 of this guide). You can add additional mileage to your ride by combining this ride with the Patapsco ride. The trail continues to be blazed yellow.

1.8 Turn right at this intersection, toward the power lines. The left branch, over the wooden bridge, will take you directly back to your car and baseball field 8.

2.0 Turn right onto the asphalt.

2.1 Turn right onto the grassy trail. The trail is clearly visible. Follow the worn path through the pines and cross the street to the trail marker on the other side. Continue into the woods.

The trails around here are pretty rooty. Be careful when it's wet.

2.7 Turn right at the T intersection. Going straight will take you back toward baseball field 8 and your car.

2.9 Follow the worn path to the right. To the left you will notice a basket for Frisbee golf.

3.0 Turn right onto the gravel road. Immediately after a tenth of a mile, turn right again and follow the gravel road to the left.

3.2 Turn right at this intersection and turn immediately left toward the wooden bridge.

3.3 Turn left immediately after crossing the wooden bridge. Notice the trailhead to the right. You will do a small loop, then return from the dirt road directly ahead and turn left onto this trail.

3.4 Immediately after passing the small stone building on the right, turn left onto the single-track.

3.5 Continue straight.

3.6 Turn left (almost a U turn) and back toward the trail you came in on. Continuing straight will take you to a small wooded section with some singletrack. These trails, however, all dead-end on private property.

3.7 Back at the stone building. Turn left, away from the way you came in. Follow this double-track back up and around the house on the top of the hill.

4.1 Turn left into the woods immediately before you cross the wooden bridge. Cross the creek and go up a short steep climb.

4.4 Continue straight through this intersection. At this point you begin to double back the way you came into this spot.

4.8 Turn right at this intersection. If you go left you will continue to backtrack the way you came in.

5.3 You're back where you started. Now that you know your way around, do it all over again to add more miles to your ride.

Additional Riding: If you are yearning for more riding, turn left and away from the parking lot. Follow the trail to a small wooden bridge. Immediately after crossing the bridge, follow the trail up and to the right to the next intersection, 1.65 miles by these directions. Turn left at the intersection and follow it under the power lines. The trail leads to Landing Road and a trailhead into Patapsco Valley State Park. There are more than 20 miles of great riding in this park.

Ride Information

Local Information

Columbia Association, Columbia, MD
(410) 715–3000
www.columbiaassociation.com/
Howard County Tourism Council, Inc. Ellicott City, MD, (410) 313–1900
www.howardcountymdtour.com

Local Events and Attractions

Howard County's local Web site
www.howardcountymdtour.com/pages/calendar/calendar.htm

Accommodations

Peralynna Manor at Rose Hill
Columbia, MD, (410) 715–4600
There are several hotels and motels in Columbia and Ellicot City, MD

17 Northern Central Rail-Trail

This converted rail-trail leads its visitors across Maryland's beautiful fields and meadows, past forests and rural farmland, and along the rushing waters of Little Falls and Gunpowder Falls. As you pedal along, you'll pass through the many historic little towns whose whole history is based upon the corridor's connection between Baltimore and Harrisburg. Celebrate the thousands of volunteers who helped make this 20-mile stretch of uninterrupted rail-trail possible by taking time to enjoy this converted and historic old rail line. Continue an additional 20.5 miles along the trail's latest extension, the York Heritage County Rail-Trail, all the way to York, Pennsylvania.

Start: Ashland parking lot
Length: 19.7 miles one way to the Pennsylvania state border. Continue an additional 20.5 miles along the York Heritage County Rail-Trail to York.
Approximate riding time: 2–3 hours one way
Difficulty: Moderate, due to length
Trail surface: Flat, hard-packed dirt trail
Lay of the land: A rail-trail ride through Maryland's scenic Piedmont region
Land status: Public right-of-way
Nearest city: Baltimore
Other trail users: Hikers, equestrians, and dogs
Trail contacts: Gunpowder Falls State Park (301) 592-2897
Rails-to-Trails Conservancy (202) 797-5400
Schedule: Open daily, from dawn till dusk
Fees and permits: None
Maps: USGS maps: Cockeysville, MD; Hereford, MD; Phoenix, MD; New Freedom, MD
ADC map: Baltimore County road map
Getting There: From the Baltimore Beltway (Interstate 695): Take Interstate 83 north 5.5 miles to Exit 20 (Shawan Road). Go east on Shawan Road less than 1 mile, then turn right on State Highway 45 (York Road). Go 1 mile and turn left on Ashland Road. Follow Ashland Road 1.5 miles, passing Hunt Valley Shopping Center on your left. Stay right on Ashland Road

(do not bear left on Paper Mill Road) to the parking lot for the southernmost starting point on the Northern Central Rail-Trail. *DeLorme: Maryland/Delaware Atlas & Gazetteer:* Page 75, D-5

Public Transportation: From downtown Baltimore, take the Central Light Rail Line north to Hunt Valley Station. Cross Highway 45 to Ashland Road and follow the driving directions to the starting point. Total distance from the station is approximately 1.8 miles.

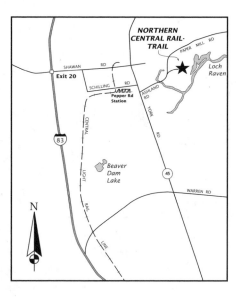

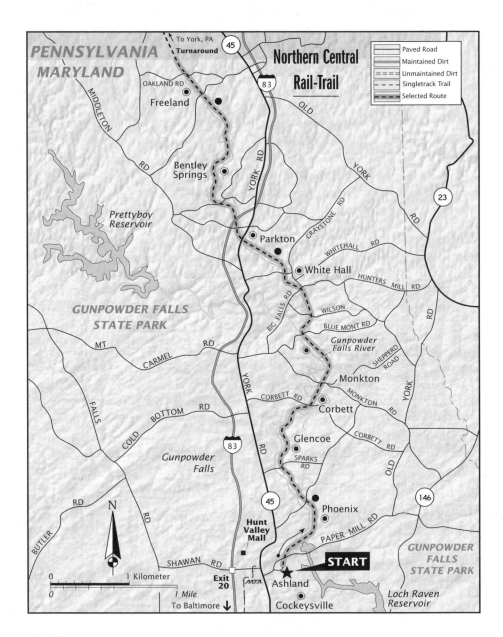

The Ride

Back when rails were king, the Northern Central Railroad was among the few rail lines dominating the Mid-Atlantic, carrying everything from milk, coal, and U.S. mail to presidents of the United States. For nearly 134 years, the Northern Central Railroad was the locomotive link that carved its way through Maryland's hilly Piedmont region and Pennsylvania's rolling farmlands. It connected Baltimore with Gettysburg, York, and Harrisburg, Pennsylvania.

Scores of small towns sprang up along the line, prospering from Northern Central's service to the large cities. Such towns as Freeland, Bentley Springs, Parkton, Whitehall, Monkton, Corbett, Phoenix, and Ashland all sent their flour, milk, paper, coal, textiles, and other goods to Baltimore markets.

The Northern Central also served in the Civil War, carrying wounded soldiers from the bloody battlefields of Gettysburg south to Baltimore hospitals. Abraham Lincoln rode the rail line north to Gettysburg to deliver his famous Gettysburg Address. It later carried his casket through Gettysburg on its way to Harrisburg, where he was buried following his assassination in April 1865 at Ford's Theatre in Washington, D.C.

▶ **The Northern Central Rail-Trail leads its visitors across Maryland's beautiful fields and meadows, past old forests and rural farmland, along the rushing waters of Little Falls and Gunpowder Falls, and through many historic little towns.**

The rail's rich history began to recede with the advent of trucks and automobiles, and in 1959 the Northern Central had to give up its local passenger service. But it was Agnes, the powerful hurricane of 1972, that dealt the final blow to the faltering rail line. Agnes washed out and destroyed many of the railroad's bridges, ultimately knocking out remaining mainline passenger services and the line's important freight transportation. Northern Central Railroad's commercial success ended, but its new identity and prosperity were just beginning.

The rail line south of Cockeysville was purchased by the state of Maryland for freight service. This left the remaining line from Cockeysville north to the Pennsylvania border open for a unique and wonderful opportunity. The residents of Baltimore County realized this opportunity in 1980 when they purchased the 20-mile corridor from Penn Central and began the backbreaking process of converting the rails to trails. After nine long, hard years of work and thousands of volunteers later, the Northern Central Rail-Trail from Ashland to the Pennsylvania border was finished.

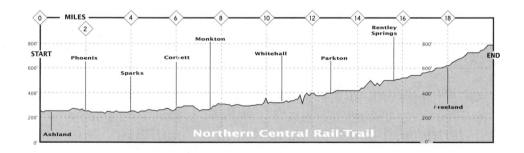

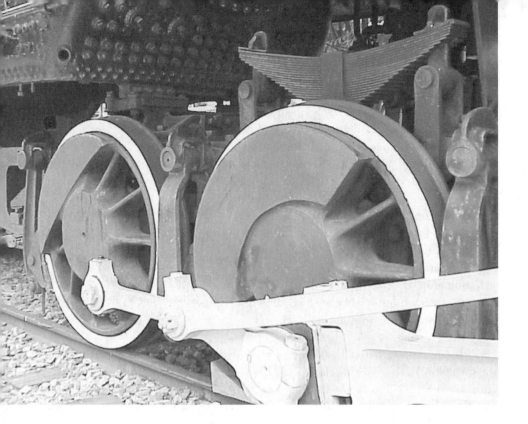

Now, more than 180,000 people visit and enjoy the trail each year. The Northern Central Rail-Trail leads its visitors across Maryland's beautiful fields and meadows, past old forests and rural farmland, along the rushing waters of Little Falls and Gunpowder Falls, and through many historic little towns.

Be warned that this once quiet treasure is gaining tremendous popularity, and parking is very limited during the prime outdoor months. Take this into account when you travel the rail-trail. Get there early.

Miles and Directions

- **0.0** **START** from the NCRR Trail parking lot in Ashland and travel north on the Northern Central Rail-Trail.
- **2.0** Pass through the town of Phoenix, site of the Phoenix textile mill, razed for Loch Raven Reservoir. The reservoir, when built in 1922, never reached the mill. The mill ruins survive, still above the waterline.
- **4.0** Pass through the town of Sparks.
- **6.0** Pass through the historic Victorian village of Corbett, listed on the National Registry of Historic Places.

7.5 Pass through Monkton, showcasing the renovated Monkton train station, now a museum and park office. Monkton is also listed on the National Registry of Historic Places. Rest rooms, telephones, and food available. Monkton Bikes rental and repair shop just off the main path.

10.8 Pass through the village of Whitehall. Telephones and parking on the left. Whitehall is a former paper mill town that used the rail to export its paper to Baltimore.

12.9 Pass through Parkton. Parkton was the railroad's hub for exporting dairy products south to Baltimore.

15.7 Reach the historic resort town of Bentley Springs. Portable toilet available.

18.0 Pass through the town of Freeland. Rest rooms and parking available.

19.7 Reach the Maryland/Pennsylvania state border. From here, you must either have arranged a car shuttle back to the Ashland parking lot or you must ride back.

(**Note:** The NCRR Trail continues as the York County Heritage Rail-Trail all the way north to York, Pennsylvania. This adds an additional 20.5 miles one way to your trip. The York County Heritage Rail-Trail was completed in the summer of 1999.)

Ride Information

Local Events and Attractions
Victorian Village of Corbett, Maryland

In Addition

Rails-to-Trails

The mission of the Rails-to-Trails Conservancy is to "enhance America's communities and countryside by converting thousands of miles of abandoned rail corridors and connecting open spaces into a nationwide network of public trails."

Every large city and small town in America, by the early twentieth century, was connected by steel and railroad ties. By 1916, the United States had laid nearly 300,000 miles of track across the country, giving it the world's largest rail system. Since then, other forms of transportation, such as cars, trucks, and airplanes, have diminished the importance of the railroad, and that impressive network of rail lines has shrunk to less than 150,000 miles. Railroad companies abandon more than 2,000 miles of track each year, leaving unused rail corridors overgrown and idle.

It wasn't until the mid-1960s that the idea to refurbish these abandoned rail corridors into usable footpaths and trails was introduced. In 1963, work began in Chicago and its suburbs on a 55-mile stretch of abandoned right-of-way to create the Illinois Prairie Path.

In 1986, the Rails-to-Trails Conservancy was founded, its mission specifically to help communities realize their dreams of having a usable rail corridor for recreation and nonmotorized travel. At the time the conservancy began operations, only one hundred open rail-trails existed. Today, more than 500 trails are open to the public, totalling more than 5,000 miles of converted pathways. The Rails-to-Trails Conservancy is currently working on more than 500 additional rails-to-trails projects.

Ultimately, its goal is to see a completely interconnected system of trails throughout the United States. If you're interested in learning more about rails-to-trails and wish to support the conservancy, please contact:

Rails-to-Trails Conservancy
1100 17th Street, NW
Washington, DC 20036
(202) 331–9696
www.railtrails.org
railtrails@transact.org

18 Gunpowder Falls State Park: Perry Hall

Riding the trails along the banks of the Gunpowder River is like stepping back in time. The large towering trees, which frame the tamed Gunpowder River, provide shelter from the surrounding urban hustle and shade on hot sunny days. With little elevation gain, and close proximity to Perry Hall and the Baltimore Beltway, this trail is the perfect getaway for a quick off-road jaunt.

Start: Trail parking area
Length: 5.4-mile loop
Approximate riding time: 1–1.5 hours (depending on skill level)
Difficulty: Easy to moderate. Mostly flat riverside trails with some technical trail sections.
Trail surface: Doubletrack and singletrack
Lay of the land: Mostly singletrack along the banks of the Gunpowder River
Land status: State park
Nearest town: Perry Hall, MD
Other trail users: Hikers, anglers, and pets (on leashes)
Trail contacts: Gunpowder Falls State Park, Kingsville, MD, (410) 592-2897
Schedule: Gunpowder Falls State Park is a day-use park only
Fees and permits: None in this area. Other areas of the park have fees and require permits. Call the park directly for specific information.
Maps: USGS map: White Marsh, MD

Getting There: From Baltimore, MD: Take Interstate 95 north to Exit 64B (on the left) for

Interstate 695 West. Immediately after entering I-695, take Exit 32B, for State Highway 1 North, toward Bel Air, Maryland. Continue on Highway 1/Bel Air Road for approximately 5.5 miles. Immediately after crossing the Big Gunpowder River, turn right into the trail parking area. The ride begins here. *DeLorme: Maryland/Delaware Atlas & Gazetteer:* Page 58, A-4

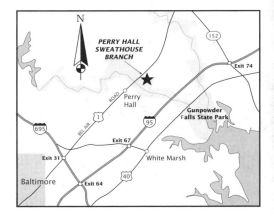

The Ride

Gateway to the Chesapeake is the term most widely used to describe Harford County. One cannot contest the importance of the Gunpowder River to the bay and the development of present-day Baltimore and Harford Counties. The present Gunpowder River, tame by most standards, used to be a wild running body of water. In 1881, when the Lock Raven Reservoir was built, the waterway was reduced to a gentle river. The river actually consists of two branches, the Great Gunpowder Falls

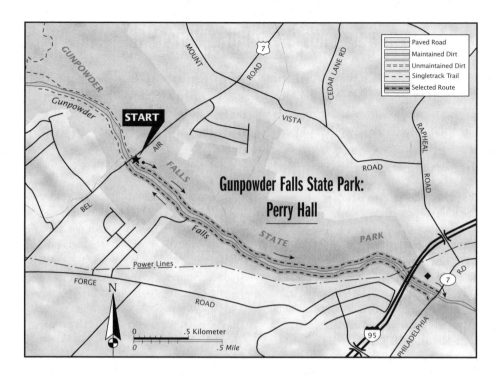

Gunpowder Falls State Park:
Perry Hall

	Paved Road
	Maintained Dirt
	Unmaintained Dirt
	Singletrack Trail
	Selected Route

in northern Baltimore County and the Little Gunpowder Falls, which forms the border between Baltimore and Harford Counties.

Great Gunpowder Falls begins its run near the Pretty Boy Reservoir in northern Baltimore County and then opens up into the large Loch Raven Reservoir. Upon exiting the reservoir, the river narrows as it approaches Kingsville and White Marsh. It then converges with Little Gunpowder Falls at Days Cove. From there, the river continues its run into the Chesapeake Bay, the largest estuary in the nation.

Hundreds of years ago, Native Americans from areas as far north as Pennsylvania roamed the lands adjacent to Gunpowder Falls in search of the hunt and riches that the Chesapeake Bay had to offer. The powerful Susquehannocks, who would terrify the smaller nomadic tribes that traveled through the region, dominated the area. During the seventeeth century, this situation changed with the arrival of European settlers.

Local legend claims that when Captain John Smith arrived to the area and English settlement began, local tribes were impressed with the power of gunpowder. The settlers had discovered saltpeter, which grew wild along the banks of the rivers and was a key ingredient in gunpowder. Supposedly, Native American tribes' interest in gunpowder led them to plant the powder itself along the banks of the river, hoping it would grow, as did the saltpeter.

In addition to saltpeter, other useful natural resources were found along the river. During John Smith's journey of 1608, he discovered deposits of iron ore. These deposits later played a role in the production of gunpowder along the banks of the rivers. As time passed, the rivers were known as the Gunpowder Falls.

By the eighteenth century, and thanks to Captain Smith's discovery, northeast Baltimore County was the site of numerous furnaces and mills; iron ore was mined throughout the river valley. A 1911 survey of the area identified eight separate mining sites in the Gunpowder region. Today, however, the Gunpowder Falls is strictly known for its winding trails, fishing holes, and occasional white-water rafting opportunities.

▶ Hundreds of years ago, Native Americans from areas as far north as Pennsylvania roamed the lands adjacent to Gunpowder Falls in search of the hunt and riches that the Chesapeake Bay had to offer.

Closest to this ride is Perry Hall, a town rich in history and closely tied to Gunpowder Falls. Originally named The Adventure, the area was owned by a wealthy planter named Harry Dorsey Gough. Gough purchased over 1,000 acres in 1774 to build a mansion and plantation. He later renamed it Perry Hall after his home in England. The mansion still stands in the northern part of the Perry Hall community.

The Gough family had a strong influence on the life of the community and dominated much of its activities until the end of the Civil War. Not only was Henry Gough a leader in the Maryland General Assembly, but he was also a founder of the American Methodist Church. With the rapid decline of plantation life in the United States, the Goughs' stronghold diminished. The Gough lands were sold in 1875 to immigrants, mostly of German origin, and Perry Hall was divided into several farms.

The new tenants quickly transformed Perry Hall into a prosperous agricultural community. The name Perry Hall eventually faded, and the community became known as Germantown. However, with growth and the arrival of immigrants of various nationalities, the Germantown name was again replaced by the title Perry Hall.

After World War II, development flourished, and the population of Perry Hall increased. With development, local residents recognized the need to form an improvement association. By the 1980s, the population of Perry Hall had nearly doubled. With the rise in population, several opportunities were brought to the area. A sprawling new mall with hundreds of stores was built in White Marsh. Several high-tech businesses joined in on the development and brought with them previously

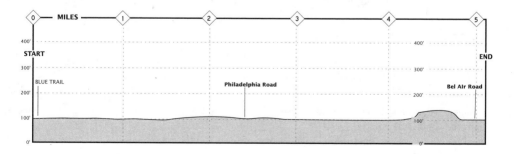

unavailable services. All this development has generated thousands of jobs in the area and has made Perry Hall an important link to the successful economy of the region.

Despite all the changes and the taming of Great and Little Gunpowder Falls, the trails that run through this area offer a glimpse of times past, when Native Americans and early settlers depended on the area's natural bounty in order to survive.

Miles and Directions

0.0 **START** at the trailhead clearly marked by a blue blaze and adjacent to the overflow parking area. Immediately after entering the trailhead, head down and bear left. Follow the blue blazes.

0.4 Continue straight at the intersection of the Yellow and Blue Trails. It is clearly marked. If you choose to take the Yellow Trail, it will bring you back to and farther up the Blue Trail.

2.3 You have reached I-95. This is a very difficult section of the trail. If you are in any way uncomfortable with this section, turn around and head back to the parking lot. The White Trail is easily accessible from there. If you choose to continue, walk your bike on the inclined concrete berm. Be very careful. The trail picks up directly on the other side.

2.5 You have reached Philadelphia Road. Turn right and cross the river.

2.6 Turn right into this driveway and then immediately right again.

2.7 Enter the woods and turn left. The trail will be clearly marked by a white blaze. The return trip on the White Trail will be a little harder than the trip on the Blue Trail. Although there is not much elevation change, the trail is rocky and technical.

2.9 Back at I-95. Continue straight, following the white blazes.

5.3 Back at Bel Air Road. Turn right and head toward the parking lot.

5.4 Turn right again and head up to the parking lot. You're done.

Advisory: Take a moment before you begin your ride to study the accurate trail map in the parking area. You will notice that there is a large area opposite Bel Air Road that is off-limits to bikes, with the exception of the White Trail. This ride will basically take you on the Blue Trail along the river, under I–95 to Philadelphia Road, and back to the parking lot on the opposite side of the river via the White Trail.

Additional Riding: If you want to do some more riding, you can pick up the White Trail for an out-and-back on the opposite side of Bel Air Road. Remember, the wildlands area is off-limits to bikes. You can also add additional distance to your ride by doing the small blue loop and riding the small yellow loop to the Lost Pond on the Blue Trail.

Ride Information

Accommodations:

Susquehanna Trading Company Guest House
Havre de Grace, MD (410) 939-4252
Vandiver Inn, Havre de Grace, MD
(800) 245-1655

19 Gunpowder Falls State Park: Sweet Air

The Sweet Air area of Gunpowder Falls State Park offers perfect intermediate trails. Located in northern Baltimore County, Sweet Air has 1,250 acres of trails. The variety of trails, from steep rocky climbs and descents to fields and flat twisty riverside trails, gives the intermediate rider the perfect stage to hone her or his skills.

Start: From the trail parking area
Length: 5.9-mile loop
Approximate riding time: 1.5 hours
Difficulty: Moderate to difficult due to elevation changes and technical trail sections. This is the perfect trail for the novice who wants to increase her or his abilities.
Trail surface: Doubletrack and singletrack loop through rolling fields and riverside trails
Lay of the land: Rolling hills and river valley
Land status: State park
Nearest town: Fallston, MD
Other trail users: Hikers, equestrians, and pets (on leashes)
Trail contacts: Gunpowder Falls State Park, Kingsville, MD, (410) 592–2897
Schedule: Gunpowder Falls State Park is a day-use park
Fees and permits: None in this area. Other areas of the park have fees and require permits. Call the park directly for specific information.
Maps: USGS map: Phoenix, MD

Getting There: From Baltimore, MD: Take Interstate 95 north to Exit 74. Turn left onto State Highway 152 (Mountain Road) and head toward Fallston, Maryland. Continue on Highway 152 for approximately 11 miles and turn left onto State Highway 165 (Baldwin Mill Road). Turn right at the second intersection onto Green Road. Continue on Green Road and turn right onto Moores Road. Take your first left onto Dalton-Bevard Road—the sign is hard to see. Continue on the gravel road until you reach a gate and a sign for Gunpowder Falls State Park-Sweet Air. Turn right and park at the top of the hill near the large trail sign.
DeLorme: Maryland/Delaware Atlas & Gazetteer: Page 75, C-6

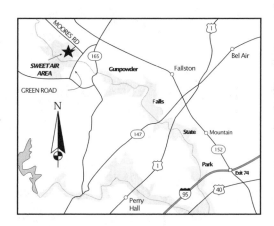

The Ride

Although not readily apparent when you start your ride, the Gunpowder Falls State Park area is part of the Chesapeake Bay watershed and its delicate ecosystem. The watershed covers 64,000 square miles and spans sections of several states, including Maryland, Virginia, West Virginia, Pennsylvania, Delaware, and New York. About

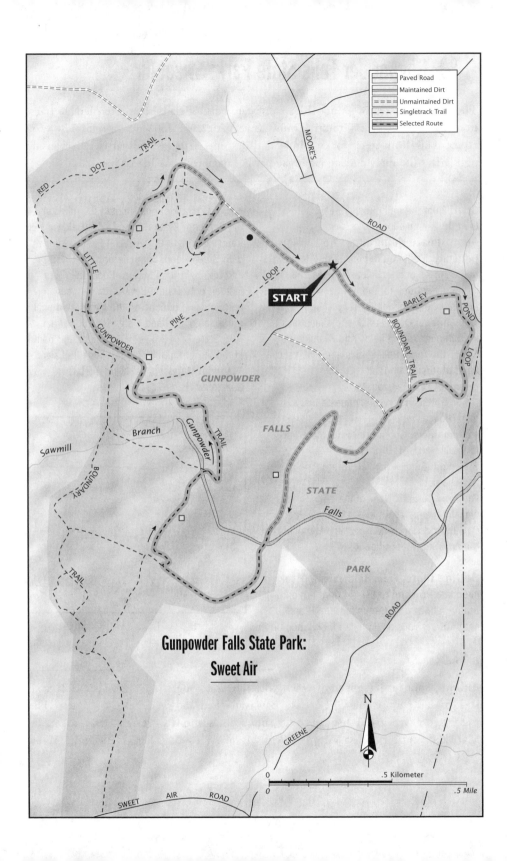

Paved Road
Maintained Dirt
Unmaintained Dirt
Singletrack Trail
Selected Route

MOORES

ROAD

START

LOOP

BARLEY

BOUNDARY TRAIL

POND

LOOP

RED

DOT

TRAIL

LITTLE

GUNPOWDER

PINE

GUNPOWDER

Branch

Gunpowder

TRAIL

FALLS

Sawmill

BOUNDARY

STATE

Falls

PARK

ROAD

TRAIL

Gunpowder Falls State Park:
Sweet Air

N

0   .5 Kilometer
0   .5 Mile

GREENE

SWEET   AIR   ROAD

The Sweet Air area offers a number of intermediate-level trails.

20,000 years ago, the sea level was more than 300 feet below what it is today. At that time, the Great Gunpowder and Little Gunpowder Falls Rivers—along with many major tributaries, such as the great Susquehanna River—emptied directly into the Atlantic Ocean. As the northern polar ice caps melted—which they still are doing, by the way—the sea level rose. Over the next thousands of years, the fertile Susquehanna River Valley filled with water, flooding to form the Chesapeake Bay.

Today the bay is one of North America's most bountiful estuaries—an estuary being a body of water where freshwater from rivers mixes with the ocean. The bay is also the richest source of seafood in the United States. Its relative shallowness and hundreds of undisturbed inlets and bays create an ideal place for aquatic life.

Native Americans lived and flourished from the bounties of the Chesapeake as far back as 10,000 B.C. In Maryland, it was the Susquehannocks who dominated the area and survived mainly on what they could draw from the water. It is unclear who was the first European to reach this specific part of the coast. Legend has it that a Spaniard, Captain Vicente Gonzales, was the first explorer to sail the head of the Chesapeake. However, in 1608, Captain John Smith sailed the Chesapeake and mapped it, thus becoming the first known settler to reach its banks.

Later, settlers came to the Chesapeake Bay area and flourished from the wealth of resources at hand. Settlers used the bay's resources for themselves and traded them with people from other regions.

Unlike the early Native Americans who believed that natural resources belonged to all, European settlers began aggressively laying claim to the lands along the bay. The settlers armed themselves with the belief that anyone could claim and own private property. Large parcels of land were cleared to make room for farms and other businesses. Unfortunately, to the detriment of the natural beauty and survival of the bay, many forests were cleared. Several animals, such as wild turkeys, bison, and various fish, became extinct, and the unintended effects have become apparent. The effects have taken a serious and quite visible toll.

Rapid development in the area, including new housing, shopping malls, and the necessary infrastructure to support them has increasingly strained the balanced ecosystem of the bay region. Today, government institutions and several citizen organizations are taking steps to ensure that future generations of Americans can continue to enjoy the resources of the Chesapeake Bay.

Miles and Directions

(**Note:** Take a moment before you begin your ride to study the trail map in the parking area. As you can see, there are several options and available loops. The following loop is by no means the only route—it's only a sampling.)

0.0   **START** at the trailhead adjacent to a gate and a large birdhouse that is directly opposite the large trail map sign in the parking area. The trail is blazed blue. This is the Boundary Trail. As its name suggests, it travels along the perimeter of the Sweet Air area.

0.3   Turn left at this intersection and continue following the yellow blazes. You are now on the Pine Loop Trail.

1.3   Continue left at this intersection. You are back on the Boundary Trail, marked by blue blazes. A right turn at this intersection will take you back up to the parking area.

1.4   Continue to the left at this intersection and head toward the brown fence and the blue blazes on the left.

1.5   Continue following the blue blazes straight into the woods.

1.7   Bear left and continue following the blue blazes.

1.8   Turn left into the woods and follow the blue blazes to the Little Gunpowder.

2.2   Turn left at this intersection. Immediately after turning, reach Little Gunpowder Falls. Cross the river and continue on the opposite side. The trail is still blazed blue.

2.4   After a short climb, turn right at this intersection.

The trails at Sweet Air give the intermediate rider the perfect stage to hone his or her skills.

2.6 Come out onto an open field. The trail continues to the right on the perimeter of the field.

2.8 Turn right at this intersection. Follow the trail into the woods. The trail will immediately come out into an open field. Turn right and continue riding along the edge of the field on the wood line. **(Option:** You can turn left when you come out onto the field and follow the perimeter until you reach the blue trail marker to continue on the Boundary Trail.)

3.0 Turn right and away from the field, onto the doubletrack and one of the connector trails.

3.3 You have reached Little Gunpowder Falls again. Cross it and continue following the trail to the right.

3.4 Turn left onto the White Trail. Get ready for some great singletrack.

4.0 Continue on the White Trail to the left. The Red Trail to the right will take you back toward the Barley Pond Loop and eventually the parking area. Follow the white blazes.

4.3 You've reached the intersection of the Blue Trail and White Trail. Turn right and then immediately left to continue on the White Trail.

4.5 Turn right at this intersection. The Red Dot Trail is a hiking-only trail.

4.8 Bear left at this intersection and follow the blue-blazed trail.

5.1 Turn right at the intersection of the Red Dot Trail and continue to follow the blue blazes along the doubletrack.

5.3 Turn right at this intersection for a quick and twisty little detour along the White Trail and Yellow Trail. If you choose, skip it and continue straight past all intersections until you get back to the parking area.

5.4 Bear left at this intersection and away from the White Trail.

5.5 Turn left at this intersection. You are now on the Yellow Trail.

5.6 Turn right at this intersection. Continue straight past all intersections to the parking area.

5.9 Finish at the parking area.

Ride Information

Accommodations

Spencer Silver Mansion, Havre de Grace, MD
(800) 780–1485
Currier House Bed & Breakfast, Havre de
Grace, MD (800) 827–2889

Southern Maryland

T he state of Maryland has an immense variety of terrain available to mountain bikers, ranging in extremes from the rocky, technical, mountainous terrain of western Maryland (for hard-core riding) to the bay shores and sandy beaches of southern Maryland, offering a uniquely pleasant environment in which to pedal one's steed. In between lies the Maryland Piedmont, with its fields, streams, and valleys.

Unlike the other regions of Maryland, southern Maryland is generally flat. But don't let this fool you. A challenging variety of trails awaits the adventurous rider.

Mostly rural, southern Maryland has several state forests and reserves open to and enjoyed by mountain bikers of all skill levels. Novice riders enjoy the generally wide and easy trails of the Patuxent Research Park. This park was once part of Fort George G. Meade, and many of the trails there today were once old army training grounds.

Farther south, near Waldorf, fat-tire enthusiasts enjoy the twisting singletrack trails in Cedarville State Forest. Popular among cyclists of all levels, Cedarville is an ideal destination for novice cyclists. They can acquaint themselves with twisty narrow trails along with the luxury of flat terrain and plenty of escape routes back onto wide dirt roads. The relatively nonexistent elevation gain or loss in this part of the state makes these trails an inviting destination for riders of all ages.

Farther south in Maryland, riders can delight in the lakeshore trails of Saint Mary's River State Park. A bit more challenging than Cedarville and other southern Maryland destinations, Saint Mary's is a preferred riding area for more advanced riders. Advocacy groups in southern Maryland work hard to keep this trail system open to cyclists. Their efforts are clearly visible in the trail's relatively good condition. Countless hours of maintenance have gone into these paths to ensure they are enjoyed by all for years to come.

The predominant landmark in southern Maryland is the Chesapeake Bay, a 200-plus-mile estuary harboring an exorbitant amount of wildlife and ecosystems. And

to the east of the bay are the flatlands of the Eastern Shore. Bordered by the Chesapeake Bay to the west and the Atlantic Ocean to the east, the Eastern Shore offers
very little elevation change. But don't let this fool you into thinking there's nothing
worth pedaling here. The relative flatness of the area lends itself to strong head winds
and thus the sense of going uphill all day long. All is not lost, however. What places
like Pocomoke River State Park lack in elevation is made up for by soft sandy sections of trail that will make your legs work harder than will a Blue Ridge climb.

20 Susquehanna River Ride

This challenging ride meanders through the varying topography of the Susquehanna River Valley, taking you through such diversity as heavy forest cover and open fields. Apart from its natural diversity, Susquehanna State Park offers a unique glimpse into the past, with several historic landmarks located within its boundaries, including the only working gristmill in Harford and Cecil Counties. Home to several mountain bike races, the trails in this park do not make for an easy ride. So bring your best pair of legs and all the bike handling skills you can muster, and be ready to have some fun.

Start: Picnic area
Length: 7 miles
Approximate riding time: 1 hour
Difficulty: Moderate to difficult due to winding singletrack through dense woodlands
Trail surface: Singletrack, paved roads
Lay of the land: Dense forest and open fields along the Susquehanna River
Land status: State park
Nearest town: Bel Air, MD
Other trail users: Hikers and equestrians
Trail contacts: Susquehanna State Park, (410) 557-7994
Schedule: Day-use only, dawn to dusk
Fees and permits: No fees
Maps: USGS maps: Conowingo Dam, MD-PA; Delta, MD-PA
Susquehanna State Park trail map

Getting There: From Baltimore: Take Interstate 95 north to Exit 89 (State Highway 155 West) toward Bel Air. Turn right on State Highway 161 (Rock Run Road) and follow the brown signs to the Rock Run Gristmill Historic Area. Turn left at Stafford Road toward the Deer Creek Picnic Area. As you drive into the picnic area, drive directly to the far right corner of the lot. The trail begins here. *DeLorme: Maryland/Delaware Atlas & Gazetteer:* Page 76, A-3

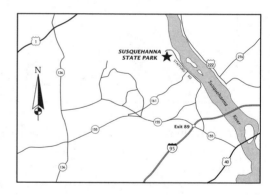

The Ride

The setting for this ride is Susquehanna State Park, 30 miles north of Baltimore near the Pennsylvania state line. First inhabited by the Susquehannock Indians, this area later became a center for the Maryland and Pennsylvania Railroad. Today, all that remains of the railroad are abandoned structures from a past when the rail line helped farms and quarries of northern Harford County prosper. Also present is a network of trails and recreation areas for folks to enjoy year-round.

This ride takes you along five of Susquehanna State Park's many different trails. Cyclists will ride through the river valley, beneath heavy forest cover to huge rock

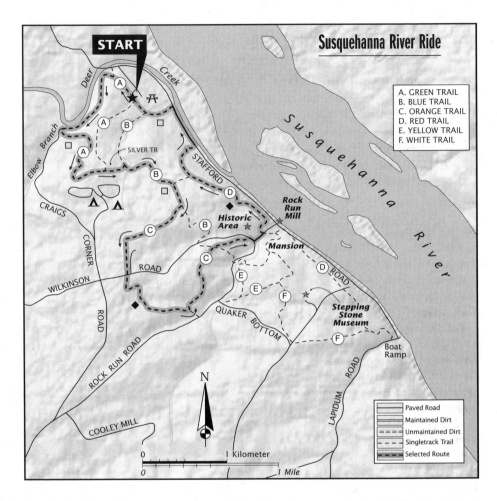

START

Susquehanna River Ride

A. GREEN TRAIL
B. BLUE TRAIL
C. ORANGE TRAIL
D. RED TRAIL
E. YELLOW TRAIL
F. WHITE TRAIL

Deer
Creek
Elbow Branch

SILVER TR

STAFFORD

Susquehanna River

CRAIGS CORNER

ROAD

WILKINSON

ROAD

Historic Area

Rock Run Mill

Mansion

ROAD

Stepping Stone Museum

Boat Ramp

QUAKER BOTTOM

ROCK RUN ROAD

LAPIDUM ROAD

COOLEY MILL

N

0   1 Kilometer
0   1 Mile

Paved Road
Maintained Dirt
Unmaintained Dirt
Singletrack Trail
Selected Route

outcroppings, and across wide-open fields. The ride also passes by Harford and Cecil Counties' only working gristmill, one of the many historic points of interest on this ride.

As you enter the park, you will clearly see evidence of the past. Make time for a walking tour of the gristmill area or explore the park's several buildings, all of which were built between 1794 and 1815. They include the Rock Run Gristmill, a spring-house, a carriage barn, and a tollhouse. Each of these unique and historic buildings offers a glimpse into the lifestyle of the 1800s.

This particular mountain bike tour begins at the Rock Run Gristmill. Built in 1794 by John Stump, a successful Harford County businessman, the mill served as the center of activity in the community. In addition to providing milling services and buying and selling grain, the mill also housed the local post office. Still in operation today, the mill features a twelve-ton, eighty-four-bucket wheel, powered by water running down Mill Race, a man-made stream draining from a small dammed pond on higher ground.

The power from the gristmill wheel's rotation operates a complex set of pulleys, belts, and gears that can be quickly adjusted by the miller to determine the grain's consistency. As you walk inside the mill, pay close attention to the flood level markers, especially the one from 1889. It's hard to imagine that nearly the entire first floor of this structure was at one point completely submerged. Pictures of past floods, storms, and ice floes that greatly affected and shaped this area are also on display.

The next stop on the tour is the springhouse. Built in 1804, the house's main purpose was to cover drinking water used at the gristmill and to serve as a cold storage house for dairy products and foods. Continue to the carriage house and the "three holer," a small stone building adjacent to the carriage house. This structure was once an outhouse with accommodations for three people—thus the name.

▶ As you enter the park, you will clearly see evidence of the past. Make time for a walking tour of the gristmill area or explore the park's several buildings, all of which were built between 1794 and 1815.

The tollhouse, perhaps one of the most important buildings at the historic area, was built in the early 1800s as part of a project by the Rock Run Bridge and Bank Company. This project included the 1-mile bridge that crossed the Susquehanna River. Intended to replace the ferry as the primary means across the river, the bridge was used extensively from its completion in 1815 until 1823, when a fire destroyed it. The bridge was then rebuilt and used for twenty more years, until it was partially destroyed by the rhythmic motion of crossing cattle. A final blow to the bridge's integrity came in 1856, when a damaging ice floe down the river completely destroyed the bridge. If you look out on the river, you can still see the stone footings that once supported this structure, the first of its kind to span the Susquehanna.

The ditch adjacent to the mill and parallel to the river was once a very important canal that extended 45 miles from Havre de Grace to Wrightsville. The original Canal Company was chartered in 1783 and had the authority to purchase all the lands required for construction. Initially, the canal was to have grain warehouses and sawmills along its banks to accommodate the developing town of Baltimore. When

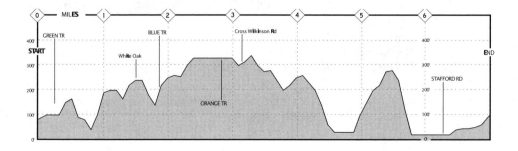

completed, the canal was 20 feet wide and up to 12 feet deep. It contained twenty-nine locks that raised and lowered boats from 29 feet at Havre de Grace to 1,000 feet at Wrightsville. With the flood of 1889, the canal suffered substantial damages, and the Canal Company was faced with extensive financial losses. The canal's usefulness waned, and it soon became obsolete. Today, all that is left of the canal within the park are three of its massive granite locks.

If your thirst for information on the area's history has not been quenched, you might consider visiting Havre de Grace and the Susquehanna Museum of Havre de Grace at the Lock House. Over the past few years, the museum has been undergoing an extensive restoration program. Its goal is to re-create a working lock to help people fully understand and interpret the canal's operations. In addition, a display house to show preserved gates, artifacts, and information on the local history of Havre de Grace and the surrounding tidewater region is also envisioned. There are four other museums, numerous shops, and fine restaurants along the promenade and waterfront, as well as several historic homes, some of which have been converted into wonderful bed-and-breakfasts.

Miles and Directions

0.0   **START** at the picnic area from the intersection of the Red and Green trails. A "Walk Zone" sign marks the entrance. Turn right and follow the green blazes.

1.0   Reach the point where you can see the intersection of Craig's Corner Road and Stafford Road. Continue following the green blazes. This is a popular access point for tubing down Deer Creek.

1.8   The intersection marked "White Oak" to the left will take you to a small opening where you can admire Maryland's state tree. This particular white oak grew from a small acorn at the time of the Revolutionary War. This is a perfect spot for a water break or picnic.

1.9   Reach the intersection of the Green and Silver Trails. Continue straight through this intersection following the Silver Trail. The Green Trail continues to the left and heads back to the picnic/parking area.

2.1   Reach the Blue Trail. Turn right, cross the creek, and follow the blue blazes. This trail will take you out of the woods through an open field.

2.7   Just before the Blue Trail turns back into the woods, there is an Orange Trail marker in the ground. Turn right onto the Orange Trail and begin following the orange blazes.

3.1   Pass the park office and maintenance complex. Continue straight. This area also serves as the equestrian parking lot.

3.5   Reach the first intersection of the Orange (Ivy Branch) Trail and Wilkinson Road. Cross the road. The Orange Trail picks up directly on the other side. After a short ascent, you will be treated to some of the best singletrack in the park. Continue following the orange blazes.

4.8   Reach an intersection with the Blue Trail. Continue straight, following the orange blazes. Ahead of you is a short, twisty, exciting descent.

Rock Run Gristmill is where this ride begins.

5.1 Reach Wilkinson Road again. Turn right on Wilkinson Road, then immediately left on Rock Run Road. Head toward the historic area.

5.2 Turn left at the connection with the Red Trail. Follow the red blazes across the creek and get ready to climb.

6.3 Reach the intersection of Stafford Road and the Red Trail. Turn left and follow Stafford Road for approximately three-tenths of a mile.

6.6 Turn left at the brown gate in the open field and follow the Red Trail toward the woods.

6.8 Cross the wooden bridge and bear left, continuing to follow the red blazes.

7.0 Reach the end of the ride.

Ride Information

Local Information

Havre de Grace Chamber of Commerce/Tourism Board, (410) 939–3303
Harford County's Web site, with information about local events and attractions:
www.co.ha.md.us

Accommodations

Camping is available from the first weekend in May to the last weekend in September
The Everything and More Inn, Delta, PA (717) 456–7263

21 Fair Hill Natural Resource Management Area

Known primarily for its rich equestrian heritage, the Fair Hill area does not conjure up images of mountain biking. However, this northern Maryland natural resource management area has some of the most enjoyable singletrack in the state. Similar to the trails in Patapsco Valley State Park, the Fair Hill area offers a superb network of trails sure to satisfy the most demanding riders.

Start: From the parking lot adjacent to the covered bridge on Tawes Road
Length: 8.3-mile loop
Approximate riding time: 1.5 hours
Difficulty: Twisty, technical singletrack with elevation changes makes this a moderate to difficult trail.
Trail surface: Singletrack, doubletrack, and gravel roads
Lay of the land: Singletrack trails that run through rolling fields and forests
Land status: Natural resource management area—Department of Natural Resources
Nearest town: Elkton, MD
Other trail users: Hikers, equestrians, anglers, and pets (dogs must be kept on leashes)
Trail contacts: DNR Office, Fair Hill, MD, (410) 398-1246

Delaware Trail Spinners, Bear, DE
www.trailspinners.org
Schedule: Varies. Call park manager's office directly for information, (410) 398-1246
Fees and permits: None
Maps: USGS map: Newark West, MD
Fair Hill maps—available for $1.00 at the DNR office

Getting There:

From Baltimore, MD: Take Interstate 95 north to Exit 109A. Get on State Highway 279 south to Elkton. Continue on State Highway 279 to the intersection with State Highway 213. Turn right onto Highway 213. Follow it for approximately 6 miles and turn right at the Fair Hill Inn, immediately before the intersection of Highway 213 and State Highway 273. Take an immediate right onto Ranger Skinner Drive. The DNR office will be to your immediate right. Follow Ranger Skinner Drive through the traffic circle and parking lots and continue to the left. Ranger Skinner Drive will run parallel to Highway 273 on your left and the Fair Hill Race Track on your right. Continue on Ranger Skinner Drive for approximately three-quarters of a mile and turn left on Training Center Road. Continue for half a mile and turn right onto Tawes Drive. Follow Tawes Drive for about 1 mile to the parking area immediately before the covered bridge. The ride begins here. *DeLorme: Maryland/Delaware Atlas & Gazetteer:* Page 78, A-1

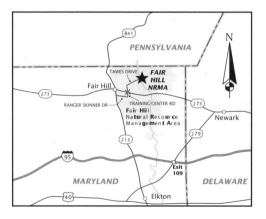

Sethe Bluestone's roadhouse was constructed in the Fair Hill area for the movie Beloved, *starring Oprah Winfrey.*

The Ride

The earliest known settlers of the Fair Hill area were the Susquehannock Indians. They belonged to the Iroquois Confederacy. Looking for a peaceful home, the Susquehannocks left the Seneca Nation and settled in this area because of the natural abundance the northern Chesapeake River and the Susquehanna River had to offer. In the early 1600s, Captain John Smith traveled these areas, bartering with the Native Americans and exploring the region. The charter of Maryland to Lord Cecil Calvert by King Charles I of England, in 1632, marked the beginning of European exploration and settlement in the area.

In 1926, William du Pont Jr. bought his first of many parcels of land in the area. After acquiring the land, du Pont brought his hounds from Montpelier, Virginia, and hired a huntsman to establish his kennels. An avid hunter and equestrian, he hunted three times a week, usually before breakfast. Despite du Pont's passion for horses and racing, he did not build the Fair Hill Racetrack until the 1930s. The racetrack was fashioned after the Ainsley Track in England, and it firmly established Fair Hill's equestrian tradition.

William du Pont's 5,700-acre estate would become one of the largest holdings in the East. Soon after his death in 1965, his heirs sold the property to Maryland's Department of Natural Resources. Since then, the Department of Natural Resources has managed and maintained the land, continuing the rich equestrian tradition that William du Pont Jr. began.

Not only is the Fair Hill area famous for its horse races, but it was chosen as the location for Oprah Winfrey's 1998 movie *Beloved*. In 1997, while flying concentric circles from Philadelphia in search of a movie location, producers for *Beloved* noticed a large secluded parcel of land marked by vast open hay fields and wooded sections. Upon further investigation, and several ground visits, Oprah and company would choose this area as one of their primary filming locations. The movie, which is based on the 1988 Pulitzer Prize–winning novel by Toni Morrison, stars Oprah Winfrey and Danny Glover, and is set in nineteenth-century rural Cincinnati. Winfrey plays Sethe Bluestone. In an effort to accurately reproduce nineteenth-century living, the film producers hired local contractors and craftsmen to build the movie set, including Sethe Bluestone's roadhouse. In addition, they trucked in several additional buildings bought from a broker in South Carolina.

▶ In 1926, William du Pont Jr. bought his first of many parcels of land in the Fair Hill area. After acquiring the land, du Pont brought his hounds from Montpelier, Virginia, and hired a huntsman to establish his kennels.

Intended as temporary structures, the buildings still stand and line part of your ride. Local interest and hundreds of visitors each year prompted the managers of Fair Hill to keep the structures standing. In addition, for their support of the movie and use of the land, the Fair Hill Natural Resource Management Area received well over one million dollars in much-needed revenue.

Fair Hill is nothing short of breathtaking, and this ride clearly reveals the beauty of the area. As you ride in and out of the woods and through the open fields, you'll soon forget about the rest of the world and begin to see why the Susquehannocks chose this area as their home. You will also see why William du Pont Jr. chose Fair

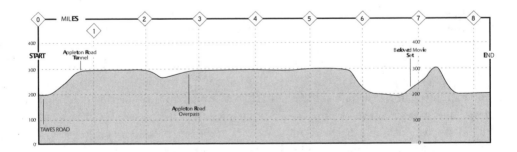

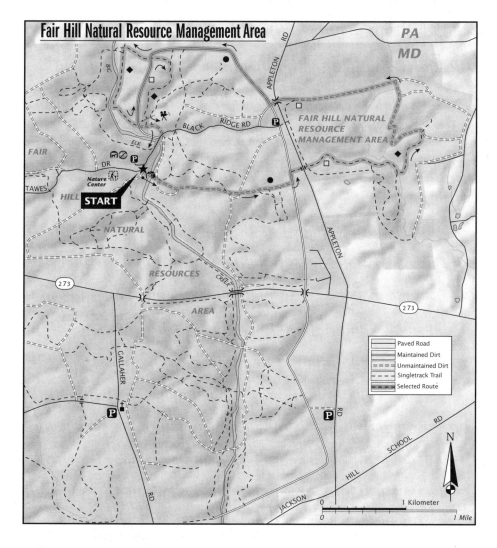

Fair Hill Natural Resource Management Area

	Paved Road
	Maintained Dirt
	Unmaintained Dirt
	Singletrack Trail
	Selected Route

Hill as his home and hunting site. The natural splendor, beauty, and quality and quantity of trails in the area make it a great place to mountain bike.

Note that there are many trails to choose from in this area, and the small loop presented here is only one of the countless riding possibilities available in the park's 5,600 acres. There is an extensive 75-mile trail system made up of singletrack and dirt roads. The loop and ride possibilities in the Fair Hill area are numerous. A trail map is available from the Fair Hill park office.

Miles and Directions

0.0   **START** from the parking lot and turn left on Tawes Road. Go through the covered bridge and follow the road for approximately 1 mile.

1.1   Turn left at the T intersection. Immediately turn right after crossing a small dip. Follow the beaten path through the tunnel beneath Appleton Road.

1.6   The trail curves left and forks. Turn right and follow the singletrack into the woods.

1.8   Turn left into the woods and follow the fork to the right. Continue down a short and steep downhill. After crossing the creek, the trail will curve to the left immediately after the creek crossing.

2.2   Turn left at this intersection.

2.5   Turn right at this intersection. Turn left after the small bridge.

2.8   Come out onto a field and follow its perimeter to the left for a short distance. Turn left into the woods and continue following the trail to the left.

3.3   Turn left onto the doubletrack. You will immediately bear right at the Y intersection into the singletrack.

3.4   Turn right at this intersection. The trail is marked by a four-by-four in the ground.

3.8   Turn left at the doubletrack. Continue following the doubletrack up a brief hill and to the left of the field. After a small downhill and creek crossing, continue following the double-track to the left.

4.1   Continue straight at this intersection and over Appleton Road.

4.9   Turn right at this T intersection and ride on the gravel road. (**Option:** You can do this loop again by turning left and riding for approximately half a mile past the Appleton Road parking lot to the tunnel that you crossed at the beginning of the ride [marker 1.10]. You can also continue a little farther and turn right on Tawes Road to finish the ride.)

5.9   Turn right at this intersection. This is a very easy intersection to miss, especially if the field has not been mowed or is overgrown. The path intersects the road perpendicularly at a point where the woods are closer to the road. If you look left you will see another path heading into the woods. You'll ride this on the way back. If you reach a large brown sign on the left side of the road that reads MCCLOSKEY AREA, you've gone too far. At the time these markers were set, there was a portable toilet and fire pit approximately 50 yards to the left from this intersection. After a short ride through the tall grass, turn left into the singletrack in the woods. What follows is a great twisty singletrack section with a couple of loose technical descents. Pay attention to the trail.

6.4   Continue straight through this intersection.

6.7   Turn left at this intersection.

6.9   Turn left at this intersection. This is the location of the *Beloved* movie set.

7.3   Turn right at this intersection. This spot is directly opposite the spot where you turned right into the woods at mile 5.9. Immediately after entering the woods, turn right and fol-low the trail through the stone ruins. Turn left immediately after the ruins. It's all downhill from here!

7.4   Bear left at this Y intersection and then turn right.

7.9 Turn right at this intersection and then turn left.

8.1 Turn right at this intersection and cross over the bridge. Immediately after crossing the bridge, bear left and follow the road to the parking lot.

8.3 Arrive at your car.

(**Note:** There are more than 100 miles of trails and roads in the Fair Hill Natural Resource Management Area. This loop is only a sampling of what this location has to offer. Time permitting, you should explore the many miles of trails in the area. An alternative parking area with additonal trailheads is adjacent to Appleton Road. Have fun and keep the rubber side down.)

Ride Information

Local Information

Cecil County's official Web site:
www.ccmagazine.org—with local information, events, and attractions

Accommodations

Fair Hill, MD, (410) 398-1246—offers primitive camping for recognized youth groups at several areas near Big Elk Creek

Garden Cottage Sinking Springs Herb Farm
Elkton, MD, (410) 398-5566

22 Patuxent Research Refuge, North Tract

If you are looking for tight switchbacks and roller-coaster singletrack, this is not the place. But if you want to freely spin on wide-open gravel roads, this is your spot. Patuxent Research Refuge is the perfect place to get acquainted with the operation of your new bicycle and its components. It's also a good area to observe some of central Maryland's wildlife. This is a great ride for the kids—especially if it's their first time off-road.

Start: From the parking lot adjacent to the contact station
Length: 7.8-mile loop
Approximate riding time: 1 hour
Difficulty: Easy, due to little elevation change
Trail surface: Doubletrack, gravel roads, some pavement
Lay of the land: Wide-open roads, minimal uphills through old army training grounds. Several old cemeteries can be seen throughout the ride.
Land status: Managed by the U.S. Fish and Wildlife Service

Nearest town: Laurel, MD
Other trail users: Hikers, anglers, naturalists, and hunters (in season)
Trail contacts: Refuge Volunteer Coordinator, Laurel, MD, (410) 674-3304
Schedule: September: 8:00 A.M. to 7:00 P.M. October: 8:00 A.M. to 6:30 P.M. November through February: 8:00 A.M. to 4:30 P.M. March: 8:00 A.M. to 6:00 P.M. April through August: 8:00 A.M. to 8:00 P.M.
Fees and permits: No fees, but you must register at the contact station and receive an access pass before riding.
Maps: USGS map: Laurel, MD

Getting There: From Washington, D.C.: Take the Interstate 495 Beltway to Interstate 95 North. Take Exit 33B (State Highway 198) east toward Laurel. Follow Highway 198 for approximately 6.5 miles. Take a right onto Bald Eagle Drive. If you reach State Highway 32, you have gone too far. Follow Bald Eagle Drive through the entrance gate and go approximately 1 mile to the contact station. *DeLorme: Maryland/Delaware Atlas & Gazetteer:* Page 47, B-6

The Ride

This ride is a wonderful introduction to both mountain biking and wildlife. The trails are wide, old roads, and the elevation changes are minimal. Unlike many of the other trails in this book, the land surrounding the Patuxent Research Refuge has remained

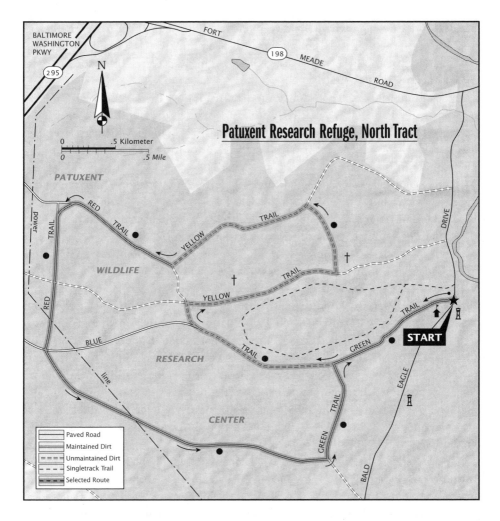

Patuxent Research Refuge, North Tract

unchanged for years. To support and promote wildlife, the Department of the Interior uses this area specifically for research, conservation, and wildlife education.

The Patuxent Research Refuge was established in 1936 by executive order of President Franklin Roosevelt, making it the nation's first wildlife research station. The refuge extends for 12,000 acres across the Patuxent River Valley, between Baltimore and Washington. It is divided into three main tracts. The North Tract, where this ride takes place, is open to the public for hunting, fishing, wildlife observation, hiking, bicycling, and horseback riding. The South Tract is the site of the National Wildlife Visitor Center—one of the largest science and environmental education centers in the Department of the Interior. The Central Tract is designated for research and the protection of wildlife; it is closed to the public.

A word of caution: The North Tract used to be a U.S. Army training facility, used for more than seventy-five years. The area still has restricted public access, mainly because of research and wildlife management activities. Remember to be careful and to not veer off the trail. Although the area has been carefully cleared of all ordnance, one can never be too sure. It is illegal to dig, use a metal detector, or remove any historic artifacts from this land.

Native Americans once occupied the area that is now Pawtuxent Research Refuge. The name Patuxent is a Native American word that means "running over loose stones." The refuge was later settled by Europeans who built small farms and mills. More recently, the U.S. Army managed the land, prior to its being transferred to the Department of the Interior.

Family cemeteries are all that remain of the early European settlers. In the cemeteries, you may notice the name Snowden. Like their neighbors to the north in Howard County, the Carrolls and the Ellicotts, the Snowdens had much to do with the growth of Laurel, Maryland, and the surrounding areas.

The Snowdens settled in this area in the late 1600s, when King Charles II granted Richard Snowden 1,900 acres. Richard Snowden would eventually own more than 16,000 acres of land along the banks of the Patuxent River. Locally, the Patuxent River was known as the Snowden River, due to the large quantity of land that he owned on both banks. Birmingham Manor, seat of the Snowden family, was a thriving plantation on the banks of the Patuxent River. Its present location is on the east side of the Baltimore Washington Parkway, opposite Laurel Airport. In its prosperous days, the plantation had twenty-four tobacco barns all in a row. Unfortunately, the Snowden home was destroyed by fire in 1891, and the surrounding outbuildings were demolished in 1953 to create the northbound lanes of the Baltimore Washington Parkway. However, rubble from the old home and two wells are still present next to the Snowden Cemetery.

Known as Fort Meade today, Fort Leonard Wood was built in 1917 adjacent to Birmingham Manor. By 1941, the U.S. Army had absorbed Birmingham Manor and many of the old structures that once defined the area. Many of these structures have since been removed, but some of the foundations still stand. In an effort to regain its past history and to document and preserve the historic richness, the Patuxent Historic Research Project was established in 1991. Rick McGill and Brian Alexander, volunteer researchers, are predominantly responsible for the preservation of these

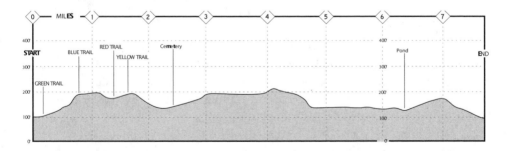

Wide trails and old dirt roads are perfect for newcomers to the sport.

cemeteries and buildings. The Patuxent visitor center and the Patuxent Research Refuge Web site both have additional information on the history of the North Tract, the Snowden Family, and other families who shaped Maryland.

Miles and Directions

0.0   **START** from the parking lot adjacent to the contact station. Go out the way you came in and make an immediate left turn. At the stop sign, turn right and follow the fork to the right onto the gravel road, away from the pavement. You are now on the Green Trail. (You must register at the contact station before beginning the ride.)

0.7   Continue straight through this intersection. Small colored arrows identify the trail. You are now on the Blue Trail.

1.5   Bear right at this intersection and follow the red marker. This will put you on the Red Trail.

1.7   Turn right at this intersection and follow the yellow marker. You are now on the Yellow Trail.

2.4   Turn left and continue on the Yellow Trail. Immediately after you turn right, you will notice a small cemetery on the right. Stones in the cemetery date all the way back to the 1600s.

2.8   Turn left to continue on the Yellow Trail. Immediately to the left, you will notice a small enclave with two small trees and a small marker belonging to Captain Dean K. Phillips, commander of the Eleventh Signal Company, Special Forces.

3.6   Turn right at this intersection. You are back on the Red Trail. (**Option:** Should you choose to do the yellow loop again, a left turn will take you back to the start of the Yellow Trail.)

4.2   Turn left at this intersection. Continue following the red marker to stay on the Red Trail.

4.9   Turn left after a brief downhill. You will be faced with an immediate fork in the road. Either way leads back to the Green Trail. However, to continue on the chapter ride, bear right onto the Blue Trail.

6.5   Turn left at this intersection. You are now on the Green Trail and on your way back to the contact station. A tenth of a mile after the turn, there is a small pond on the left.

7.4   Turn right at this intersection to continue on the Green Trail. (**Option:** You can turn left and do the loop again.)

7.7   You are back at the parking lot and contact station.

Note: You can add additional miles to the ride by taking the Wildlife Loop away from the contact station and toward Lake Allen and the Pine Trail. You can also ride along the Wildlife Loop and check out some of the observation points and lookouts along the road.

Ride Information

Local Information
Web site and phone contact for Laurel, MD
(301) 725-7800; www.laurel.md.us

Local Events and Attractions
Patuxent Research Refuge and National Wildlife Visitor Center, www.patuxent.fws.gov
(301) 497-5760

23 L. F. Cosca Regional Park

Readily accessible from the Washington Beltway, L. F. Cosca Regional Park is a deceiving place. Its small size and rather urban setting hide a great network of singletrack. This regional park in Prince George's County has that specific ingredient that makes every ride better—singletrack. The variety of possible routes in this park will undoubtedly keep you busy for a couple of hours.

Start: Clearwater Nature Center
Length: 5+ miles of trails
Approximate riding time: 1 hour
Difficulty: Easy to moderate
Trail surface: Singletrack
Lay of the land: Stream crossings and heavily wooded terrain around Cosca Lake
Land status: Regional park
Nearest town: Clinton, MD
Other trail users: Hikers and nature enthusiasts
Trail contacts: L. F. Cosca Regional Park (301) 868-1397
Clearwater Nature Center (301) 297-4575
Schedule: Open daily 7:30 A.M. to dusk, year-round
Fees and permits: Memorial Day to Labor Day, nonresidents of Prince George's or Montgomery County must pay a $5.00 fee for parking within the confines of the park
Maps: USGS map: Piscataway, MD
ADC map: Prince George's County road map
Park Service trail map

Getting There: From the Capital Beltway (Interstate 495): Take Exit 7 to State Highway 5 (Branch Avenue) toward Waldorf. Go approximately 4 miles to State Highway 223 (Woodyard Road). Turn right on Woodyard Road, taking it 0.6 miles to Brandywine Road. Turn left on Brandywine Road. Follow it south toward Clinton (0.75 miles), then turn right on Thrift Road. Thrift Road takes you south 1.5 miles to the park entrance on your right. Go right into the park to the Clearwater Nature Center on top of the hill. Parking, telephones, toilets, and small creatures can all be found at the nature center. *DeLorme: Maryland/Delaware Atlas & Gazetteer:* Page 37, B-5

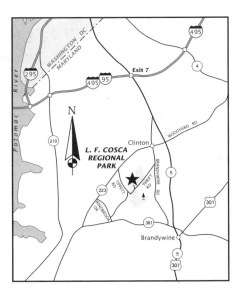

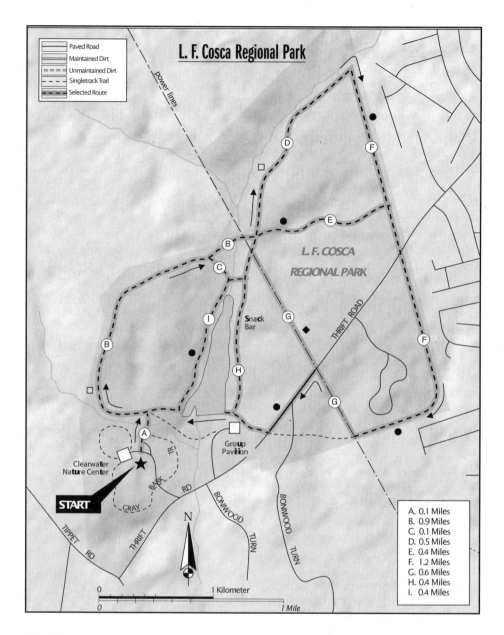

L. F. Cosca Regional Park

Legend:
- Paved Road
- Maintained Dirt
- Unmaintained Dirt
- Singletrack Trail
- Selected Route

L. F. COSCA REGIONAL PARK

Snack Bar

Group Pavilion

Clearwater Nature Center

START

power lines

THRIFT ROAD

PARK TR

GRAY RD

THRIFT RD

TIPPET RD

BONIWOOD TURN

BONIWOOD TURN

N

A.	0.1 Miles
B.	0.9 Miles
C.	0.1 Miles
D.	0.5 Miles
E.	0.4 Miles
F.	1.2 Miles
G.	0.6 Miles
H.	0.4 Miles
I.	0.4 Miles

0   1 Kilometer

0   1 Mile

The Ride

Things can often deceive you, disappoint you, and leave you feeling shortchanged. Louise F. Cosca Regional Park, just outside the town of Clinton in Prince George's County, is one such place that will, indeed, deceive you. It will not, however, leave you disappointed. For despite its small size, this park has everything off-road cyclists dream of: deep, wooded surroundings; stream crossings; a beautiful 15-acre lake; quick, rugged singletrack trails; and a variety of off-road possibilities.

Your ride starts from the parking lot at Clearwater Nature Center, one of the state's most innovative nature centers. This lava-rock building is placed deep within the woods, featuring a large greenhouse and indoor pond, complete with live occupants. From here, you'll descend quickly into the woods along the park's main trail. (Although this book guides you left, following trails around the perimeter of the park, don't hesitate to explore and create your own circuits.) The trail travels quickly along the creek, often precariously close to the water's edge, then up through the trees above the creek valley. This leads to a thrilling, narrow descent down winding singletrack to Butler Creek. Crossing Butler Creek presents a challenge, as it is a bit too wide to jump and somewhat difficult to negotiate from the bike. While descending the last hill, detour right onto Trail C and take the easy route over the creek via a small wooden bridge at the north end of the lake. Once across the creek, the ride just gets better. Whichever route you choose toward the west end of the park, you're in for a wonderful ride. The trails twist back and forth beneath the tall trees and, in the colorful fall season, can be breathtaking. Continuing around the perimeter of the park, the trails roll more gently back toward the start of the ride, allowing you to sit back and enjoy your wooded surroundings.

The variety of possible routes within Cosca's 500 acres of rolling, wooded parkland will turn your ride into much more than a quick jaunt through the woods. You can spend hours exploring the different trails, then pedal over to the snack bar and finish a great day by lounging along the shores of L. F. Cosca's Lake.

> ▶ The trails twist back and forth beneath the tall trees and, in the colorful fall season, can be breathtaking. Continuing around the perimeter of the park, the trails roll more gently back toward the start of the ride, allowing you to sit back and enjoy your wooded surroundings.

Miles and Directions

0.0 START from the parking lot at the Clearwater Nature Center and follow Trail A down wooden-plank steps into the woods.

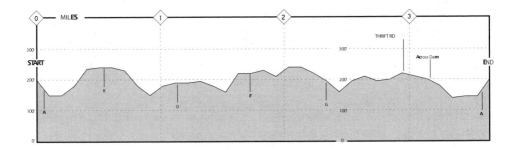

This rider is chillin' on the outer edge of the park and enjoying the wooded surroundings at trail end.

0.1 Turn left at this trail intersection with Trail B. Turning right takes you along a secondary trail toward the Group Pavilion. Heading straight on Trail B takes you up a steep hill to the lake.

0.8 You may either continue straight on Trail B down this fantastic descent or turn right on Trail C, then left on Trail H. The strategy is to connect with Trail D. The advantage of detouring on Trail C, then left on Trail H back to Trail D, is that you avoid slogging through thick brush and Butler Branch Creek, where there is no good place to cross. Take your pick.

1.0 Bear left on Trail D. This is an exciting trail, taking you up and down a quick and challenging singletrack. (**Option:** Trail E is a fun alternative here, twisting quickly through the woods along more level terrain.)

1.5 Turn right on Trail F. This trail gently rolls along a more open jeep trail.

2.0 Cross Thrift Road. Continue on Trail F.

2.7 Turn right at the power lines (Trail G).

2.9 Turn left on Thrift Road. You could follow the power lines (Trail G) all the way back into the park.

3.1 Bear right off Thrift Road to a hiking trail, which takes you past the Group Pavilion and up to the dam.

3.3 Reach the lake. Cross the dam, taking Trail B down the hill back to Trail A. Turn right to the snack bar for some food—a great diversion when you reach the lake.

3.5 Follow Trail A back up the hill to the Clearwater Nature Center parking lot.

Ride Information

Local Information
Prince George's County Parks and Recreation
www.smart.net/~parksrec/index.htm
Maryland-National Capital Park and Planning Commission, Riverdale, MD, (301) 699-2407

24 Cedarville State Forest

Tight, twisty singletrack is what you'll find when you visit Cedarville. There are over 10 miles of singletrack and doubletrack in this 3,500-acre state forest just south of Washington, D.C. Its proximity to the nation's capital and its modest terrain have made Cedarville State Forest a popular cycling destination for riders throughout the region. Unlike those in neighboring parks to the north, the trails in Cedarville are generally hard-packed dirt with very few rocks. Occasional mud holes may slow you down, but this is otherwise one of the most enjoyable mountain bike destinations in the area.

Start: Park office
Length: 7.9 miles
Approximate riding time: 1.5–3 hours
Difficulty: Easy due to flat, unimpeded trails
Trail surface: Flat, dirt trails and dirt roads
Lay of the land: Flat, woodland setting with a freshwater lake

Land status: State forest
Nearest town: Brandywine, MD
Other trail users: Campers, anglers, hikers, equestrians, and hunters
Trail contacts: Maryland Forest, Park, and Wildlife Service, (301) 888-1622
Schedule: Open daily from 8:00 A.M. to sunset most of the year. Winter schedule: 10:00 A.M. to sunset
Fees and permits: $2.00 per car
Maps: USGS maps: Brandywine, MD; Hughesville, MD
ADC maps: Prince George's County road map, Charles County road map

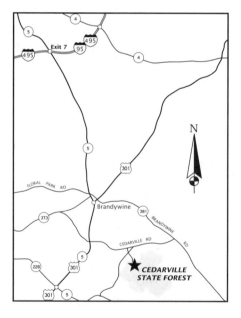

Getting There: From the Capital Beltway (Interstate 495): Take Exit 7 to State Highway 5 (Branch Avenue) toward Waldorf. Go 11.6 miles on Highway 5 (which joins with U.S. 301), then turn left on Cedarville Road. Go 2.3 miles, then turn right on the forest entrance road (Bee Oak Road). Park office and parking 1 mile down the road. Portable toilets are available. Water and telephones are not available. *DeLorme: Maryland/Delaware Atlas & Gazetteer:* Page 37, D-6

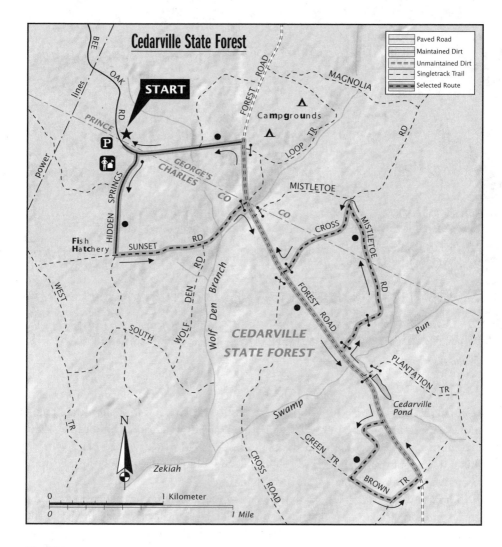

The Ride

Here's an off-road ride that rolls along forest roads and wooded trails through Prince George's and Charles Counties' quiet state forest. There are no monuments, natural wonders, or sights of great historical significance in Cedarville State Forest. Even the name may leave you wondering, as cedars are uncommon to the immediate area. (The name, in fact, was taken from a nearby post office.) What this small state forest in southern Maryland offers instead is a network of wonderful wooded trails and dirt roads that guide visitors beneath tall stands of loblolly and white pine, around groves of holly and magnolia trees, past a four-acre lake, through the headwaters of Maryland's largest freshwater swamp, and across abandoned farmland with streams and springs once used for making moonshine.

Cedarville's beauty makes for a wonderful ride for novices and experts alike.

The state acquired the land in 1930 during a period of farm abandonment and crop failures in southern Maryland. It planned to use this land to demonstrate techniques in forestry, but the land is now managed for both recreation and business. You may notice, as you ride through the park, sizable areas that have been clear-cut or thinned. The cut timber, restricted to Virginia and loblolly pine, is sold to paper mills as far away as West Virginia and Pennsylvania.

This is a wonderful ride for novices and experts alike who have a passion for the great outdoors. Cedarville's terrain is mostly flat, as is most of southern Maryland, but the beauty of its wooded forest roadways rises high above most everything else in the area.

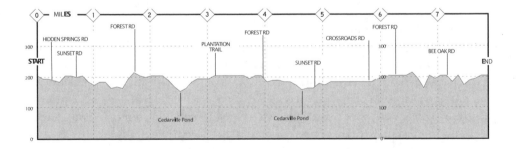

Miles and Directions

0.0 **START** at Cedarville State Forest's park office on Bee Oak Road. From the parking lot, turn right on Bee Oak Road (paved).

0.1 Turn right on Hidden Springs Road (paved).

0.7 Hidden Springs Road comes to an end. Turn left on Sunset Road. This is a rolling rutted dirt trail through the woods (fish hatchery to the right at this intersection).

1.7 Turn right on Forest Road (dirt).

2.8 Pass Cedarville Pond on the left. Go straight through the steel gate, continuing on Forest Road.

3.1 Turn right off Forest Road on Plantation Trail (Brown Trail), which loops around the south end of the park. The CCC (Civilian Conservation Corps) planted the thick growth of loblolly pine that this trail tunnels through in the 1930s.

3.6 Plantation Trail comes to a T, intersecting with Swamp Trail (Green Trail). Turn left, continuing to follow the Brown Trail signs.

4.0 Turn left on Forest Road (dirt).

4.7 Pass Cedarville Pond on the right.

4.8 Turn right on Mistletoe Road (doubletrack trail). Watch for the brown wooden street signs at each intersection along Forest Road.

5.1 Continue straight through the wooden gate on Mistletoe Road.

5.8 Turn left on Crossroads Road at this intersection (doubletrack trail).

5.9 Cross Heritage Trail. Continue straight on Crossroads Road.

6.3 Turn right on Forest Road (dirt).

7.2 Turn left on Bee Oak Road (paved).

7.9 Reach the park office.

Ride Information

Local Information

Charles County's Web site has local information, events, and attractions:
www.ccmainstreet.com

Accommodations

Structured campsites are available off Forest Road. Primitive camping is also available in the forest.

25 Patuxent River Park

Less than an hour from Capitol Hill, Patuxent River Park offers a varied network of trails suitable for cyclists of all skill levels. Winding singletrack throughout the park offers visitors a unique glimpse into the pristine natural beauty and biodiversity of the Chesapeake Bay region. And lack of any serious elevation changes makes this an ideal place for riders of all ability levels. The diversity and quality of the trails in the Patuxent River Park are bound to delight and satisfy.

Start: Park office
Length: 7 miles
Approximate riding time: 1 hour
Difficulty: Easy to moderate
Trail surface: Singletrack
Lay of the land: Wooded, rolling terrain
Land status: State park and natural area
Nearest towns: Upper Marlboro, MD; Waldorf, MD
Other trail users: Hikers, equestrians, cross-country skiers, and bow hunters

Trail contacts: Patuxent River Park (301) 627-6074
Schedule: Open daily, 8:00 A.M. to dusk
Park Office is open 8:00 A.M. to 4:00 P.M.
Fees and permits: Required park use permit (available at park office). You may purchase a seasonal visitor's pass or pay $2.00 per visit.
Maps: USGS map: Bristol, MD
ADC maps: Prince George's County road map
Department of Parks and Recreation trail map
Patuxent River Park trail map

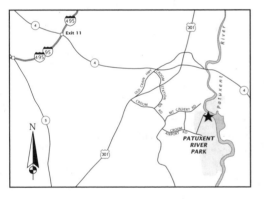

Getting There: From the Capital Beltway (Interstate 495): Take Exit 11 east on State Highway 4 (Pennsylvania Avenue). Follow Highway 4 east 6.3 miles, then exit left on Old Crain Highway, traveling south. Almost immediately, turn left on Croom Station Road. Go 2.5 miles and turn left on Croom Road (State Highway 382). Go 1.3 miles and turn left on Croom Airport Road. This takes you into Patuxent River Park. After 2 miles, turn left on Park Entrance Road and travel 1.5 miles to the end, parking at the park office. *DeLorme: Maryland/Delaware Atlas & Gazetteer:* Page 38, A-1

The Ride

The ride through this section of Patuxent River Park is a fantastic journey over wooded, rolling terrain along nearly 10 miles of woodland horse trails and twisting singletrack. The trails, open to hikers, horseback riders, and cyclists, lead you through Jug Bay's beautiful 2,000-acre limited-use natural area, providing a close-up look at a coastal ecosystem with amazing biodiversity in one of Maryland's premier greenways. Watch for snakes, turtles, bald eagles, blue herons, and rails.

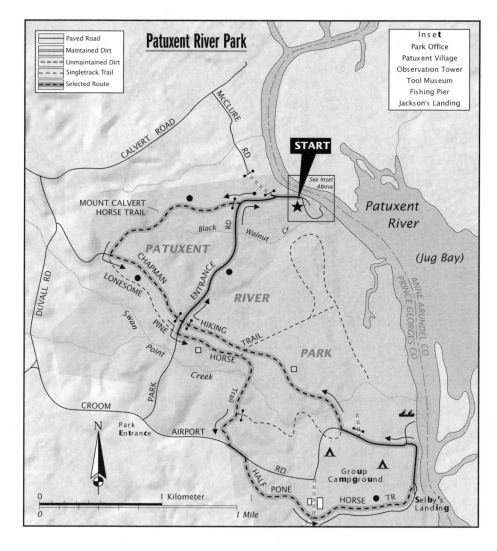

Patuxent River Park

Legend:
- Paved Road
- Maintained Dirt
- Unmaintained Dirt
- Singletrack Trail
- Selected Route

Inset
- Park Office
- Patuxent Village
- Observation Tower
- Tool Museum
- Fishing Pier
- Jackson's Landing

START

See Inset Above

McCLURE

CALVERT ROAD

RD

MOUNT CALVERT
HORSE TRAIL

Patuxent River

(Jug Bay)

Black

RD

Walnut

Cr

PATUXENT

CHAPMAN

ENTRANCE

DUVALL RD

LONESOME

RIVER

Swan

PINE

HIKING

TRAIL

PARK

Point

HORSE

ANNE ARUNDEL CO
PRINCE GEORGES CO

Creek

PARK

Trail

CROOM

N

Park
Entrance

AIRPORT

RD

HALF

Group
Campground

PONE

HORSE

TR

Selby's
Landing

0   1 Kilometer

0   1 Mile

Acquired by the Maryland Department of Natural Resources, the Jug Bay Natural Area represents Maryland's nationally acclaimed land preservation program called Program Open Space. This program was designed to preserve open land and to protect valuable natural resources.

The results of this program offer something of value to all who come to visit. Naturalists are given the unique opportunity to observe freshwater, tidal, and nontidal wetlands; historians may experience life along the river during the nineteenth century at the Patuxent Village; nature lovers can drive or pedal a 4-mile, self-guided tour through the Merkle Wildlife Sanctuary, including the thousand-foot boardwalk crossing the Mattaponi Creek; hunters enjoy bow season for squirrel, rabbit, and deer; and hikers, equestrians, and mountain bikers have miles of wooded singletrack

Chapman Trail offers excellent riding.

trails to enjoy. All hikers and riders, however, are required to register at the park office and must have a park permit before venturing onto the trails. Permits can be obtained from the park office for $2.00 a visit. A seasonal visitor's pass is also available.

This fabulous ride offers cyclists wanting to venture off the road and into the woods a fantastic opportunity to see nature up close without the grueling pressures of steep climbs and treacherous descents. Don't be fooled, though. Patuxent River Park is full of exciting trails to keep cyclists of any ability interested and entertained.

If the off-road riding isn't enough while you're here, cyclists can pedal along the 4.5-mile Critical Area Driving Tour from 10:00 A.M. to 3:00 P.M. on Saturdays throughout most of the year. The tour is open to cars on Sundays only, so cyclists will have the route to themselves. However, it is closed October through January. Visitors pedaling through the 2,000-acre Merkle Wildlife Sanctuary can see thousands of Canada geese and other waterfowl making their annual pit stop.

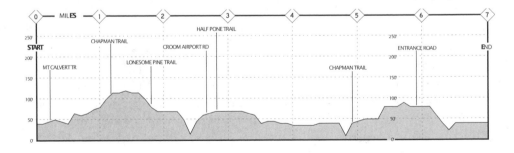

Miles and Directions

0.0 **START** from the park office at the northern end of Park Entrance Road. Travel south on Park Entrance Road.

0.4 Turn right off Park Entrance Road through a wooden gate on Mount Calvert Horse Trail. The trail is slightly hidden from the road. A wooden post with a horse trail symbol marks the trailhead.

1.2 Turn left off Mount Calvert Horse Trail on Chapman Hiking Trail. This trail leads you away from a field into the woods.

1.6 Exit the woods around a steel gate and turn right on Park Entrance Road. Look for the yellow horse-crossing sign just up the road.

1.7 Turn left on the Lonesome Pine Horse Trail just past the yellow horse-crossing sign. A wooden post with a horse-trail symbol marks this trail.

2.0 Turn right at the trail intersection, continuing downhill. Be careful of the wooden water bars laid across the trail.

2.3 Turn right at the trail intersection, continuing on the Lonesome Pine Horse Trail. Turning left takes you on a hilly ride along another horse trail to Croom Airport Road. This trail is often closed during wet seasons.

2.6 Turn left on Croom Airport Road. You should see the yellow horse-crossing sign to the left up the road. Keep your eyes peeled for this trail.

2.7 Turn right on the Half Pone Horse Trail. This trail is a bit obscure. Keep your eyes peeled for the wooden post that marks it.

3.2 Cross the dirt jeep trail, continuing straight on Half Pone Horse Trail.

3.5 Cross another dirt road. Follow Half Pone Horse Trail along the perimeter of the group campgrounds. The campgrounds and picnic area should be on your left. Continue following the trail around the right side of the cornfields. You will continue along what seems like a tractor path around the cornfields. It dumps you back on Croom Airport Road next to the Selby's Landing boat ramp.

4.6 Pass the gravel road and gate on the right.

4.9 Turn right off Croom Airport Road, back into the woods on the horse trail. This trailhead is very obscure and overgrown. It begins off the road down behind the weeds and is marked by a wooden horse-trail post. There is a post on opposite sides of Croom Airport Road at this point.

5.7 Reach the trail intersection and continue straight.

6.0 Turn right on Park Entrance Road. You can go straight on the hiking trail if you'd like.

7.0 Arrive back at the park office. Grab a soda and ride down to Jug Bay for some rest.

Ride Information

Local Events and Attractions

Merkle Wildlife Sanctuary, Upper Marlboro, MD—driving tour (Sundays from 10:00 A.M. to 3:00 P.M.) beginning at Jug Bay Natural Area: (800) 784-5380

Accommodations

Makai Pierside Bed & Breakfast, Deale, MD (410) 867-0998

Tidewater Treasures, Chesapeake Beach, MD (410) 257-0785

In Addition

Chesapeake Bay

Certainly, one of the most prominent features in this region is the Chesapeake Bay—the largest inlet on the Atlantic coast of the United States. The unique character and identity of eastern Maryland and Virginia are woven inexplicably around the bay's coastal environment and economy, giving this region a flavor all its own.

The Patuxent River, along which the Patuxent River Park is located, travels nearly 100 miles to reach the bay and is one of the many broad, deep tidal rivers to pour into this vast waterway. Other major rivers feeding the bay are the Susquehanna, Patapsco, Severn, Potomac, Rapahannock, York, and James. The Chesapeake Bay is actually the "drowned" river valley of the lower part of the Susquehanna River, which pours into the bay at its head near the Maryland/Pennsylvania border.

In all, the bay measures nearly 195 miles long, ranges from 3 to 25 miles wide, and is deep enough to accommodate oceangoing vessels. It has about 27,000 miles of shoreline and covers 3,237 square miles of water. The Chesapeake Bay is considered one of the most important commercial and sportfishing grounds in the United States. It is famous for its oysters, crabs, and diamondback terrapins.

Another unique feature associated with the bay is the Chesapeake Bay Bridge-Tunnel, stretching between Cape Charles (the southern tip of Virginia's Eastern Shore) and a point east of Norfolk, Virginia. The bridge-tunnel carries motorists over and under 17.6 miles of uninterrupted ocean.

One of the nice things about traveling to Patuxent River Park is the classic eastern Maryland scenery and character that you are bound to experience along the way. As you drive down U.S. Highway 301, you should have plenty of opportunities to purchase fresh blue crabs from roadside vendors or to stop at one of the many seafood restaurants serving nothing but the freshest catch.

26 Saint Mary's River State Park

Boasting more than 8 miles of pristine singletrack, Saint Mary's Lake is an Eastern Shore destination. The ride's lack of serious elevation change makes this trail ideal for beginning to intermediate riders. The advanced rider should not be discouraged, however, as the winding singletrack trails make for great fun. Enjoy the variety of terrain that this trail has to offer.

Start: Main parking lot at the boat ramp
Length: 8.15 miles
Approximate riding time: 1.5 hours
Difficulty: Easy to moderate with flat, winding singletrack
Trail surface: Singletrack
Lay of the land: Wooded acres and fields, swamps and small streams
Land status: State park
Nearest town: Waldorf, MD
Other trail users: Hikers, anglers, hunters, and canoeists
Trail contacts: Saint Mary's River State Park, care of Point Lookout State Park, Scotland, MD (301) 872-5688 or www.dnr.state.md.us/publiclands/southern/stmarysriver.html
Schedule: Open 6:00 A.M. to sunset daily from March 1 through the third weekend in November
Fees and permits: There is a $2.00 fee per car from May to September
Maps: USGS maps: Hollywood, MD; Solomon Island, MD

Getting There: From Waldorf: Take State Highway 5 south to Leonardtown. Continue for approximately 5 miles and turn left on Camp Cosoma Road (follow signs to Saint Mary's River State Park). Follow Camp Cosoma Road until it ends. Park at the far right corner (as you drive in) by the rest rooms. A sign marks the trailhead. *DeLorme: Maryland/Delaware Atlas & Gazetteer:* Page 30, C-3

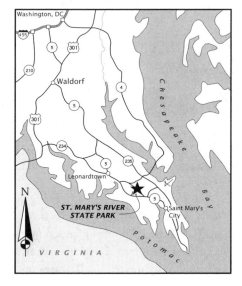

The Ride

Southern Maryland does not usually conjure up images of great mountain biking terrain. However, near Lexington Park, north of Saint Mary's City in Saint Mary's County, is a small treasure not too many off-road cyclists know about—Saint Mary's River State Park. Located between Leonardtown and Lexington Park, near the mouth of the Chesapeake Bay, this remote park boasts over 8 miles of pristine singletrack.

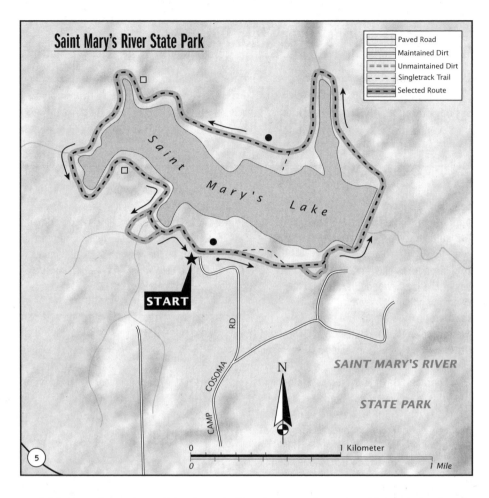

Saint Mary's River State Park

	Paved Road
	Maintained Dirt
	Unmaintained Dirt
	Singletrack Trail
	Selected Route

Saint Mary's Lake

START

COSOMA RD

CAMP RD

N

SAINT MARY'S RIVER

STATE PARK

0   1 Kilometer

0   1 Mile

5

Making a short trip to Saint Mary's City, designated a national historic landmark, is well worth the time. On March 25, 1634, some two hundred colonists sent by Lord Baltimore of England landed on the shores of Saint Clements Island. Two days later, they sailed their ships, the *Ark* and the *Dove,* up what is now the Saint Mary's River and bought close to 30 square miles of land. This land, purchased from the local Native Americans, included the Yeocomico Village, establishing what is now Saint Mary's City.

Prior to the landing of England's colonists and as far back as 3,000 years ago, several Indian tribes, including the Piscataway-Conoy, Algonquins, and Susquehannocks, called this area home. Evidence of their existence can still be found along the banks of the river in the form of arrowheads, pottery, and ax heads.

As the first capital of Maryland and the fourth permanent English settlement in the New World, this area on the Eastern Shore was a busy pioneer community. In 1637, Saint Mary's County was established, and it became known as the "Mother

County of Maryland." Saint Mary's County was also the first county to establish peaceful relations with the local Indians and was home to Maryland's first state house.

Today, much of what used to be Saint Mary's City no longer exists. By the time the state house was moved to Annapolis in 1695 and the American Revolution had ended, Lord Baltimore's capital was gone. However, during the commemoration of Maryland's 300th anniversary in 1934, the original Maryland state house was reconstructed. In 1984, for Maryland's 350th anniversary, other original sites were reconstructed. As time passes, more of Maryland's original buildings and points of interest are identified by more than 150 active archaeological excavations. Today, Saint Mary's City and County are living museums of Maryland's past.

In the 1970s, the state began purchasing land north of Great Mills, named for the mills operating along the banks of the Patuxent River. By 1979, it had completed a dam designed to protect the 5,600-acre watershed from spring floods. In 1981, this area was opened to the public as a state park.

Located on the northern edge of the Saint Mary's River watershed, the park is divided into two sites. Our ride is located on Site 1, which holds the 250-acre Saint Mary's Lake. This area has become a popular freshwater fishing spot and is currently designated as a trophy bass lake. Of more importance to cyclists, Saint Mary's Lake is circled by an 11.5-mile trail, of which 8 miles are mapped for your ride. As you pedal through the forest, notice the variety of habitats ranging from wooded acres and grass fields to swamps and streams. Currently, the park is in its early stages of development, so read the main bulletin board for special announcements and information on areas that may be closed to the public.

Miles and Directions

0.0 **START** from the parking area and enter at the trailhead (marked by a hiker sign). Immediately after your start, follow the right fork. The left fork will lead you to the same place, but the right one is more fun.

0.18 Turn right at this trail intersection. If you choose the left fork, continue straight.

0.2 Cross a small wooden bridge. Follow the trail to the right.

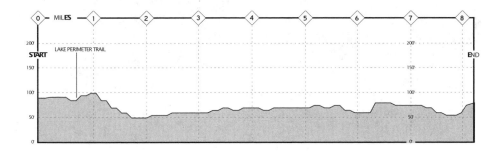

Mountain biking keeps you close to nature.

0.4 Turn left at this intersection and follow the waterline toward the dam. If you chose to go left at the previous fork, you will arrive at this intersection 10 yards to your left.

0.46 Cross the dam.

1.0 Turn left on the singletrack. The trailhead is shortly before the road curves up and to the left.

1.6 After a short downhill, cross another small wooden bridge and continue straight. The trail is now blazed white.

2.1 Cross the creek and turn left.

3.0 Bear right at this intersection. The left fork will take you to a small point overlooking the lake—a nice spot for a picnic.

3.4 Bear left and cross another small wooden bridge.

3.45 Continue to the left and over another wooden bridge.

5.1 Cross the creek. The trail continues on the other side. This is a muddy area.

5.3 Locals have built a corduroy bridge over a swampy area.

5.6 Cross yet another small wooden bridge.

5.65 Continue to the left.

7.1 Turn right at this intersection. If you choose to go left, follow the markers in parentheses.

7.2 Turn left, then cross the creek. This trail is marked with orange tape.

7.7 Cross a series of small wooden bridges. The trail continues to the left.

8.15 Arrive back at the parking lot.

Ride Information

Local Information
Historic Saint Mary's City, St. Mary's City, MD (301) 862-0990

Local Events and Attractions
Southern Maryland Online—a local Web site with information about events and attractions in St. Mary's, Charles, and Calvert Counties: www.somd.com

Accommodations
Myrtle Point B&B, California, MD (301) 862-3090

Local motel and hotel references: www.somd.com/travel/hotels.htm

In Addition

Mountain Biking with Your Dog

Many people love to bring their canine companions along on mountain bike trails. Our furry friends make great trail partners because they're always good company and they never complain. If you take your dog mountain biking with you or are considering it, there are a number of important items to keep in mind before hitting the trails.

Getting in Shape

It would be no better for your dog than it would be for you to tackle running a marathon without first getting into good physical condition. And if your pet has been a foot warmer much of his life, you will need to train him into reasonable shape before taking him along on those long weekend bike rides.

You can start your dog's training regimen by running or walking him around the neighborhood or, better yet, a local park. Frisbees and balls are also great tools to help get your dog physically fit for those upcoming mountain bike rides. Always remember that on a trail, your dog probably runs twice as far as you ride. Build your dog's exercise regimen based on the mileage you plan to ride each time you head out. If you're going on a 5-mile trail, assume your dog needs to be in shape for a 10-mile trail. Gradually build up your dog's stamina over a two- to three-month period before committing him to arduous afternoons of trying to keep up with you as you pedal along on your bike.

Training

Teaching your dog simple commands of obedience may help keep both you and your dog out of a heap of trouble while out there on public trails. The most important lesson is to train your dog to come when called. This will ensure he doesn't stray too far from the trail and possibly get lost. It may also protect him from troublesome situations, such as other trail users or perhaps coming in contact with local wildlife. Also teach your dog the "get behind" command. This comes in especially handy when you're on a singletrack trail and you run into other bikers. Teaching your dog to stay behind you and your bike and to follow your lead until the trail is clear can be a valuable and important lesson. Remember also to always carry a long leash with you in case, after all your prior training, you still have to tie your dog up to a tree at a campsite or succumb to local leash laws on crowded trails.

There are a number of good dog training books on the market that should help train you and your dog to stay out of trouble with other trail users. Also look to your local SPCA or kennel club for qualified dog trainers in the area.

Nutrition

Nutrition is important for all dogs. Never exercise a dog right after a meal. Feed your pet a high-quality diet such as Hills Science Diet or Iams. These products have higher-quality ingredients and are more nutritionally balanced than generic grocery store dog foods. They may be more expensive than some generic brands, but your dog doesn't need to eat as much to get the same nutrition and calories. If you insist on feeding your dog a grocery store diet, stick with the Purina brand, as it is better for your dog than most others in this class.

Trail Tips

Try to pick your riding trails near lakes or streams. The biggest threat to your dog when biking is the heat, and water is essential to keep him cool. If the trail doesn't have water nearby, then you need to bring as much liquid for him as you would drink yourself. A small lightweight plastic bowl can be used to give your dog water, or you can purchase a collapsible water bowl made from waterproof nylon (call Ruff Wear, 541–388–1821). You can also use a waterbottle to squirt water into your dog's mouth.

- Try not to take your dog riding with you on a really hot day—above eighty degrees. Take your dog riding in the early morning or evening when the air is cooler and safer for your pet.
- Watch for signs of heat stroke. Dogs with heat stroke will pant excessively, lie down and refuse to get up, and become lethargic and disoriented. If your dog shows any of these signs, immediately hose him down with cool water and let him rest. If you're on the trail and nowhere near a hose, find a cool stream and lay your dog in the water to help bring his body temperature back to normal.
- Avoid the common foot pad injuries. Don't run your dog on hot pavement or along long stretches of gravel road. Always bring a first aid kit that includes disinfectant, cotton wrap, and stretchy foot bandage tape so you can treat and wrap your dog's paw if it becomes injured. You might also want to look into purchasing dog booties, useful for protecting your dog's pads and feet during long runs outdoors.
- Be sure to keep your dog's nails trimmed. If your dog's nails are too long, they might catch on an object along the trail, leading to soft tissue or joint injuries.
- Don't take your dog on crowded trails and always carry a leash with you. Remember, just because you love your dog doesn't mean other people will.

27 Pocomoke State Park

Algonquin for "black water," the Pocomoke River flows southwesterly through Maryland for nearly 55 miles to the Chesapeake Bay. Along its banks, in the south, near the town of Snow Hill, Maryland, lies Pocomoke State Park. The Pocomoke ride takes place in a relatively flat area designated for off-road-vehicle use. What this ride lacks in elevation, however, is made up for by the terrain surface. Loose sandy areas will make pedaling a challenging endeavor. Don't let this discourage you, though. The trail's wide surface is perfect for family rides, and the abundant wildlife will make the ride an enjoyable adventure. Over 172 species of birds make this area home. If you're lucky, you may even catch a glimpse of bald eagles gliding over the open river. After your ride, visit historic Snow Hill. You can also see this area's Cypress Swamps while flat water canoeing. If you happen to visit in July, take a drive over to Assateague Island, where you can watch the famous pony river crossing to Chincoteague.

Start: Nature Center parking lot
Length: 5.5-mile loop
Approximate riding time: 1–2 hours
Difficulty: Easy to moderate
Trail surface: ORV trails and dirt roads
Lay of the land: Wooded acres and fields, swamps and small streams
Land status: State park
Nearest town: Pocomoke City, MD

Other trail users: Boaters, campers, anglers, flat water canoeists, hikers, 4WD motorists, sightseers
Trail contacts: Pocomoke River State Forest, Snow Hill, MD, (410) 632-2566
Schedule: Open daily from dawn to sunset year-round
Maps: USGS maps: Snow Hill, MD; Girdletree, MD-VA

Getting There: From Cambridge, MD: Take U.S. Highway 50 through Salisbury. Pick up State Highway 12 to Snow Hill, Maryland. Once in Snow Hill, turn left on Market Street (State Highway 394) and follow it to U.S. Highway 113. Shortly after Highway 394 merges onto U.S. Highway 113, turn right into Pocomoke State Park. Take your first right and follow the signs to the nature center. *DeLorme: Maryland/Delaware Atlas & Gazetteer:* Page 27, A-4

The Ride

Welcome to way-down southeastern Maryland in Snow Hill—one of the friendliest areas on Maryland's Eastern Shore. Located in Worcester County along the banks of the Pocomoke River, approximately 3.5 miles south of Snow Hill, are the Pocomoke River State Forest and Park. The Pocomoke River—Algonquin for "black water"—originates in the Great Cypress Swamp on the Maryland-Delaware border. It then meanders southwesterly for nearly 55 miles through Maryland before flowing into Pocomoke Sound and the Chesapeake Bay.

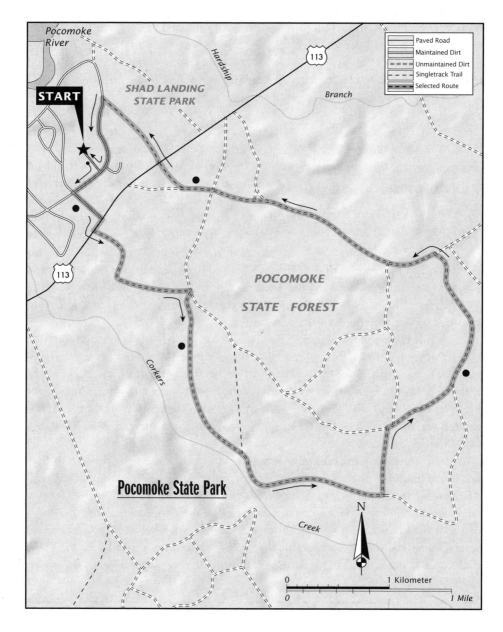

Map legend:
- Paved Road
- Maintained Dirt
- Unmaintained Dirt
- Singletrack Trail
- Selected Route

Pocomoke River

START

SHAD LANDING STATE PARK

Hardship

Branch

113

113

POCOMOKE STATE FOREST

Corkers

Pocomoke State Park

Creek

N

0   1 Kilometer
0   1 Mile

English settlers founded historic Snow Hill in 1642—later declared a royal port by William and Mary of England. As such, Snow Hill was the home of a thriving ship-building industry, a busy commerce center, and, by 1742, the Worcester County seat.

The Pocomoke River became a heavily traveled trade route, and overnight travel services to Baltimore and Norfolk, Virginia, emerged. Hotels, boardinghouses, and a very successful lumber company—the Richardson, Smith, and Moore—were founded. For a time, Snow Hill thrived. Then, with the end of the Civil War and the arrival of the railroad and modern transportation, river transportation became outdated. Snow Hill's reign as a successful river city began to wane, its people turning from shipbuilding and commerce to agriculture. Today, Snow Hill remains a historic town and is quietly becoming a popular respite from the big cities to the north. Its proximity to the ocean, the ever-popular Assateague Island, and the scenic Pocomoke River have made Snow Hill a popular vacation destination.

▶ As you enter the park, take your first right and park your car by the nature center. The trailhead is directly across from the park entrance and clearly marked with a large wooden sign reader Chandler Trail.

The combination of swamp and upland in this area offers a wide variety of plant and animal life as well. White dogwoods and pink laurels are present throughout the spring months, and visitors may spot playful river otters in the Pocomoke or cast lines out for the more than fifty species of fish. The area has also been described as one of the best environments for bird life along the Atlantic coast. Evidence of this is clear from the 172 species of birds spotted throughout the region, including the bald eagle, often seen gliding over the open river.

This ride takes you through 5.5 miles of off-road-vehicle tracks on the south side of the Pocomoke River, through stands of loblolly pine. What this ride lacks in elevation will be made up for by its riding surface. Sections of trail are loose and sandy, making pedaling a chore. Other sections are deep with water and swampy, challenging yet enjoyable to ride. The entire route takes place on a small parcel of land designated for off-road-vehicle use. Keep alert, because you may cross paths with a four-wheeler or motorcycle.

As you enter the park, take your first right and park your car by the nature center. The trailhead is directly across from the park entrance and clearly marked with a large wooden sign reading CHANDLER TRAIL. This is where the fun begins. The ride takes you through the forest in a counterclockwise direction along nearly 5.5 miles of ORV tracks. Although you are limited to the off-road-vehicle tracks, there are several unmarked trails along this ride that are off-limits to motorized vehicles. These trails can add mileage to your ride and offer some exciting alternatives to this route.

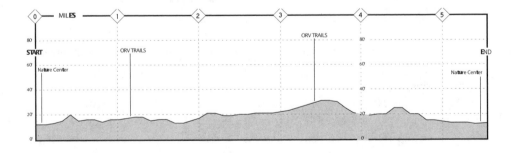

Don't expect any long climbs or speeding descents. This ride is mostly flat and leisurely, providing you with a great opportunity to enjoy the beauty of the forest and its wildlife.

Make sure to take some time out to visit nearby Snow Hill and soak in the history of Maryland's past. There are plenty of other activities to do in the area. Flat water canoeing is very popular and gives visitors a chance to experience the Pocomoke River and its Cypress Swamps, this area's biggest attraction. In addition, Assateague Island is only minutes away. This unique spot on the Eastern Shore is home to wild horses, made famous by their annual July swim across the river to Chincoteague. Also in Assateague is a 3-mile Wildlife Loop trail, restricted to foot and bicycle traffic from dawn until 3:00 P.M.

Although southeastern Maryland is not a mountain biking mecca, there is a wide variety of activities to keep even the hardiest of mountain bikers busy. If you are traveling to the beach and are in dire need of an off-road ride, stop by Snow Hill and the Pocomoke River State Forest. You won't be disappointed.

Miles and Directions

0.0 **START** from the parking area and head back to U.S. Highway 113. Cross U.S. Highway 113. The trailhead is directly across from the park entrance; begin here. Enter the trail marked "Pocomoke River State Forest, Chandler LUV Track."

0.1 Bear right at this intersection.

0.25 Turn left here.

0.57 Turn right on the first road of this three-way intersection.

2.17 Turn left at this intersection.

2.44 Turn right at this intersection.

2.47 Continue straight.

2.81 Continue straight through this and the next intersection.

3.45 Turn left at this intersection. Continue straight.

4.25 Bear left at this intersection.

4.5 Continue straight at this intersection.

4.7 You're back at U.S. Highway 113. Cross the road and pick up the trail on the other side. Four vertical logs and a WEAPONS PROHIBITED sign mark the trail.

5.2 Turn left on the road and bear left at the next intersection.

5.47 Bear to the right and follow the sign to the nature center. You're done.

Ride Information

Local Amenities and Attractions

Boat launch, boat rental, campfire programs, campsites, fishing, flat water canoeing, hiking trail, playground, and swimming.

Honorable Mentions

Southern Maryland

Here is an index of great rides in southern Maryland that didn't make the list this time around but deserve recognition. Check them out and let us know what you think. You may decide that one or more of these rides deserves higher status in future editions, or perhaps you may have a ride of your own that merits some attention.

E Calvert Cliffs

Located on the western side of the Chesapeake Bay, the cliffs at Calvert Cliffs State Park dominate the shoreline. Rising more than 100 feet from the shores of the Chesapeake, these 15-million-year-old cliffs contain over 600 species of fossils from the Miocene period. Calvert Cliffs State Park is located in Calvert County on State Highways 2 and 4, 14 miles south of Prince Frederick. There are over 13 miles of foot and mountain bike trails here. Bicycles are allowed on the service road. For more information and directions to open riding areas, call Blue Wind in California, Maryland, at (301) 737–2713. *DeLorme: Maryland/Delaware Atlas & Gazetteer:* Page 31, B-4.

F Tuckahoe State Park

Located just east of Maryland's Bay Bridge in Talbott County, Tuckahoe State Park has a surprisingly great trail system. The park has two main sections of trails. The first and longest is located below the dam and travels parallel to Tuckahoe Creek. This trail switches between hiking trails, equestrian trails, and a wide hard-surfaced path. The second trail is far shorter and runs along the creek above the lake. This section is far more challenging than the lower trail, offering more obstacles and a few sharp drop-offs with steep sections along gullies. For more information, call or write Tuckahoe State Park at 13070 Crouse Mill Road, Queen Anne, MD 21657, (410) 820–1668. *DeLorme: Maryland/Delaware Atlas & Gazetteer:* Page 50, C-3

G Wye Island Natural Resource Management Area

Wye Island is located in Queen Anne's County near Queenstown, Maryland. The island is located between the Wye and Wye East Rivers in the tidal recesses of the Chesapeake Bay. Approximately 2,450 of the 2,800 acres are managed and maintained by the Department of Natural Resources and the Maryland State and Park Forest Service. There are over 6 miles of trails, some of which are open to bicycles. For more information, call or write Wye Island Natural Resource Management Area at 632 Wye Island Road, Queenstown, MD 21658, (410) 827–7577. *DeLorme: Maryland/Delaware Atlas & Gazetteer:* Page 50, D-1

Northern Virginia

Traffic! Is there really anything more to say about Northern Virginia? Most of us in the Northern Virginia area are stuck in it going one direction, the other, or both, and it's only getting worse (do they really think building more roads will solve the problem?). So what's the deal? Can you really find a good place to ride a bike in this overdeveloped suburb of D.C.? Absolutely!

Look no further than Wakefield Park and Lake Accotink, just a quarter mile off the Beltway. Here you'll find great off-road riding for a variety of skill levels, including everything from taxing singletrack to sluggish dirt paths. The ride is guaranteed to keep cyclists who are just leaving work, tired of rush hour, and in need of a quick fix before heading home, in just the right mind-set.

But that isn't all. Northern Virginia is actually loaded with great places to pedal off-road. Cyclists just need to be creative. Some of the rides are in fairly standard places, such as Burke Lake Park with its meandering pathway around the lake, great for novices and families. Other mountain bike trails had to be built, such as the trails in Fountainhead Regional Park, planned by the Northern Virginia Regional Park Authority in close collaboration with the Mid-Atlantic Off-Road Enthusiasts (MORE). The trail system at Fountainhead is a great circuit of tightly wound singletrack going up and down the hilly banks of the Occoquan Reservoir through a lush canopy of woods. However, cyclists will find some of the best singletrack (huge steeps and rugged terrain) where they may least expect it—power lines. Some of the area's power line right-of-ways offer up spectacular off-road terrain that even the most hard-core cyclists will love. For a great example, check out the Centerville Power Line ride. I'm sure you'll come back smiling and exhausted.

So even though it may take you a few nerve-racking hours to drive 10 miles through Northern Virginia traffic just to get to some of these rides, once you get out on the trails described in this book, all that frustration and energy will be well served on what is certainly some of the most fun riding in the region.

28 Waterford Dirt Ride

With no singletrack in sight, this backcountry ride along quiet dirt and gravel roads makes for a perfect ramble through Northern Virginia's hunt country. Cyclists should bring along a pair of well-conditioned legs to help them through the ride's length and smattering of small climbs. Don't forget the camera, though, as this route takes you through some of the prettiest countryside and most historic towns west of the Beltway.

Start: Loudoun County High School
Length: 27.5 miles
Approximate riding time: 2.5–3 hours
Difficulty: Moderate to challenging due to length and many small climbs
Trail surface: Rolling dirt and gravel roads
Lay of the land: Rolling backcountry roads through Leesburg's scenic countryside

Land status: Public roads
Nearest town: Leesburg, VA; Waterford, VA
Other trail users: Motorists
Trail contacts: None available
Schedule: None available
Fees and permits: Not applicable
Maps: USGS maps: Purcellville, VA; Lincoln, VA; Leesburg, VA; Waterford, VA
ADC map: Loudoun County road map

Getting There: From the Capital Beltway (Interstate 495): Take Exit 10, U.S. Highway 7 (Leesburg Pike), west all the way to Leesburg (28 miles). At the Leesburg city limits, stay on U.S. Highway 7 (Market Street) through Leesburg. Turn left on Catoctin Circle. At the third light, turn left on Dry Mill Road. Loudoun County High School is on your right. Park here. *DeLorme: Virginia Atlas & Gazetteer:* Page 79-80, D-1

The Ride

When Amos Janney led a small group of Quakers in 1733 from Bucks County, Pennsylvania, to the fertile land just west of the Catoctin Mountain along South Fork Creek, he may never have imagined that someday the land he sought out would become some of Virginia's most beautiful horse country. And more significantly for bicyclists, the land would become an ideal setting for some exceptionally scenic off-road bicycle rides.

But then again, perhaps he did. Janney and his group of Quakers yearned to be free from the persecutions of the Old World and wished to escape Pennsylvania's

Old Waterford Road is particularly scenic.

ever-increasing population. They sought the solitude and peace of this expansive valley between Catoctin and the Blue Ridge Mountains.

Today, unpaved roads climb along Catoctin Mountain, then roll leisurely along the valley floor. Panoramic views of the green countryside and the mountains beyond are a wonderful backdrop to the horse and dairy farms spread throughout the valley. The Waterford-Hamilton-Leesburg area, just as Amos Janney and his group of settlers discovered, is still the perfect location to escape the masses, to be free of the oppressive daily grind of our "new world," and to discover an undisturbed, peaceful haven.

▶ **This route is comprised primarily of unpaved dirt and gravel roads, perfect for the off-road tourist looking for more than ballistic singletrack and rugged trails.**

This route is comprised primarily of unpaved dirt and gravel roads, perfect for the off-road tourist looking for more than ballistic singletrack and rugged trails. Stop in the historic town of Waterford and have a look around. Amos Janney settled this Virginia town and called it Milltown. An Irish cobbler whose hometown was Waterford, Ireland, later renamed it. Cross the Washington & Old Dominion Trail into the town of Hamilton for a break, then be on your way, heading south toward Mount Gilead before riding north again to Leesburg. Be sure to notice the spectacular homes along Loudoun Orchard Road and Mount Gilead Road, and be careful not to bump into the deer residing in force throughout this area.

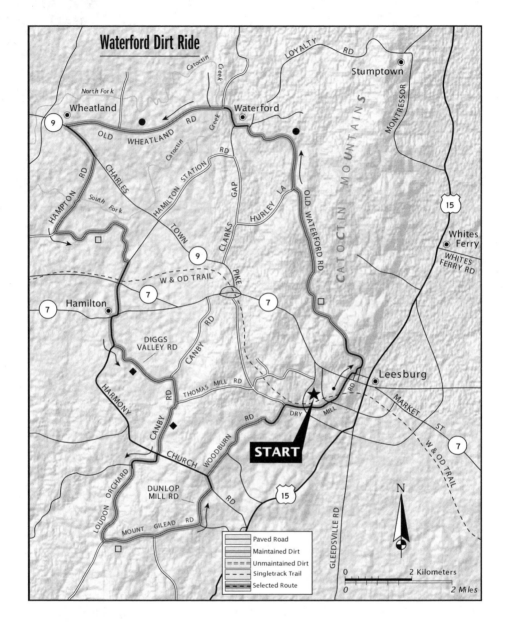

Waterford Dirt Ride

Miles and Directions

0.0 **START** at the Loudoun County High School parking lot off Dry Mill Road. Turn left on Dry Mill Road. Follow the yellow bike route signs (paved).

0.3 Cross over Washington & Old Dominion trail. Continue straight.

0.5 Cross Loudoun Road.

0.6 Cross Market Street.

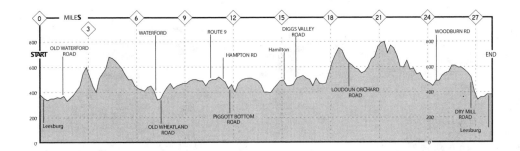

0.7   Turn right on Cornwall Street (paved).

0.8   Turn left on Memorial Drive. Memorial Drive stays to the right side of Memorial Hospital, heading toward Gibson Street (paved).

0.9   Turn right on Gibson Street (paved).

1.1   Turn left on Old Waterford Road (paved). Graveyard on the right.

2.3   Old Waterford Road turns to gravel (unpaved).

5.3   Stay right on Old Waterford Road at the intersection with Hurley Lane (unpaved).

7.2   Turn left on Main Water Street (paved). Arrive in the historic town of Waterford.

7.4   Turn left on Old Wheatland Road (paved).

7.7   Old Wheatland Road turns to gravel (unpaved).

10.6   Turn left on Charles Town Pike (State Highway 9) (paved). Be careful along this road. The speed limit for cars is 55 miles per hour.

11.2   Turn right on Hampton Road (unpaved).

11.8   Turn left on Piggott Bottom Road (unpaved).

12.2   Bear left at the stop sign, continuing on Piggott Bottom Road.

14.0   Turn right on Hamilton Station Road (paved).

14.3   Cross Washington & Old Dominion trail.

15.1   Turn right on Colonial Highway (paved). Arrive in the historic town of Hamilton.

15.2   Turn left on Harmony Church Road (paved).

15.8   Bear left on Diggs Valley Road (unpaved).

17.2   Diggs Valley Road comes to a four-way intersection. Turn left, continuing on Diggs Valley Road (unpaved).

17.4   Turn right on Canby Road (unpaved). Stay on Canby all the way to Harmony Church Road.

19.0   Cross Harmony Church Road on Loudoun Orchard Road (paved).

19.7   Bear left, continuing on Loudoun Orchard Road (paved).

20.1   Loudoun Orchard turns to gravel (unpaved).

21.4   Turn left on Mount Gilead Road (unpaved).

23.3   Turn left on Dunlop Mill Road (unpaved).

24.1   Turn left on Harmony Church Road (paved).

24.3   Turn right on Woodburn Road (unpaved).

26.7 Turn right on Dry Mill Road.

27.5 Arrive at Loudoun County High School.

Ride Information

Local Information

Loudoun Tourism Council (800) 752-6118

Local Events and Attractions

Leesburg calendar of events
www.leesburgonline.com
Waterford Homes Tour and Crafts Exhibit
in October, (540) 882-3085
www.waterfordva.org

Accommodations

Loudoun County Guild of Bed-and-Breakfasts
(800) 752-6118
www.vabb.com

Organizations:

Waterford Foundation www.waterfordva.org

29 Ball's Bluff Canal Ride

This ride, which begins at Ball's Bluff, offers a real variation in terrain to cyclists. Traveling first in Virginia, the course alternates between paved and unpaved roads, starting out flat, then rolling, before getting very hilly as it crosses over Catoctin Mountain. On the Maryland side, you can relax along the all flat, all dirt C&O Canal Towpath, which meanders along the scenic Potomac River. Along the way, you will cross over the Monocacy Aqueduct, the largest aqueduct along the 185-mile canal. Catch the ferry at Whites Ferry to cross back over to the Virginia side and return to the start of the ride.

Start: Ball's Bluff National Battlefield Park
Length: 31.1 miles
Approximate riding time: 3+ hours
Difficulty: Difficult, due to length of ride and mountain climb
Trail surface: Dirt roads, canal towpath
Lay of the land: Hilly
Land status: Public roads
Nearest town: Leesburg, VA
Other trail users: Tourists and motorists
Trail contacts: C&O Canal headquarters (301) 739-4200
Schedule: Ball's Bluff National Cemetery is open from dawn to dusk
Whites Ferry is open from 6:00 A.M. to 11:00 P.M. each day
Fees and permits: Whites Ferry: $3.00 per vehicle for ferry ($5.00 round-trip) or $.50 per bicycle
Maps: USGS maps: Leesburg, VA; Waterford, VA; Point of Rocks, MD; Poolesville, MD
ADC maps: Loudoun County, VA; Montgomery County, MD

Getting There: From the Capital Beltway (Interstate 495): Take Exit 10, U.S. Highway 7 (Leesburg Pike), west all the way to Leesburg (28 miles). At the Leesburg city limits, take U.S. Highway 15 north approximately 1.5 miles, then turn right on Ball's Bluff Road. This will take you 0.8 miles to Ball's Bluff National Cemetery and Battlefield. Park here and begin your ride. *DeLorme: Virginia Atlas & Gazetteer:* Page 80, C-1

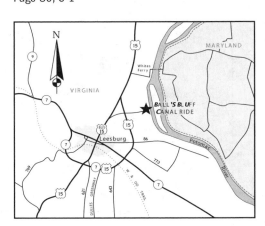

The Ride

Following what he believed were instructions from General George McClellan to push south, Union General Charles P. Stone set in motion a series of events on the night of October 20, 1861, that would result the next evening in carnage on the wooded bluff above the Potomac River.

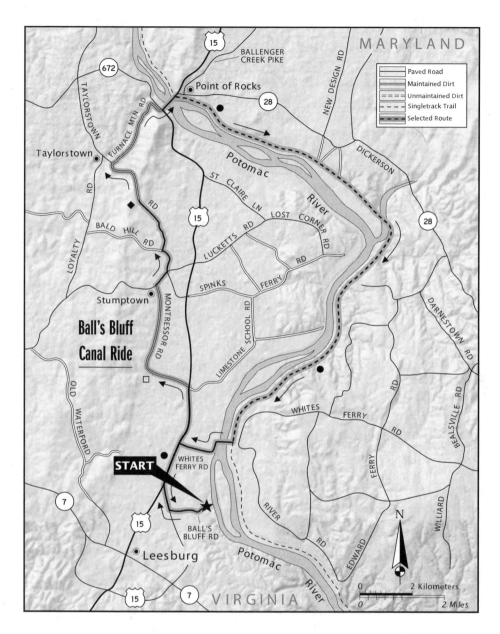

MARYLAND

BALLENGER
CREEK PIKE

15

672

Point of Rocks

28

NEW DESIGN RD

DICKERSON

Taylorstown

TAYLORSTOWN

FURNACE MTN RD

Potomac

River

28

ST CLAIRE LN

LOST CORNER RD

15

RD

BALD HILL RD

LUCKETTS RD

RD

LOYALTY RD

SPINKS

FERRY

DARNESTOWN RD

Stumptown

MONTRESSOR RD

LIMESTONE SCHOOL RD

**Ball's Bluff
Canal Ride**

RD

WHITES

FERRY

BEALSVILLE RD

OLD WATERFORD

WHITES
FERRY RD

FERRY

START

RIVER RD

WILLIARD

7

15

N

BALL'S
BLUFF RD

Leesburg

Potomac

RD

EDWARD

River

0   2 Kilometers

15

7

VIRGINIA

0   2 Miles

Reconnaissance reported to General Stone an ill-guarded Confederate camp outside Leesburg, Virginia. Eager for the opportunity to destroy it, Stone positioned his men at Conrad's (Whites) Ferry, Harrisons Island, and Edwards Ferry. Movement across the swollen Potomac began at midnight, but Stone's men found no camp at the reported site. Instead, they found only a moonlit grove of trees, mistaken by his men the previous night for tents.

They chose to continue toward Leesburg and, early that morning, met resistance from a Confederate outpost just north of Leesburg near Ball's Bluff. After hearing of skirmishes with Union soldiers, four companies of Confederate infantry were sent from Leesburg to the previously small outpost just west of Ball's Bluff, pushing the Union troops back toward the river. Throughout the afternoon, a series of advancements and attacks by a continually reinforced Confederate line forced the ill-fated Union troops near the edge of a steep drop to the rocky banks of the Potomac. When Union reinforcement did arrive by climbing a path at the side of the bluff, there was confusion among the officers over who was in command. A decision finally was made to fight their way through Confederate lines, since the only alternative was to retreat off the bluff, 90 feet down to the river below. But just as the Union troops attempted their advance, Confederates launched a murderous attack, blocking both the path that Union reinforcements had previously climbed and any chance for their retreat. Federal troops were suddenly forced to choose between furious Confederate gunfire and a suicidal leap to the rocks far below. Nearly 1,000 Union soldiers were lost that afternoon, dealing a severe blow to the Northern army, which was still reeling from its recent defeat at the first Battle of Bull Run. Ball's Bluff National Cemetery and Battlefield, the country's smallest national battlefield, remains today a quiet testimony to America's most violent era.

Miles and Directions

0.0 **START** at Ball's Bluff National Battlefield Park. Follow Ball's Bluff Road to U.S. Highway 15 (Leesburg Pike).

1.0 Turn right on U.S. Highway 15 (Leesburg Pike) heading north. Be sure to ride on the shoulder. This is a busy road.

4.1 Turn left on Montressor Road (State Highway 661) (unpaved).

5.0 Bear right, continuing on Montressor Road.

7.2 Turn right on Stumpton Road (State Highway 662) (paved).

7.7 Turn left on New Valley Church Road (State Highway 663) (paved).

8.2 Turn right on Taylorstown Road (State Highway 663) (paved).

9.9 Taylorstown Road turns to gravel and begins a steep ascent (unpaved).

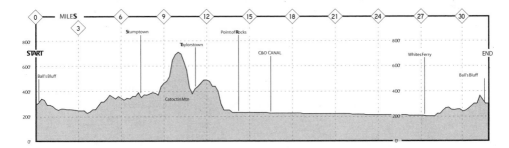

10.7 Reach the summit of this climb. Begin a fast, gravelly descent.

11.3 Turn right on Furnace Mountain Road (State Highway 665) at the bottom of the descent (unpaved). Food 0.2 miles ahead on Taylorstown Road.

13.7 Turn right on Lovettsville Road (State Highway 672) (paved).

13.75 Turn left on U.S. Highway 15 (north) and cross the bridge over the Potomac. Use the sidewalk across the bridge.

14.3 Once across the bridge, turn right on State Highway 28 (paved) into Point of Rocks, Maryland. There's a general store 1 block up the road. Immediately turn right on Commerce Street (a small street that goes behind the houses on Main Street). Follow this street across the railroad track, then over the wooden bridge to the C&O Canal Towpath (paved).

14.4 Turn left on the C&O Canal Towpath, heading downriver (unpaved).

27.1 Turn right on Whites Ferry Road to Whites Ferry (paved). Take the ferry across the Potomac. Remember to have the toll with you (50 cents for bicycles).

28.4 Turn left on U.S. Highway 15 (James Monroe Highway). Be sure to ride on the shoulder. This is a busy road.

30.1 Turn left on Ball's Bluff Road (paved) toward the battlefield.

31.1 Arrive back at Ball's Bluff National Battlefield.

Ride Information

Local Information

Whites Ferry, Dickerson, MD
(301) 349-5200
www.vdest.com/dc/WhitesFerryLoudoun
Tourism Council, (800) 752-6118

Local Events and Attractions

Ball's Bluff Battlefield Regional Park
(703) 779-9372
www.nvrpa.org/ballsbluff.html

Ball's Bluff Tavern, (703) 777-7757
www.ballsbluff.com
Civil War Reenactment in Leesburg, VA
August, (703) 777-1368

Accommodations

Tarara Winery and Bed-and-Breakfast
(703) 771-8157

30 Middleburg Vineyard Tour

Virginia is quickly becoming renowned worldwide for its wine. And Loudoun County is home to a number of the Old Dominion's finest wineries. This mostly non-paved (gravel and dirt) ride is set up to lead cyclists through the area's beautiful rolling horse country, connecting (or passing nearby) a number of Northern Virginia's most productive vineyards. Make plenty of time for this trip and stop often to taste the latest wine.

Start: Middleburg Elementary School
Length: 23.1 miles
Approximate riding time: 2–3 hours (not counting stops at vineyards)
Difficulty: Moderate to difficult (due to length)
Trail surface: Unpaved dirt and gravel roads
Lay of the land: Mostly easy rolling
Land status: Public roads
Nearest town: Middleburg, VA
Other trail users: Motorists and wine tasters
Trail contacts: None
Schedule: Meredyth Vineyard 10 A.M. to 5 P.M., seven days a week
Piedmont Vineyard 10 A.M. to 4 P.M., seven days a week
Swedenburg Vineyard 10 A.M. to 4 P.M., seven days a week
Fees and permits: $3.00 to $5.00 per winery for wine tastings. Call in advance for current prices.
Maps: USGS maps: Rectortown, VA; Middleburg, VA
ADC map: Loudoun County road map; Fauquier County road map

Getting There: From the Capital Beltway **(Interstate 495):** Take Interstate 66 west 8.5 miles to Exit 57, U.S. Highway 50 West. Go 23 miles on U.S. Highway 50 West into Middleburg. U.S. Highway 50 (John Mosby Highway) becomes Washington Street within the Middleburg town limits. From Washington Street, turn right on State Highway 626 (Madison Street). Go 0.1 miles and turn right into the Middleburg Elementary School parking lot. *DeLorme: Virginia Atlas & Gazetteer:* Page 75, A-7

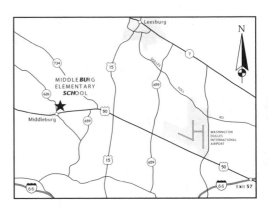

The Ride

This ride travels through some of Virginia's finest wine country, where visits to the vineyards are always welcome and wine tasting is just part of the tour.

You start in the historic town of Middleburg, a small touristy outpost in the middle of Hunt Country. Horses abound in this magnificent countryside. A town with a rich history, Middleburg has enjoyed its share of good fortune. Established in 1787,

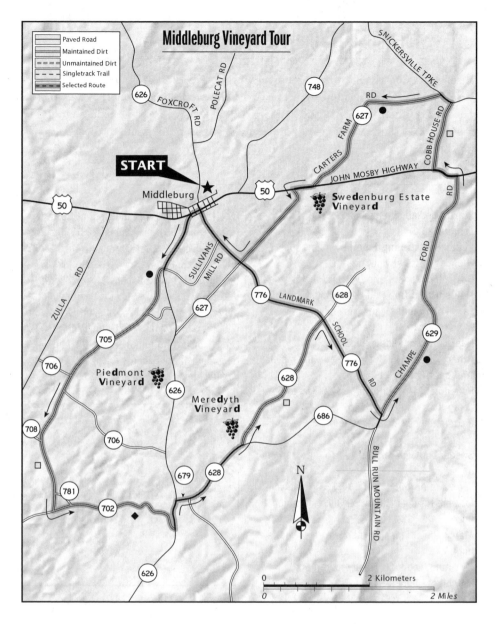

Middleburg Vineyard Tour

Paved Road
Maintained Dirt
Unmaintained Dirt
Singletrack Trail
Selected Route

START

Middleburg

Swedenburg Estate
Vineyard

Piedmont
Vineyard

Meredyth
Vineyard

0   2 Kilometers

0   2 Miles

N

this centuries-old town was even graced by a U.S. president when the Kennedy family attended the local Catholic church and built a home just outside town.

The ride starts on a route toward Piedmont Vineyard but breaks off from the main road onto backcountry dirt, perfect for an off-road tourist. This first section rolls comfortably past small estates and low-key horse farms. But when you turn east, the roads lift you into the hills. You'll pass some of the old and new—abandoned stone houses and state-of-the-art homes—then head toward Meredyth Vineyard to lavish in the land of the well-to-do. Gorgeous estates rest on acres of open land, where thoroughbreds graze in the warm sun. What a wonderful place to ride and dream. But don't forget to stop at the vineyard. (Its hours are from 10:00 A.M. to 4:00 P.M.) The rest of the ride rolls up

▶ **You start in the historic town of Middleburg, a small touristy outpost in the middle of Hunt Country. Horses abound in this magnificent countryside.**

and down below Bull Run Mountain, taking you past one more vineyard, the Swedenburg Estate, before leading you back into Middleburg.

If the wine doesn't get the best of you, enjoy the endless dirt roads scattered throughout this region. This is excellent off-road riding for cyclists looking for a change of pace and scenery.

Miles and Directions

0.0 **START** at the Middleburg Elementary School parking lot. Turn left on State Highway 626, Madison Street (paved).

0.1 Turn right on Washington Street (U.S. Highway 50) (paved).

0.3 Turn left on Plains Road (State Highway 626). Follow the purple vineyard sign (paved).

1.1 Turn right on State Highway 705 (paved).

1.2 State Highway 705 changes to dirt (unpaved).

3.2 Stay straight on State Highway 705 at this intersection. State Highway 706 turns right.

3.4 Stay right on Highway 705 at this intersection. Highway 706 turns left.

4.2 Turn left at the T, continuing on Highway 705. State Highway 708 goes right (unpaved).

5.3 Turn left at the stop sign on State Highway 702 (unpaved).

7.6 Turn left on Highway 626 (paved).

7.9 Bear right on State Highway 679 at the bottom of the descent. This turns into State Highway 628.

9.1 Turn left on Highway 628 (unpaved). This is slightly hidden. The turn comes after a long rock wall on the left, just past a large brick house with three chimneys.

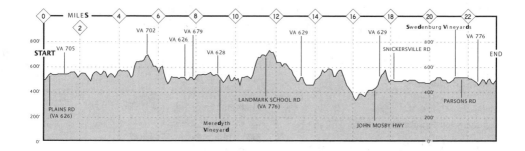

Riding through Virginia's wine country is especially beautiful.

9.4   Meredyth Vineyard on the left. Stop in for a tour. Hours are from 10:00 A.M. to 4:00 P.M.

11.5   Turn right on Landmark School Road (State Highway 776) (paved). For those who have had enough, you can turn left on Landmark School Road and take the shortcut back to Middleburg (2.4 miles).

13.2   Turn left on Champe Ford Road (State Highway 629) (unpaved).

17.1   Turn left on John Mosby Highway (U.S. Highway 50). Be careful of traffic (paved).

17.5   Turn right on Cobb House Road (State Highway 629) (unpaved).

18.5   Turn left on Snickersville Road (paved).

18.8   Turn left at the bottom of the hill on Carouters Farm Road (State Highway 627) (unpaved).

21.3   Turn right on John Mosby Highway (paved). Pass Swedenburg Estate Vineyard. Stop for a sip of wine before continuing on.

21.5   Turn left on Parsons Road (Highway 627) (unpaved).

22.6   Turn right on Landmark School Road (State Highway 776) (paved).

23.0   Arrive back in Middleburg. Cross Washington Street to Madison Street.

23.1   Turn right into the school parking lot. Drink too much wine?

Ride Information

Local Information
Loudoun Tourism Council, (800) 752-6118

Local Events and Attractions
Meredyth Vineyard, (540) 687-6277

Piedmont Vineyard, (540) 687-5528
www.piedmontwines.com

Swedenburg Estate Vineyard,
(540) 687-5219

In Addition

Mountain Biking and Wine

If my assumption is correct, many of you are like me and have never really refined your tastes in good wine. After all, we're mountain bikers for heaven's sake! If such is the case, then you may also find yourselves feeling about as silly and uneducated as I have been when the proprietor of a winery serves samples of the vineyard's great variety of wines. You may understand little to none about what this person is talking about. If you're like me, you politely sip the wine, nod your head at each flavor's description, and wonder how they can arrive at so many names for such similar tastes. Before subjecting yourself to this unnecessary display of embarrassing ignorance and vacant wine tasting, educate yourself a bit and enjoy tasting some of the vineyard's fine products. Hopefully, after reading some of the following information before cycling up to a winery's door, you may quite miraculously understand some of what the proprietor is telling you about the latest flavors and enjoy the samples that much more.

Wine is the fermented juice of grapes. Nearly all the wine made throughout the world comes from one species of grape—Vitis vinifera. As many as 4,000 varieties of grapes have been developed from this one species. Each differs, sometimes only slightly, from the others in size, color, shape of the berry, juice composition, ripening time, and resistance to disease. Only about a dozen of the 4,000 or more varieties of grapes are commonly used for wine making. Chief among them are Chardonnay, Riesling, Cabernet Sauvignon, Sauvignon Blanc, Pinot Noir, Gewurztraminer, and Muscat.

The main reason the varieties of *Vitis vinifera* are used throughout the world in wine production is their high sugar content when ripe. Wine with an alcohol content of 10 percent or slightly higher is produced from the grapes' natural sugar after fermentation. Wines with less alcohol are unstable and subject to bacterial spoilage.

Wine Colors

We're all familiar with colors of wine: white wine, rosé, and red wine. But why the different colors and what's the big deal anyway?

- White wine is produced when only the juice from the grape is used. The skin is removed before fermentation begins. The juice is normally colorless, though some varieties have a pink to reddish color. Because only the grape's juice is used, white wine tends to be much sweeter, thus much easier on the palate for most people unfamiliar with drinking wine.

- A rosé is produced when the skins of red or black grapes are removed after fermentation has begun.

- Red wine is produced when whole, crushed red or black grapes are used, including the skins. Red wine is often more bitter than white wine, with a stronger taste.

What are we supposed to eat with this stuff, anyway?

It's suggested that we drink white wines with light foods such as salads, chicken, and fish. Red wines are recommended for heavier flavored foods such as red meat. The reasons are strictly for the palate. A strong tasting red wine may overwhelm the light flavors of chicken or fish, while the sweeter, lighter flavor of white wine may get lost on a hearty, juicy steak. What should cyclists drink with their spaghetti? Either one is fine. Heck, who cares? It's wine!

Where does it come from?

Although Italy produces more wine, the world's leading wine producer in terms of quality is France, with outstanding products from Bordeaux and Burgundy, the Loire and Rhône Valleys, and Alsace. Other major producers are Spain, the United States, Germany, Chile, Argentina, South Africa, and Australia. In the United States, California is the leading wine-producing region. Central Virginia is a close second.

The process of making wine—in short

White wine: Red and white grapes are de-stemmed and crushed before going into a horizontal press for more crushing (end plates in the horizontal press move toward each other and crush the grapes). The juice (sans skin) then flows to a vat for fermenting. The juice has not had time to pick up color from the skins, leaving it white.

Red and rosé wines: The crushed grapes go directly into fermenting vats with their skins. After fermenting, the unpalatable red press wine is mixed with free-run wine.

The dry skins and pulp (called marc) can be distilled into cheap brandy.

Fermentation starts when wine yeast on the skins of ripe grapes comes in contact with the grape juice. After running off into casks, the new wine then undergoes a series of chemical processes, including oxidation, precipitation of proteins, and fermentation of chemical compounds. Each of these processes creates the wine's characteristic bouquet (aroma). After periodic clarification and aging in casks, the wine is ready to be bottled.

31 Great Falls National Park

Great Falls National Park is a natural haven for thousands of Washingtonians seeking solitude from the daily grind of gridlock and government. Trails abound throughout this park on the river, offering cyclists, hikers, and equestrians alike rugged terrain. Some portions of the park's trails are wide, dirt carriage roads dating back through history and meandering through the scenery, while others are steep, rocky, and narrow, keeping even agile cyclists on the tips of their seats. Come one and all to this park of presidents, dignitaries, and commoners and enjoy what folks throughout time have been enjoying along the rapids of the Potomac.

Start: Visitor center
Length: 6.8 miles
Approximate riding time: 1-1.5 hours
Difficulty: Moderate due to occasional steep, rocky singletrack
Trail surface: Rocky, dirt trails and carriage roads
Lay of the land: Wooded, rocky, and hilly terrain along the banks of the Potomac River
Land status: National park
Nearest town: McLean, VA
Other trail users: Hikers, equestrians, climbers, kayakers, and tourists
Trail contacts: National Park Service, (703) 759-2915
Schedule: Park is open from 7:00 A.M. to sunset
Fees and permits: $2.00 entrance fee
Maps: USGS maps: Vienna, VA; Falls Church, VA
ADC map: Northern Virginia road map
National Park Service Official Trail Map and Guide

Getting There: From the Capital Beltway (Interstate 495): From Exit 13 northwest of McLean, take State Highway 193 (Georgetown Pike) west toward Great Falls. Go about 4 miles, then turn right on Old Dominion Road, which becomes the park entrance road. Go 1 mile to the end of this road and park at the visitor center. Telephones, water, food, rest rooms, and information available inside the visitor center. *DeLorme: Virginia Atlas & Gazetteer:* Page 76, A-4

The Ride

Great Falls is one of the nation's most popular national parks. How appropriate then for it to be located just 14 miles from our nation's capital. And what a thrill for cyclists to know that mountain biking is not only allowed at the park—it's welcome.

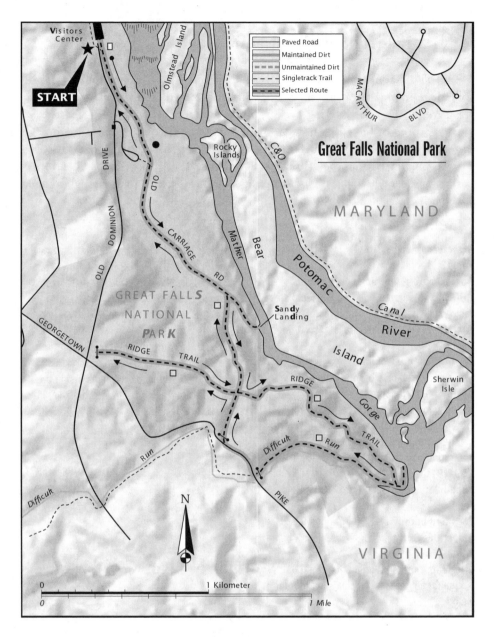

Great Falls National Park

Paved Road
Maintained Dirt
Unmaintained Dirt
Singletrack Trail
Selected Route

Visitors Center
START

Olmstead Island

Rocky Islands

OLD DOMINION DRIVE

GEORGETOWN

GREAT FALLS NATIONAL PARK

RIDGE   TRAIL

CARRIAGE   RD

Mather

Bear

C&O

Sandy Landing

MACARTHUR BLVD

MARYLAND

Potomac

Canal

River

Island

RIDGE

Gorge

Sherwin Isle

TRAIL

Difficult   Run

PIKE

Run

Difficult

N

VIRGINIA

0   1 Kilometer
0   1 Mile

Along with hikers, historians, rock climbers, and kayakers, off-road cyclists come in droves to enjoy the park's public resources. There are over 5 miles of designated trails to enjoy in this park, all of which conveniently intersect to create hours of off-road adventure. The trails vary in intensity, ranging from rolling forest roads beneath tall oaks and maples to steep, rocky singletrack overlooking the dramatic

Mather Gorge. The park's unequaled beauty, proximity to Washington, and accessible trails combine to make Great Falls National Park Northern Virginia's most popular off-road cycling haven.

The ride begins at the visitor center parking lot and travels south along Old Carriage Road through the middle of the park. Old Carriage was used in the 1700s to carry settlers to their dwellings at Matildaville, ruins of which still stand. Henry Lee, a Revolutionary War hero and friend of George Washington's, developed this small town. Named after Lee's first wife, Matildaville lasted only three decades before fading into history.

▶ During the winter months, breathtaking views of the gorge show through deciduous trees. The trail then descends quickly to the Potomac (another great view) and follows along Difficult Run before heading north again back toward the start.

The route bends deep into the park and travels up and down the rocky pass along Ridge Trail. During the winter months, breathtaking views of the gorge show through deciduous trees. The trail then descends quickly to the Potomac (another great view) and follows along Difficult Run before heading north again back toward the start.

Great Falls has always been a popular place to visit for locals and world tourists alike. Some have come to survey the river's rapids. George Washington formed the Patowmack Company in 1784 to build a series of canals around the falls. Theodore Roosevelt came to Great Falls to hike and ride horses during his presidency. Today, thousands come to enjoy Great Falls as well. But they don't come to build canals, develop towns, make trade, or seek solitude from the presidential office. They come only to ride the park's great trails, kayak the rapids, climb the steep cliffs, and bear witness to the magnificent scenery at Great Falls National Park.

Miles and Directions

0.0 **START** at Great Falls Visitor Center. Follow the horse/biker trail south along the entrance road.

0.4 Bear right at the rest rooms and go around the steel gate on Old Carriage Road (unpaved).

1.1 Bear left down the trail to Sandy Landing.

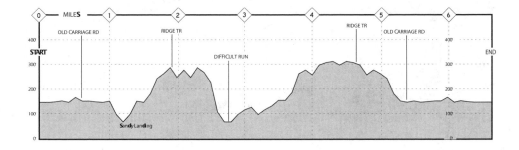

Difficult Run Trail offers many spots for a brief respite and a look around.

1.3 Arrive at Sandy Landing, a beautiful spot along the river, great for viewing Mather Gorge. Return to Old Carriage Road.

1.5 Turn left, continuing on Old Carriage Road. Begin a steady uphill.

1.9 Turn left near the top of this climb on Ridge Trail.

2.7 Turn left after the steep descent on Difficult Run Trail. Head toward the Potomac.

2.9 Arrive at the Potomac River. This is another great spot to view Sherwin Island, where Mather Gorge and the Potomac River converge. Turn around and follow Difficult Run Trail west along Difficult Run Creek toward Georgetown Pike.

3.6 Turn right on Georgetown Pike. Be careful with traffic and ride on the dirt shoulder.

3.8 Turn right on Old Carriage Road. This is the first dirt road you come to along Georgetown Pike. Go around the gate and begin climbing.

4.0 Turn left on Ridge Trail. Follow this toward the entrance road.

4.7 Reach the park entrance road (Old Dominion Road). Turn around and continue back on Ridge Trail.

5.4 Turn left on Old Carriage Road.

6.4 Go through the gate at the beginning of Old Carriage Road and head back to the parking lot at the visitor center.

6.8 Arrive back at the visitor center and parking lot.

Ride Information

Local Information

Fairfax County Convention and Visitors Bureau
(800) 7FAIRFAX
www.visitfairfax.org

Local Events and Attractions

Colvin Run Mill, (703) 759-2771

Wolf Trap Farm Park for the Performing Arts
(703) 255-1800

Restaurants

Evans Farm Inn & the Sitting Duck Pub
(703) 356-8000

32 Difficult Run

This 12-mile point-to-point route from Reston, Virginia, to Great Falls National Park may define what could someday become a new form of non-paved trail systems through the ever-growing and increasingly paved suburban landscape of Northern Virginia. Combining a mixture of clay-surfaced singletrack, bike paths, public parkland, and creek corridors, this ride follows what is perhaps the longest, most interesting trail system in the Washington, D.C./Baltimore region. Mountain bikers will love it.

Start: Twin Branches Nature Trail
Length: 12 miles from Reston to Great Falls National Park; 24 miles round-trip
Approximate riding time: 2 hours one way
Difficulty: Moderate to difficult due to length and muddy, technical sections
Trail surface: Mostly singletrack with a few paved bike paths
Lay of the land: Rolling, wooded terrain tracing the banks of the creek
Land status: Regional parkland
Nearest city: Reston, VA
Other trail users: Hikers and horseback riders
Trail contacts: Fairfax County Park Authority (703) 324-8700; National Park Service (703)

759-2915; Reston Association (The Glade) (703) 437-7658
Schedule: Parks and trails open from dawn to dusk year-round
Fees and permits: None
Maps: USGS maps: Vienna, VA; Falls Church, VA
ADC maps: Northern Virginia road map
Lake Fairfax park and trail map
Great Falls map and trail guide

Getting There: From the Capital Beltway (Interstate 495): Take the Washington-Dulles Access Road (toll road) west for 7 miles to Exit 5, Hunter Mill Road. Go south on Hunter Mill Road to Sunrise Valley Road and turn right. Go half a mile and turn left on South Lakes Drive. Turn left on Twin Branches Road. Follow Twin Branches Road to Glade Drive and park. Twin Branches Trail starts here. *DeLorme: Virginia Atlas & Gazetteer:* Page 76, A-3
Public Transportation: Take the Metro Orange Line to the Dunn Loring Metro Station. From the station, follow the narrow bike path on Gallows Road to the W&OD Rail-Trail. Proceed west on the rail-trail until the trail joins the ride at mile 0.9. **Note:** This option will add approximately 7 miles each way to the ride total.

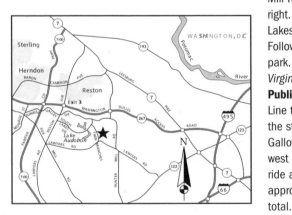

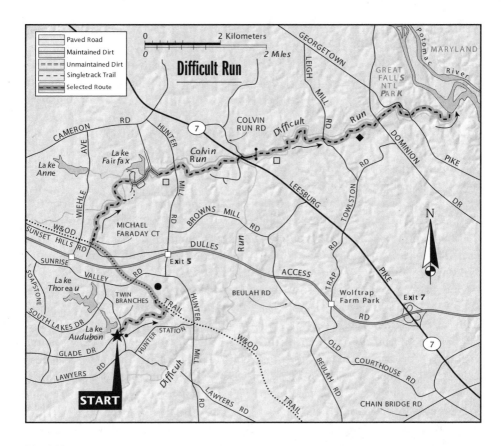

The Ride

As Northern Virginia continues to pave itself into one of most congested metropolitan areas in the nation, outdoor enthusiasts trapped in the suburban sprawl will delight in this system of interconnected dirt trails, pathways, and creek corridors. All of these trails and pathways are remnants of a time, not long ago, when Reston, Colvin Run, and Great Falls were little more than wooded landscapes, rolling farmland, and horse pastures. As suburban sprawl gobbled up every bit of land in sight, somehow the pathways along these creek corridors survived, leaving what is today one of the most impressive non-paved pathways in the region.

▶ **Difficult Run Trail is the only trail connecting the Northern Virginia suburbs with Great Falls National Park and the Potomac River.**

The first half of the ride weaves its way through Reston, Virginia, once a leader in community planning. One of the unique features setting this small city apart is its intricate network of public walkways, designed to lead residents anywhere they want to go within the community without having to get in their cars and brave the roadways.

You'll begin this ride at the trailhead for Twin Branches Nature Trail on Twin Branches Road and head east toward the Potomac. Should you be interested in exploring Glade Stream Valley Park, simply head west at this starting point and ride downhill along the paved path. This path will lead you alongside the Glade, a trickling creek at the southern edge of the Reston development. You can choose to ride on a natural surface trail or an asphalt path, both of which parallel the creek for 3 miles to Colts Neck Road. Along the Glade, visitors are treated to preserved natural habitats and a bounty of whistling feathered companions.

▶ **Start your ride and head east on the all-dirt singletrack along Twin Branches Nature Trail.**

Start your ride and head east on the all-dirt singletrack along Twin Branches Nature Trail. This rugged trail system will lead you all the way to the Washington & Old Dominion Bike Trail, a converted rail-trail travelling 45 miles from Shirlington near Interstate 395 all the way to Purcellville in Loudoun County. Turn left on the W&OD and follow it for a few miles to Michael Faraday Court, where another trail, beginning at the end of the court, takes you winding along Colvin Run through Lake Fairfax Park. You may wish to stop for lunch at this 479-acre park and enjoy the lake, take a train ride on the miniature train, or even go for a swim. Down the hill to the southeast side of the park, the trail resumes its course along Colvin Run, well marked with white blazes for horseback riding. It then continues east, across Leesburg Pike to Difficult Run. The trail comes to a scenic end at the Potomac River in Great Falls National Park, where you can watch the turbulent water rushing through Mather Gorge.

Please be aware of the rapidly deteriorating conditions of the trailway along Difficult Run. In recent years, this scenic, wooded path, tracing the banks of the creek, has been deformed into a muddy bog, slogging its way along a course of disaster for anyone hoping to use this creek corridor in the future. Be very delicate on this trail, and ride only when the ground is dry. Your help in preserving this trail will stand to benefit everyone in years to come. Contact the Fairfax County Park Authority or National Park Service to help maintain the trail, then gather a group of friends together on a Saturday afternoon and, with park-service guidance, put some sweat into maintaining the trail.

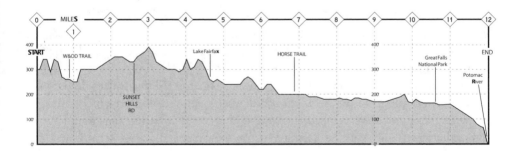

The trail north of Leesburg Pike can get muddy. Use your best judgment before proceeding.

HELP!
The section of trail along Difficult Creek to Great Falls is in great need of attention. For it to remain open to public use, it must be treated delicately. You will encounter a great deal of mud and trail erosion, so use your best judgment before proceeding the rest of the way to the Potomac.

1. Avoid riding here when the ground may be wet, especially after a rainstorm or during the thawing season.

2. Always stay on the trail. It's better to walk your bike through the muddy sections than to ride around them, widening the trail even further.

3. Contact the Fairfax County Park Authority or the National Park Service and help repair and maintain this important off-road trail.

Miles and Directions

0.0 **START** from the Twin Branches Nature Trail trailhead on the east side of Twin Branches Road. The trailhead on the west side of the road takes you along Glade Trail. From the trailhead, split left, following Twin Branches Nature Trail downhill into the woods.

0.8 Twin Branches Nature Trail comes to a T just after crossing a small wooden bridge. Turn left toward the Washington & Old Dominion Bike Trail. Turning right leads you into private property.

0.9 Turn left on the Washington & Old Dominion Bike Trail.

2.0 Cross Sunrise Valley Drive.

2.3 Go underneath Dulles Access Road.

2.6 Cross Sunset Hills Road.

2.9 Turn right into Michael Faraday Court. Go to the end of the court and look for a small dirt trail that leads up a little grassy hill into Reston Industrial Park. Bear left through this park onto Colvin Run Trail, marked by a wooden post with a white band and a horseshoe on it. This trail descends rapidly to Colvin Run.

3.8 Colvin Run Trail crosses over a little creek and comes to a T. Turn left at this split, following the Lake Fairfax Nature Trail up to the camping grounds and playing fields of Lake Fairfax.

4.3 Turn right up the gravel road to the playing fields. Playing fields on the right, group camping on the left. Follow the gravel road to Lake Fairfax Dam.

4.7 Cross Lake Fairfax Dam into the main park area. Food, drinks, rest rooms, a working train, and a park office all are available. Take a break for lunch if you wish. To continue on, follow the horse trail, beginning in front of the park office, down the hill south of the dam and back toward Colvin Run.

5.5 Cross Hunter Mill Road. Follow the marked horse trail (white blaze with horseshoe) along Colvin Run. This trail takes you all the way to Great Falls National Park.

6.7 Turn left on Carpers Farm Way to the light at Leesburg Pike (U.S. Highway 7). Cross Leesburg Pike, then turn immediately right, following this unimproved road to the end. **NOTE:** You must cross Difficult Run a number of times on this last section of trail. The creek is pretty wide, and you are almost guaranteed to get wet. If you would rather stay dry, do not continue. Return to Twin Branches Road the same way you came.

(Continuing from Leesburg Pike to Great Falls)

6.9 Follow the Horse Trail (white blaze) at the end of this road into the woods. This leads you along Difficult Run toward the Potomac.

7.5 Cross Difficult Run. The trail continues on the other side of the creek (Fairweather crossing).

8.5 Cross Leigh Mill Road. Continue straight on Difficult Run Trail. An equestrian park is on the right.

9.5 Cross at the low point in the creek from the right side of Difficult Run to the left side. The trail along the right side of the creek ends.

10.6 Go underneath Old Dominion Road.

10.8 Cross Difficult Run again. Smooth concrete layers the creek bottom here. Be careful crossing.

11.0 Cross Difficult Run.

11.2 Follow Difficult Run to the right, which takes you underneath Georgetown Pike and continues to the Potomac.

12.0 Reach the Potomac River at the southern end of Mather Gorge.

There is a great network of trails through Great Falls, all of which are open to bikes. Look to Ride 31 for maps of Great Falls National Park.

Ride Information

Local Information

Fairfax County Convention and Visitors Bureau
(800) 7FAIRFAX
www.visitfairfax.org

Local Events and Attractions

Meadowlark Gardens Regional Park
(703) 255-3631
Kidwell Farm at Frying Pan Park
(703) 437-9101

33 Centreville Power Lines

They may not be scenic mountain roads or offer endless backcountry exploration, but the rugged trails beneath the crackling wires of the power lines make for the ultimate suburban off-road adventure. Power lines have it all—rocks, ditches, hills, dirt, and, most important, open land on which to ride. For a quick and tough ride to help burn off that long, congested commute home from the office, this is it.

Start: Centreville Elementary School
Length: 7.8 miles
Approximate riding time: 1.5–2 hours
Difficulty: Difficult due to sections of very rugged terrain
Trail surface: Rugged singletrack and paved bike paths
Lay of the land: Suburban cycling through power line rights-of-way
Land status: Public and private rights-of-way
Nearest towns: Centreville, VA; Manassas, VA
Other trail users: Power line repairmen, 4WD motorists
Trail contacts: Virginia Power Company
Schedule: None
Fees and permits: None
Map: USGS map: Manassas, VA
ADC map: Northern Virginia Road Map

Getting There: From Interstate 66: Take Exit 53, heading south on State Highway 28

(Sully Road). Sully Road changes to Centreville Road across Lee Highway (U.S. Highway 29). Follow Centreville Road for about 2 miles, then turn left into the Centreville Elementary School parking lot.

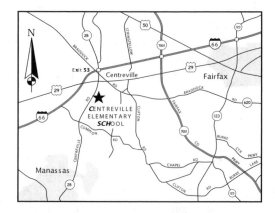

The Ride

Like so many communities in Northern Virginia, Centreville has seen its share of suburban sprawl. In fact, in the past few years, this once small town has been all but swallowed up by the ever-expanding suburbs of Northern Virginia. Surprisingly, though, this incredible growth was once not so easy to come by, and Centreville struggled to get to where it is today.

Centreville had been trying to grow for some time, but for a while was having an altogether tough time of it. Since its establishment in 1792, this small trading center, located nearly equidistant from Leesburg, Warrenton, Middleburg, Washington, Georgetown, and Alexandria, had tried diligently to become more than just a rest stop along Braddock Road.

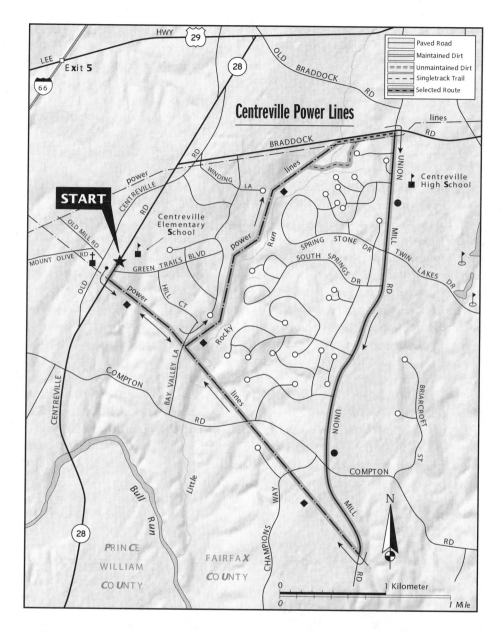

Centreville Power Lines

When construction began on Little River Turnpike in the late eighteenth century, for example, the townspeople hoped this trade highway, stretching west from Alexandria, would be built to pass through their community. At the time, Alexandria was the Potomac's largest market town. Developers, however, routed Little River Turnpike north in favor of smoother, more even terrain, bypassing the town altogether. The town later tried to house the district court of Virginia, which served

Fairfax, Fauquier, Loudoun, and Prince William Counties. This idea was also rejected in favor of Dumfries in Prince William County. Ever persistent, Centreville founded what it hoped would become a prestigious academy to attract outside scholars to take up residence in local homes. This effort also went without much success. At one time, Centreville was even a local center for slave rental and trade. But into the twentieth century, this small town remained nothing more than the unimposing rest stop it had always been.

As you pass through Centreville today, however, much of this history may seem very distant and unfamiliar, because the town has suddenly become a sprawling community of subdivisions, shopping centers, and Beltway commuters. And it continues to expand at a phenomenal rate farther and farther west.

Centreville is not unlike many communities surrounding the Washington, D. C./ Baltimore area that have, in the last ten to twenty years, seen tremendous growth. This explosive growth has, in most cases, virtually wiped out the small-town flavor that dominated the region west of the cities. Towns and villages, desperate for so long to attract more people and new businesses, could never have anticipated the recent boom in development, which has transformed these small hamlets into huge bedroom communities for the Washington, D. C./Baltimore megalopolis.

With this growth, precious back roads and trails were permanently lost, forcing local off-road cyclists to look even harder for places to ride. Thus, the discovery of the power lines! They may not be scenic mountain roads or offer endless backcountry exploration, but the rugged trails beneath these crackling wires make for the ultimate suburban off-road adventure. Power lines have it all—rocks, ditches, hills, dirt, and, most important, open land on which to ride. You'll find yourself crashing down rocky descents, slogging through muddy streambeds, then up and over steep, rutted climbs that snake back and forth beneath the super-charged black cables that bring power to the surrounding homes and neighborhoods.

The most important thing to remember when riding the power lines is that there is always a way through the obstacles. Sometimes you just have to find it. Have fun!

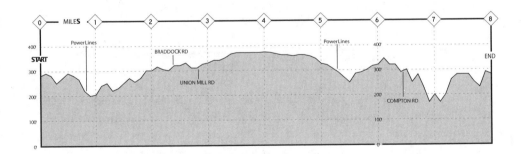

Riders tackle the trails beneath the power lines.

Miles and Directions

0.0 **START** at Centreville Elementary School. Travel south along the asphalt path parallel to Centreville Road. This leads you directly to the power lines.

0.2 Turn left off the asphalt path and hit the dirt trails beneath the power lines. Follow the trail on the left side.

0.75 Cross Bay Valley Lane.

0.8 Turn left at the small fenced-in substation, following the secondary power lines that run north along Little Rocky Run Creek to Braddock Road.

2.0 Pass a small park with tennis courts.

2.2 After passing the park, reenter the trail on the right side of the power lines.

2.4 Climb up the embankment at Braddock Road and turn right on the asphalt path. At this point, the trail beneath the power lines disappears as the power lines parallel Braddock Road.

2.8 Turn right on the asphalt bike path along Union Mill Road.

3.1 Centreville High School is on the left.

4.3 The bike path ends. Continue riding along the shoulder. Be careful of traffic.

4.8 At this intersection with Compton Road, go straight through the stop sign, continuing on Union Mill Road. Union Mill Road continues into a new housing development. Follow this road to the power lines.

5.3 Turn right off Union Mill Road and ride to the power lines, heading west back to Centreville Road.

6.4 Cross Compton Road.

7.0 Pass the small fenced-in power station on the right. Continue straight. Cross Bay Valley Lane.

7.7 Reach Centreville Road. Turn right on the asphalt bike path back toward the school.

7.8 Arrive back at Centreville Elementary School. Tough ride, huh?

Ride Information

Local Information

Prince William County/Manassas Conference and Visitors Bureau, (800) 432–1792
www.visitpwc.com

Local Events and Attractions

Civil War weekends in Manassas, VA
July, August, (800) 432–1792

Manassas National Battlefield Park
(703) 361–1339
www.nps.gov/mana/online.htm
Splashdown Water Park, (703) 361–4451

34 Wakefield Park/Accotink Trail

Host to countless mountain bike races and cross-country races throughout the season, Wakefield Park has become somewhat of a local stronghold for mountain bike excitement in Northern Virginia. With the nearby power lines behind Wakefield Park and trails that are perfect for a quick workout as you exit the Beltway from a long day's grind, this area is a sweet spot in the local off-road scene. And from here, cyclists less interested in mashing out their frustrations on technical track can instead leisurely pedal along a flat, dirt path, beneath Braddock Road and over to Lake Accotink Park. Here, a scenic, woodland preserve, as well as an abundance of short, steep hills, tree roots, quick dips, and fast turns, awaits. Stop off after work and get out of traffic for this great mountain bike locale.

Start: Wakefield Park Recreation Center

Length: 6.1 miles

Approximate riding time: 1 hour

Difficulty: Main loop is rated easy. Offshoot trails are more difficult

Trail surface: Singletrack and dirt trails

Lay of the land: Wooded and relatively flat, next to the Capital Beltway

Land status: County parks

Nearest cities: Annandale, VA; Alexandria, VA

Other trail users: Hikers

Trail contacts: Fairfax County Park Authority (703) 324-8700
Lake Accotink Park, (703) 569-7120
Wakefield Park, (703) 321-7081

Schedule:
Open daylight to dark all year

Fees and permits: None

Maps: USGS maps: Annandale, VA
ADC map: Northern Virginia road map
Fairfax County Park Authority trail map

Getting There: From the Capital Beltway **(Interstate 495):** Exit west at Exit 54A onto Braddock Road. In less than 0.2 miles, turn right on Wakefield Park's entrance road. Go 0.6 miles to the parking and recreation center on the left. Phones, water, rest rooms, and food are available at Wakefield Recreation Center. *DeLorme: Virginia Atlas & Gazetteer:* Page 76, B-4

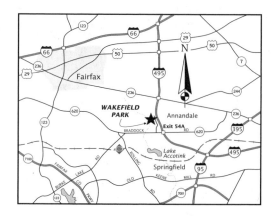

The Ride

Sometimes it's interesting to see where you find singletrack. Typically, great mountain bike trails lie west or far north of the Washington suburbs. Out there—usually a "long drive" from where most of us live—singletrack and forest roads trace the landscape in

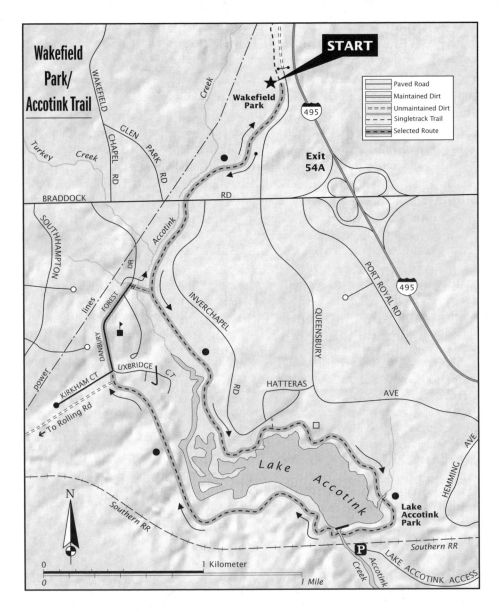

Wakefield Park/Accotink Trail

START

Wakefield Park

Creek

WAKEFIELD

495

Exit 54A

GLEN CHAPEL RD

PARK RD

Turkey Creek

BRADDOCK RD

Accotink

SOUTHHAMPTON

DR

FOREST

lines

DANBURY

power

KIRKHAM CT

UXBRIDGE CT

← To Rolling Rd

INVERCHAPEL

RD

HATTERAS

QUEENSBURY

PORT ROYAL RD

495

AVE

HEMMING AVE

Lake Accotink

Lake Accotink Park

Southern RR

N

0   1 Kilometer
0   1 Mile

P

Southern RR

LAKE ACCOTINK ACCESS

Accotink Creek

	Paved Road
	Maintained Dirt
	Unmaintained Dirt
	Singletrack Trail
	Selected Route

all directions. The dirt's the limit. "If only we lived closer to the trails," goes the suburban cyclist's woeful anthem.

But a closer inspection reveals that we do live near the trails—thanks to the Fairfax County Park Authority. Wakefield and Lake Accotink Parks, less than half a mile from the Capital Beltway in Fairfax County, are filled with a network of fun, technical singletrack. Most of these singletrack trails are offshoots from the park's main loop, a wooded dirt trail around Accotink's scenic seventy-acre lake.

The Accotink Trail was once part of the Orange and Alexandria Railroad's original roadbed, built in the early 1850s. The rails and ties, of course, have since been removed, and a new rail was laid farther south along a straighter route.

▶ **The Accotink Trail was once part of the Orange and Alexandria Railroad's original roadbed, built in the early 1850s.**

Lake Accotink's history began in the 1930s, when the U.S. Army Corps of Engineers dammed Accotink Creek to create a reservoir for Fort Belvoir, nearly 5 miles downstream. The lake and surrounding land were given to Fairfax County in 1965 by the federal government for park and recreational use. The park's great trails, open to bicycling, have been "maturing" ever since.

This ride begins from Wakefield Park and travels south along the Accotink Trail around the lake, then back to Wakefield. There are even some great trails that go north from Wakefield and cross challenging routes beneath the power lines.

For thrill seekers, there is an abundance of short, steep hills, tree roots, quick dips, and fast turns. For the off-road cyclist with a lighter touch, Accotink Trail takes you through a scenic woodland preserve, quiet and relaxing in the spring and summer, breathtaking in the fall. Who says you have to drive far to get out of the gridlock and into the woods? For Beltway commuters, Accotink is less than a stone's throw away.

Miles and Directions

0.0 **START** at Wakefield Park Recreation Center near the big green recycling bins. The trail begins near the park entrance road and heads south through Wakefield toward Braddock Road.

0.2 Cross the athletic fields parking lot. Accotink Trail continues on the other side of the parking lot.

0.6 Cross under Braddock Road.

0.7 Just across Braddock Road, bear left, continuing on the main trail.

1.0 Stay left at the fork in the trail and follow the wooden Accotink Trail post.

2.1 Trail comes to a T. Turn right, following Accotink Trail. The creek should be on your right. This part of the trail winds up and down through the woods. A lot of fun.

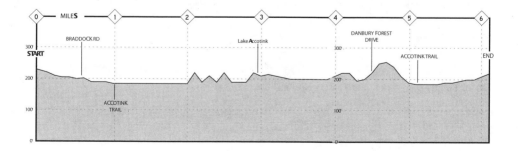

Zipping downhill past the Lake Accotink Dam is a rush.

2.9 Arrive at Lake Accotink's marina. You'll find food, drinks, putt-putt golf, and canoe and boat rentals. Stay right, crossing the parking lot toward the dam.

3.0 Cross Lake Accotink Dam. Following the bike path, which parallels the train trestle, head toward the woods opposite the dam.

3.3 Reenter the woods, up a steep climb, on Accotink Trail.

4.5 Turn hard right off the dirt path on an asphalt trail, which takes you down Danbury Forest Drive in the neighborhood of Danbury Forest. Kings Glen Elementary School on the right.

4.9 Reenter Accotink Trail on the right, just after Lonsdale Drive. This is a steep descent alongside the concrete steps into the woods.

5.0 Turn right off the asphalt path, following Accotink Trail across a wooden footbridge over Accotink Creek.

5.1 Turn left on Accotink Trail.

5.5 Cross under Braddock Road.

6.1 Arrive back at the parking lot of Wakefield's recreation center.

Ride Information

Local Information

Fairfax County Convention and Visitors Bureau
(800) 7FAIRFAX; www.visitfairfax.org

Local Events and Attractions

The Athenaeum in Alexandria
(703) 548-0035

Memorial Day Jazz Festival in Alexandria
(703) 838-4844
Torpedo Factory Art Center, (703) 838-4565
West End Dinner Theater, (800) 368-3799
www.wedt.com

35 Burke Lake Loop

This ride isn't designed for thrill seekers and singletrack lovers. Instead, it reveals the lighter side of off-road bicycle riding, leading cyclists on a pleasant off-road trip past flower gardens and lakeside vistas. The route is mostly flat and smooth, traveling along well-maintained dirt paths around Burke Lake or meandering along South Run on a paved bicycle path. If you get eager to take on some rough stuff, simply cut out from the South Run bicycle path near South Run District Park and take on the rugged, hilly singletrack beneath the power lines. There's plenty for off-road cyclists to do along this easy route to and from Burke Lake, so bring the family and enjoy the ride.

Start: South Run District Park
Length: 7.3 miles
Approximate riding time: 1-1.5 hours
Difficulty: Easy
Trail surface: Asphalt and dirt trails
Lay of the land: Wooded and flat
Land status: Regional park
Nearest town: Springfield
Other trail users: Hikers, boaters, anglers, naturalists, and picnickers
Trail contacts: Fairfax County Park Authority (703) 324-8700
Burke Lake Park, (703) 323-6601
Schedule: Open daily from dawn to dusk, mid-March to mid-November. Trail is open year-round.
Fees and permits: $3.50 per car for nonresidents of Fairfax County at Burke Lake
Maps: USGS maps: Fairfax, VA; Occoquan, VA
ADC map: Northern Virginia road map
Burke Lake Park trail map

Getting There: From the Capital Beltway (Interstate 495): Take Interstate 95 south toward Richmond. Go only about 0.5 miles and take Springfield Exit 57, State Highway 644 (Old Keene Mill Road). Follow Old Keene Mill Road west 3 miles, then turn left on Huntsman Boulevard. Follow Huntsman Boulevard 1.5 miles to the Fairfax County Parkway. Turn right on the Fairfax County Parkway, travel about 0.3 miles, and turn left into South Run District Park. Parking, water, phones, rest rooms, and showers are available at the South Run Recreation Center. *DeLorme: Virginia Atlas & Gazetteer: Page 76, B-3*

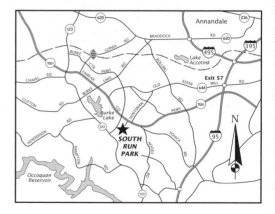

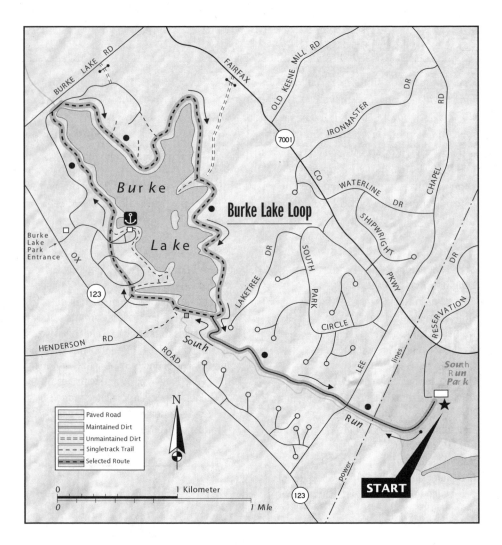

The Ride

> This spring the government chose Burke for the new airport. The whole
> town was shocked. 4,500 acres has been condemned. The town hasn't
> been the same since. Over 100 families are forced to find new homes by
> May 1, 1952.
>
> —*Virginia Lee Fowler*
> *October 11, 1951*

This was the mood of the people of Burke, who were told in the early 1950s that
the U.S. government planned to build a huge space-age airport in the town of
Burke, Virginia. Had it not been for some great leaders in the town's fight against

this proposal, what is now Dulles International Airport would have been built on the exact parcel of land you see in this map. Having lost the battle, the U.S. government reconsidered its original plan and decided instead on a large tract of undeveloped land in Chantilly. As we know, Dulles Airport is now one of the nation's largest international airports.

▶ Surrounded by wooded parkland, it's easy to agree that Burke Lake, Fairfax County's largest lake, is also one of the region's prettiest, most peaceful places for a bike ride.

The government publicly auctioned the parcels of land set aside for the original Burke airport site on Saturday, June 13, 1959. Nearly 900 acres were given to the Fairfax County Park Authority, which in the 1960s dammed streams and flooded 218 acres to create Burke Lake.

This ride begins behind the fieldhouse at South Run District Park and follows South Run north to Burke Lake. Unique and colorful gardens grow along the South Run trail, tilled by the residents of South Park Circle.

Surrounded by wooded parkland, it's easy to agree that Burke Lake, Fairfax County's largest lake, is also one of the region's prettiest, most peaceful places for a bike ride. The gravel and dirt trail around the lake is flat—meandering along the shoreline. From this trail, you can view hundreds of birds as they come and go to their temporary home during the spring and fall migrations.

This ride does not have to start from South Run District Park, and can easily be altered to begin at Burke Lake. But be prepared for a $3.50 per car fee for to nonresidents of Fairfax County.

Miles and Directions

0.0 **START** at South Run District Park behind South Run Recreation Center (main building at the park). Follow the paved path, starting behind the fieldhouse, down the hill into the woods.

0.2 Reach the bottom of the hill and follow the asphalt bike path along South Run. The stream should be on your left.

0.4 Cross underneath the power lines.

0.6 Cross underneath Lee Chapel Road.

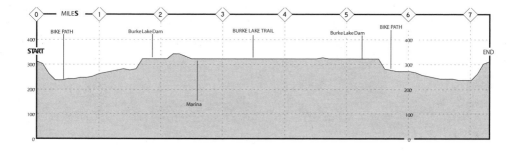

1.5 Arrive at Burke Lake and turn left, crossing the dam.

1.7 Reach the other side of the dam. Continue along the gravel bicycle and walking path, following the park trail signs.

2.0 Reach a small parking lot and boat ramp at the end of the cove. Follow the park trail signs.

2.2 Cross a small open field. Stay to the right side of the field. The trail picks up on the other side. (Trail markings are obscure here, so keep a sharp eye.)

2.4 Cross the park road leading to Burke Lake Park's marina. Follow the park trail signs across the road, back into the woods. A concession stand with food and drinks, boat rentals, rest rooms, and more are available at the marina. To continue on, stay left on the trail, going around the Frisbee golf course.

3.3 The trail drops out on the paved park road. Turn right on this road, cross the bridge, then reenter the trail back into the woods. (Burke Lake Road is on your left.) Continue following the trail around the lake.

6.0 Reach the dam. The loop around Burke Lake is complete. Stay to the left and follow the asphalt bicycle path along South Run back to South Run District Park.

7.1 Cross underneath the power lines.

7.3 Bear left up the asphalt path to South Run Park.

7.5 Reach South Run Park's recreation center.

Ride Information

Local Information

Fairfax County Convention and Visitors Bureau
(800) 7FAIRFAX; www.visitfairfax.org

Local Events and Attractions

Burke Lake Park offers fishing, boating, and a great Frisbee golf course.

36 Fountainhead Regional Park

Here's your chance to ride trails designed by mountain bikers for mountain bikers. As soon as your ride begins, you'll notice the thought that went into these trails. Curves and twists in the landscape will require your total concentration. Thanks to the efforts of the local mountain bike advocacy group MORE (the Mid-Atlantic Off-Road Enthusiasts), riders in the Washington area can enjoy this great network of singletrack trails along the Occoquan Reservoir. Although short in length at just 4.5 miles, the rugged and challenging trails will more than satisfy the hard-core cyclist in you.

Start: Fountainhead Park
Length: 4.5 miles
Approximate riding time: 1 hour
Difficulty: Moderate to difficult
Trail surface: Technical singletrack and doubletrack
Lay of the land: Wooded and hilly
Land status: Northern Virginia Regional Park
Nearest town: Springfield, VA
Other trail users: Hikers, boaters, swimmers, equestrians, campers, and anglers
Trail contacts: Northern Virginia Regional Park Authority, (703) 352–5900
Fountainhead Regional Park, (703) 250–9124
MORE (Mid-Atlantic Off-Road Enthusiasts), (703) 502–0359
Schedule: Open daily from dawn to dusk, March to November
Fees and permits: $3.50 per car at Burke Lake Regional Park for nonresidents of Fairfax County
Map: USGS map: Occoquan, VA
ADC map: Northern Virginia road map

Getting There: From the Capital Beltway (Interstate 495): Take Exit 5 west onto Braddock Road. Head south on State Highway 123. Continue past Burke Lake Park to the Fountainhead Regional Park sign on the right side of the road. Turn right at this sign on Hampton Road. Follow Hampton Road to the park entrance on the left. Park in the first parking lot on the right. The trailhead is to your left. *DeLorme: Virginia Atlas & Gazetteer:* Page 76, C-3

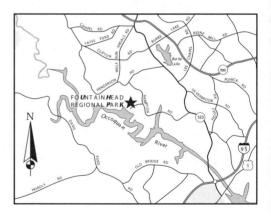

The Ride

Thanks to the hard work of local advocacy groups, Virginians now have a host of new trails available for mountain biking. And the Fountainhead Regional Park Mountain Bike Trail is one of the best. Located in southern Fairfax County, right next to the Occoquan Reservoir, this trail offers a wide variety of terrain for riders of all skill levels.

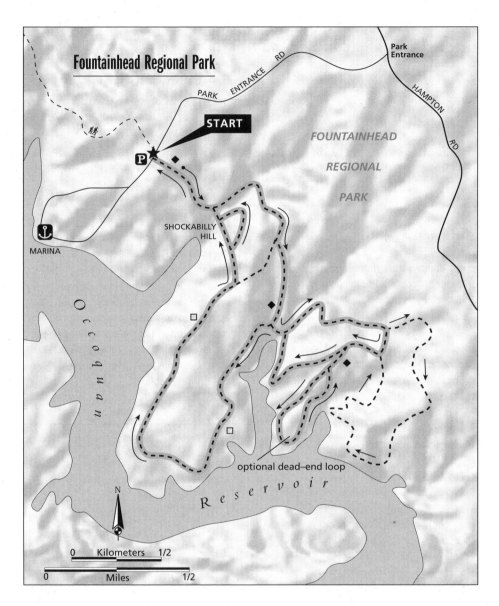

Fountainhead Regional Park

Park Entrance

PARK ENTRANCE RD

HAMPTON RD

START

FOUNTAINHEAD REGIONAL PARK

SHOCKABILLY HILL

MARINA

Occoquan

optional dead–end loop

Reservoir

N

| 0 | Kilometers | 1/2 |
| 0 | Miles | 1/2 |

The Doag Indians were the first to inhabit this area because of its abundance of natural resources. They called it Occoquan—"at the end of the water"—because of its proximity to the river. As with most eastern American Indians, the Doags soon succumbed to English settlers, leaving the name Occoquan as one of the few legacies of their existence. During the Civil War, this area served as a strategic line of defense between the North and South. Such famous Civil War battlegrounds as Bull Run are just a few miles upstream.

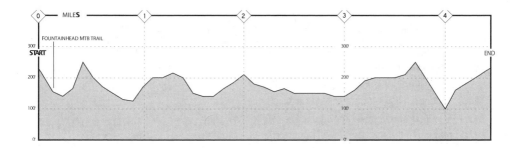

Today, the area serves as part of the larger Bull Run Recreation Area and is managed by the Northern Virginia Regional Park Authority (NVRPA). This off-road bicycling trail is the first of its kind for mountain bikers in northern Virginia. The NVRPA envisions it as an example for the region—a pilot program of sorts. If no user conflicts arise from this experiment, the NVRPA will consider opening more trails for off-road cyclists in the region. Let's set a good example here and help ensure the growth and acceptance of off-road bicycling trails throughout this area.

Your ride starts in the main parking lot as you head toward the marina. From the lot, pedal toward the trail entrance (staging area). This trail is one-way traffic only, so don't plan to travel it in any direction but clockwise. After a brief, fast, and technical downhill, you will bear left at the first trail intersection. Be sure to avoid the right fork in this trail—it's for equestrians and hikers only. A small technical stream crossing leads you to the first turn and the beginning of the loop. The trail takes you around and back on a series of small loops offering up to 5 miles of technical, challenging singletrack. If, after your first or second loop, you're still up for it, head out to the marina and rent a boat or even play a game of miniature golf.

While you're here, don't miss the quaint, historic downtown of Occoquan, rich with history, antiques shops, arts and crafts, and great restaurants. You'll also find the nation's first automated gristmill. And don't forget to check out a host of historic homes and businesses, some of which have been in operation for over 200 years.

Miles and Directions

0.0 **START** at the Red Trail trailhead, approximately 10 yards to the left of the Nature Trail.

0.2 Turn left at this intersection and continue downhill toward the creek crossing. The trail, clearly marked as a bike trail, briefly joins a hiking trail.

0.26 Take a left before a major creek crossing. Remember this is a one-directional trail. This is the only way to go. On your way back, you will have to negotiate Shockabilly Hill with its steep drop-offs. This hill is visible on the other side of the creek.

0.35 Cross the small creek and continue following the red blazes. Get ready to climb.

0.5 After a series of twists and one challenging ascent, turn left at the trail intersection, continuing down a gradual descent. Pay close attention to the exposed roots and stumps—unless you want to sample the soil! Turning right will take you to Shockabilly Hill.

0.84 There is a sharp sudden left switchback toward the bottom of the hill. Continue following the red blazes away from the reservoir. Do not go across the creek.

0.86 Turn right at this point and cross the small creek. Continue back toward the reservoir.

0.9 After a short steep hill, you will be directly across from the previous switchback. Continue left, following the red blazes. The direction is clearly marked.

1.16 Continue following the trail signs and red blazes.

1.37 Turn right at this trail intersection. The trail to the right is an equestrian-only trail.

1.53 Turn left, following the trail toward the Optional Dead End Loop. Prepare for a fun descent. This is a two-way section, so be careful.

1.61 Bear right onto the singletrack. After a twisty descent, the trail curves to the left, offering a great view of the reservoir.

2.1 You have completed the Optional Dead End Loop. Turn right and continue up the two-way traffic section of trail.

2.2 Turn left at this intersection and continue down a fast descent. Keep alert, because you will have to turn left abruptly.

2.3 Follow the trail to the left.

2.4 Follow the switchback to the right. The trail continues to be blazed red.

2.66 Follow the trail to the left at another sign pointing to the parking lot. Go over the small wooden bridge and continue following the red blazes.

4.16 Reach Shockabilly Hill. Continue straight down this hill only if you are an expert. These directions lead you to the right, following the "easier" alternate route.

4.3 Turn right over the wooden bridge. At this point, if you choose, turn right immediately after the bridge and do the loop again. If not, continue straight toward the red/yellow blazes.

4.35 Turn right over the small wooden bridge.

4.5 Arrive back at the trailhead.

Ride Information

Local Information

Occoquan's Web site for local information
www.occoquan.com
Fairfax County Convention and Visitors Bureau
(800) 7FAIRFAX; www.visitfairfax.org

Local Events and Attractions

Historic town of Occoquan www.occoquan.com
Harbor River Cruises in Occoquan
(703) 385-9433

Historic Occoquan Spring Arts & Crafts Show
(703) 491-2168

Accommodations

Bennett House Bed & Breakfast, 9252 Bennett Dr., Manassas, VA 20110-5031
(703) 368-6121
Sunrise Hill Farm B&B, 5590 Old Farm Inn, Manassas, VA 20110-2118
(703) 754-8309

Here's a trail specifically designed by mountain bikers for mountain bikers.

THE FOUNTAINHEAD TRAIL PROJECT: A GROUNDBREAKING EVENT

The Fountainhead Regional Park Mountain Bike Trail was opened in the spring of 1997. Before then, bicycles were not permitted on any of the trails within the park. The trail is a single-direction trail (clockwise), clearly marked with trail signs and red blazes. If at any point the red blazes are on the back of the trees rather than on the front, then you are going in the wrong direction and should turn around.

The Fountainhead Regional Park Mountain Bike Trail represents an important opportunity and major breakthrough for cyclists in the Washington metropolitan area. It was planned by the Northern Virginia Regional Park Authority (NVRPA) in close collaboration with the Mid-Atlantic Off-Road Enthusiasts (MORE) and initially funded, in large part, by REI (Recreational Equipment, Incorporated). This flagship mountain bike trail project was designed specifically by mountain bikers for mountain bikers and will serve as a real litmus test for other park officials who may be interested in constructing and maintaining mountain-bike-specific trailways at their parks.

A paved trailhead and two-way access trail are lined with a split-rail fence to resist erosion and discourage "trail braiding." The trail was designed to take advantage of the area's elevation and terrain, and water bars are widely employed on its steeper grades, including new rubber belt-style devices popular in California. Overall trail usage is expected to be very high, quite possibly exceeding 500 users per month. Please take extreme measures when riding here to ensure this trail's success and durability. The trail is built. Now it's up to us to make sure it stays open.

The number (703) 250–2473 is a dedicated trail line with daily updated messages about trail conditions, closings, and openings. Cyclists should always call this number before heading out to the trail. The Fountainhead Regional Park number is (703) 250–9124.

37 Prince William Forest Park

Down here in Prince William County lies a relatively large park, preserved as one of the few remaining piedmont forest ecosystems in the National Park Service. Within its 18,000 acres are 35 miles of hiking trails, hundreds of acres open to primitive camping, a scenic paved road looping through the park (incidentally named Scenic Drive Road), and a plethora of wildlife and plant life for city folks to enjoy. Four miles of the Scenic Drive have a dedicated bike lane providing a paved, relatively flat surface ideal for beginning bicyclists. More experienced cyclists have the option of off-road biking on any of the ten fire roads in the park.

Start: Prince William Forest Park visitor center
Length: Varies, depending on route chosen. (There are 8.2 miles of unpaved roads open to cyclists.)
Approximate riding time: Varies, depending on route chosen
Difficulty: Moderate
Trail surface: Paved and unpaved park roads
Lay of the land: Hilly piedmont and coastal plains
Land status: Administered by the National Park Service
Nearest town: Dumfries, VA
Other trail users: Hikers, motorists, nature lovers, and pyrite collectors
Trail contacts: Prince William Forest Park Visitor Center, (703) 221-7181
National Park Service, (703) 759-2915
Schedule: Open daily from dawn to dusk. Registered campers and cabin campers have access twenty-four hours. Visitor center is open between 8:30 A.M. and 5:00 P.M.
Fees and permits: A three-day family pass is $4.00 per vehicle within park, $2.00 for cyclists and walk-ins
Maps: USGS map: Joplin, VA
ADC map: Prince William County road map

Getting There: From the Capital Beltway (Interstate 495): Take Interstate 95 south toward Richmond for 20 miles. Take Exit 150, State Highway 619 (Joplin Road) west. Turn right from Joplin Road in one-tenth of a mile to the park entrance road. The visitor center is about 1 mile down this road. You'll find a telephone, rest room, park information, and trail maps. *DeLorme: Virginia Atlas & Gazetteer:* Page 76, D-3

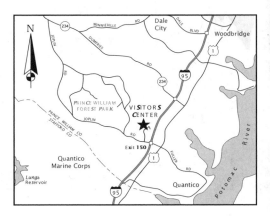

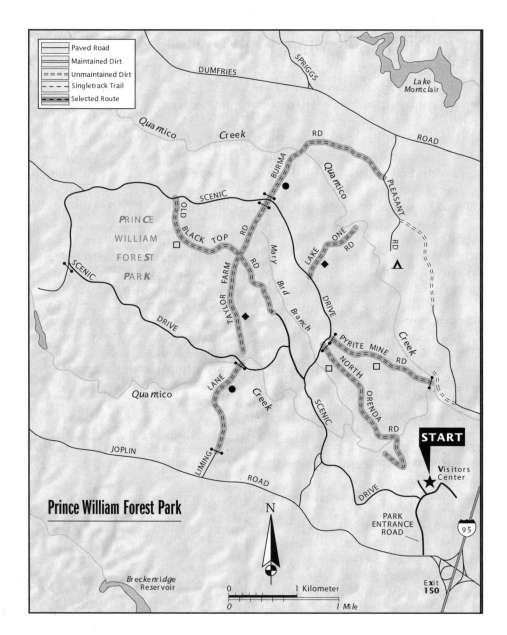

Legend

	Paved Road
	Maintained Dirt
	Unmaintained Dirt
	Singletrack Trail
	Selected Route

Prince William Forest Park

START

Visitors Center

PARK ENTRANCE ROAD

Exit 150

N

0   1 Kilometer
0   1 Mile

The Ride

At one time, Prince William Forest Park's thousands of acres of forestland was extensively farmed for tobacco. Then, when the hills eroded and the earth could no longer support their crops, farmers turned to dairy farming, already well established throughout the county. But for those living in the Quantico Creek area, this business also failed. The Civil War was equally taxing for those already struggling here. The Confederates blockaded the Potomac, requiring large numbers of troops for support. Those living in the vicinity of the blockade were required to provide the troops with timber and food and found that what little they had before the war was no longer enough.

In 1889, mining operation near the confluence of the north and south branches of Conduce Creek provided a much-needed boost to the area's economy. But a strike over wages closed the high-grade pyrite ore mine in 1920, bringing down with it any hope for the area's recovery. It was soon thereafter that the U.S. government bought the land, resettling nearly 150 families. With the help of the Civilian Conservation Corps, they began the effort to "return the depleted land to an ecological balance."

Originally established as the Chopawamsic Recreational Demonstration Area by an act of Congress in August 1933, Prince William Forest Park, a unit of the National Park Service, is mandated to "conserve the scenery and the natural and historic objects and the wildlife therein and to provide for the enjoyment of the same in such manner and by such means as will leave them unimpaired for the enjoyment of future generations." The park contains the largest example of an eastern piedmont forest ecosystem in the National Park System and is a sanctuary for native plants and animals in the midst of this rapidly developing metropolitan area.

All kinds of outdoor activities, including bicycling, are available within the park. Riding on park trails, unfortunately, is prohibited. However, there are many unpaved, dirt roads throughout the park that can be used by cyclists. Many of these roads are separate out-and-back fire roads, in which case you may need to ride along the paved Scenic Drive Road to create loops. Scenic Drive Road is very well maintained and even has its own dedicated bike lane. Road cyclists from all around often come to Prince William Forest Park just to ride this paved loop through the forest, getting quite a workout from its hilly terrain.

FALL LINE Prince William Forest Park lies along the border between two physiographic zones: the Piedmont and the Coastal Plain. Many of the faulted rocks represent the fall line, a unique geological feature. Streams form falls or rapids as they leave the harder rocks of the Piedmont and enter the softer rocks of the Coastal Plain.

To witness the progress the forest has made in reclaiming what was once depleted and eroding farmland is a wonderful experience. And riding your mountain bike along the forest roads through the park gives you an up-close look at this process in action.

Folks looking to do more than just bike can explore as many as 35 miles of hiking trails along ridges, into valleys, and beside the two main creeks in the park. Scenic Drive Road provides access to all of the trails and features within the park. Bicycles are not allowed on any of the park's hiking trails.

POTOMAC MILLS SHOPPING CENTER

Around here, in this metropolitan area, it's hard to really get away from it all no matter how hard you may try. And this point is never more evident than when you drive a bit farther south of Prince William Forest Park on I–95 to one of Virginia's greatest tourist attractions, Potomac Mills shopping center, a destination shopping attraction that brings in over 13,000 bus tours each year. Potomac Mills was reported in the *Washington Post* on September 8, 1991, as the top-rated tourist attraction in the state of Virginia, ahead of both Colonial Williamsburg and Busch Gardens.

With its more than 52 acres of parking and 1.7 million square feet of fully enclosed shopping space, it's easy to understand how this super-regional specialty mall brings in the foot traffic. The mixture of outlet stores and off-price retailers draw cost-conscious shoppers from around the globe. It's really somewhat bewildering to wander Potomac Mills's crowded walkways past its hundreds of shops and thousands of people. The thought of getting back on the bike and pedaling to Prince William Forest Park becomes all the more enticing. But, hey, if you're down in the area anyway, why not head to the largest, most crowded single-floor shopping mall on the planet? Buy some Power Bars and Lycra shorts, then head back north and hit the trails.

Miles and Directions

Liming Lane Fire Road, 0.8 miles long. This forest road is, for the most part, moderately easy. It begins from the parking lot on Scenic Drive Road and takes you out of the park's boundaries to Joplin Road.

Taylor Farm Road, 1.5 miles long. From the northern part of Scenic Drive Road, Taylor Farm Road is mostly level until it drops sharply to the south branch of Quantico Creek. The first nine-tenths of this road are part of the 9.7–mile South Valley Trail, which travels the circumference of this part of Prince William Forest Park.

Burma Road, 1.5 miles long. Burma Road starts out as an easy forest road, then crosses over a series of hills, making this section moderately difficult. This forest road crosses Quantico Creek and takes you to Pleasant Road. From here, you can create a loop back to Scenic Drive Road. Following Pleasant Road past Cabin Camp, you can gather "fool's gold" at the site of the old pyrite mine. Cross Quantico Creek again and take Pyrite Mine Road back to Scenic Drive Road.

Pyrite Mine Road, 1.0 miles long. This forest road takes you from Scenic Drive Road to Quantico Creek, the North Valley Trail, and the old pyrite mine. The trail is moderate in the beginning, then becomes steep at the end.

This is one of the short fire roads in the park.

North Orenda Road, 1.2 miles long. This is a moderate forest road that takes you down to the south branch. Across the creek is the South Orenda fire road, which leads you back to the visitor center.

Lake One Road, 0.6 miles long. Lake One Road starts from the parking lot along Scenic Drive Road and takes you down a moderately steep hill to Quantico Creek.

Old Black Top Road, 1.6 miles long. Old Black Top Road starts from the Turkey Run parking area and travels north, crossing Taylor Farm Road, then connects with Scenic Drive Road. The terrain is moderate and offers a good challenge through the middle of the park.

Ride Information

Local Information

Prince William County Convention and Visitors Bureau, (800) 432-1792
www.nps.gov/prwi/

Local Events and Attractions

Lazy Susan Dinner Theater, (703) 550-7384
Waterworks Water Park
www.pwcces.com/waterworks
Historic town of Occoquan
www.occoquan.com
Harbor River Cruises in Occoquan
(703) 385-9433

Historic Occoquan Spring Arts & Crafts Show
(703) 491-2168

Accommodations

Oakridge Campground, $10 a night
Turkey Ridge Run Campground, $30 a night
Cabin Rental, (703) 221-5843

Organizations

Friends of Prince William Forest Park
www.bmsi.com/fpwfp

Washington, D.C.

t's tough to say a whole lot about mountain biking in the city, as no more than two rides originate here and just one finishes in D.C.—and in Anacostia at that! But surprisingly, both of these trails offer up some of the best off-road adventures in the book.

Starting in Georgetown, the C&O Canal is the longest and perhaps most scenic uninterrupted off-road ride not only in the state of Maryland but quite possibly in the whole East Coast, measuring in at just under 185 miles long. Despite the fact that it's a dead-flat ride along the Potomac River from Georgetown to Cumberland, Maryland, cyclists who have pedaled the distance throughout the years have logged miles and miles of countless sights and adventures. Cruising the C&O Canal in its entirety can be a real endeavor, so take it in pieces and ride it one section at a time. Or simply pedal this scenic national historic landmark along the same section day after day. Whatever you do, you won't be disappointed.

The Fort Circle Park ride is quite different from the C&O Canal, both in its location and its topography. This ride rolls along a hilly greenway through southeast D.C. and Anacostia, connecting a number of old Civil War forts, once part of a series of fortifications surrounding the city in defense against the South. Indeed, this area is probably better known for its crime than its singletrack, but the Fort Circle Park oasis that cuts through the heart of Anacostia will surprise most any cyclist who pedals through deep green woods along the hilly and well-maintained hike/bike trail. The history of the area isn't bad either, so don't forget to make a stop at Fort Dupont Park to learn more.

D.C. is too small and too crowded to host many mountain bike trails. And besides, who wants to ride over suspect terrain with all those lawyers around? But don't overlook what it does have to offer off-road enthusiasts and make sure to give both these rides a try.

38 Fort Circle Trail

Winding through a forested oasis, Fort Circle Trail is both a pathway through history and a greenway into the future of park systems. This dirt and gravel trail system travels up and down the hilly terrain east of Anacostia River, connecting a series of old Civil War fortifications built to protect Washington, D.C., during the war. The greenway is a surprisingly well-maintained park, kept up by the National Park Service, slicing through the heart of D.C.'s Anacostia neighborhoods. Allow plenty of daylight for this ride (you don't want to get caught here at night) and bring along a good map. Despite its location, visitors to this greenbelt will love it here.

Start: Smithsonian Museum of African-American History
Length: 12.2 miles out and back
Approximate riding time: 1–2 hours
Difficulty: Difficult
Trail surface: Singletrack and gravel
Lay of the land: Hilly
Land status: Administered by the National Park Service
Nearest city: Washington, D.C.
Other trail users: Hikers
Trail contacts: National Capital Park East (202) 426–7723
National Park Service, (202) 426–7745
www.nps.gov
Schedule: Open from dawn till dusk, year-round

Fees and permits: None
Maps: USGS map: Washington, D.C.–East Anacostia, MD
ADC map: Prince George's County
Fort Circle Parks historical map
Fort Dupont Park

Getting There:
From the Capital Beltway (Interstate 495):
Exit north on State Highway 5 (Branch Avenue) toward Washington. Go 2.8 miles, then turn left on Suitland Parkway. Go 1.8 miles, then turn right at the light on Stanton Road. Take the immediate right up Gainesville Street, then left up 18th Street. At the top of the hill, turn right on Erie Street and park at the Smithsonian Museum of African-American

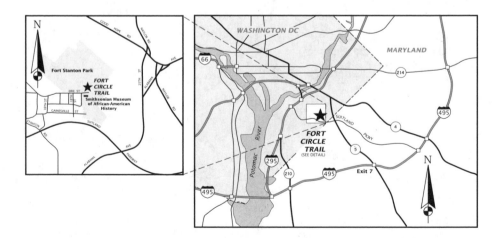

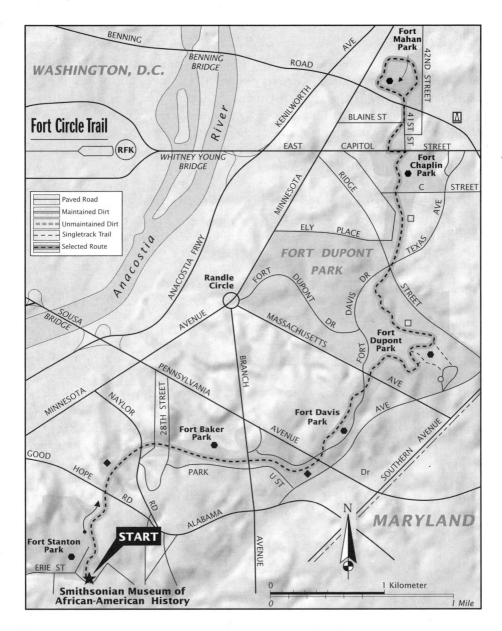

Fort Circle Trail

Legend:
- Paved Road
- Maintained Dirt
- Unmaintained Dirt
- Singletrack Trail
- Selected Route

WASHINGTON, D.C.

Fort Mahan Park

BENNING

BENNING BRIDGE

ROAD

KENILWORTH AVE

BLAINE ST

42ND STREET

41ST ST

M

RFK

WHITNEY YOUNG BRIDGE

EAST CAPITOL STREET

Fort Chaplin Park

C STREET

RIDGE AVE

MINNESOTA

ELY PLACE

TEXAS

FORT DUPONT PARK

Randle Circle

FORT

DUPONT

DAVIS DR

DR

STREET

ANACOSTIA FRWY

SOUSA BRIDGE

AVENUE

MASSACHUSETTS

DR

Fort Dupont Park

FORT AVE

PENNSYLVANIA

BRANCH

28TH STREET

MINNESOTA

NAYLOR

Fort Baker Park

Fort Davis Park

AVE

AVENUE

GOOD HOPE RD

PARK

U ST

AVENUE

Dr

SOUTHERN AVENUE

RD

ALABAMA

AVENUE

N

MARYLAND

START

Fort Stanton Park

ERIE ST

Smithsonian Museum of African-American History

0   1 Kilometer
0   1 Mile

History. Phone, water, and rest rooms are available. *DeLorme: Virginia Atlas & Gazetteer:* Page 77, B-6

From the Baltimore Washington Parkway (Interstate 295): Exit west on Suitland Parkway. Go 1.2 miles, turn left at the first light on Stanton Road. Continue with directions above.

Public Transportation: Take the Metro Blue Line to Benning Road (44th Street). Travel west on Benning Road for 3 blocks and pick up the ride on the right side of the road at mile 5.7 across from 41st Street.

The Ride

After Confederates overwhelmingly defeated the Union army at the first battle of Manassas in July 1861, Union General George McClellan, aware of Washington's vulnerability, ordered heavy fortifications built around the virtually defenseless Union capital. At the time, Fort Washington, nearly 12 miles downriver, was all that guarded Washington. But by the spring of 1865, a ring of sixty-eight forts, ninety-three batteries, and nearly 200 cannons and mortars surrounded the capital, making it the most heavily fortified city in the nation.

The only challenge to Washington's defenses came in July 1864, with a daring attack by Confederate general Jubal A. Early. Choosing a route through the northern perimeter of the city's defense, Early fought his way from Frederick, Maryland, to Silver Spring. But Union forces rushed reinforcements to the northern garrisons above Washington and successfully routed Early's troops. The Confederates were forced to retreat across the Potomac at Whites Ferry and Edwards Ferry, ending the first and only action against the city.

Most of the forts and batteries were dismantled after the Civil War, and the land returned to its prewar owners. Nonetheless, remains of several of these fortifications were preserved by the National Park Service and now make up the Fort Circle Parks. Among those under the care of the National Park Service are several forts built on hilltops overlooking the Anacostia River. Fort Mahan, Fort Chaplin, Fort Dupont, Fort Davis, and Fort Stanton were some of the strongholds guarding Capitol Hill.

Today, the corridor between these forts along the Anacostia River makes a wonderful greenway, complete with a well-maintained and clearly marked hiker-biker trail that connects Fort Stanton with Fort Mahan. Long sections of narrow single-track and twisting trails take you up and down the steep hills on which the forts were built. Cyclists must allow plenty of daylight for this ride and should study directions and maps carefully before starting. While this trail winds through a forested oasis, it's also in some of Washington's rougher neighborhoods, notorious for their high crime rates. Be safe, wear your armor, and have fun, because this is absolutely one of Washington's greatest mountain bike rides!

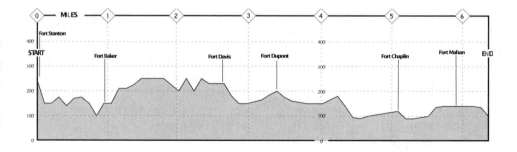

Happily cruising along the Fort Circle Trail, a rider takes a break.

WASHINGTON, D.C., AND L'ENFANT

Washington, D.C., one of only a few planned cities in the world, was designed by Pierre L'Enfant. The cornerstone for the city was laid in 1793. Its original design in the shape of a diamond was created to be both geometrically and geographically precise. In 1847, however, the southwest quadrant was returned to Virginia. The city centers on the Washington Monument, where the north-south and east-west axes of the diamond converge. The Potomac River separates the city from Virginia on the southwest side, while Maryland borders the northwest, northeast, and southeast sides of the city. The district's other major river, the Anacostia, flows through the southeastern part of the city into the Potomac and eventually the Chesapeake Bay. The entire area of Washington, D.C., measures nearly 69 square miles, while the constantly growing metropolitan area measures in at more than 400 square miles. Today, estimates bring the Washington, D.C./Baltimore area close to 6.9 million people, making it the fourth largest metropolitan area in the United States.

Miles and Directions

0.0 **START** in the parking lot of Anacostia's Smithsonian Museum for African-American History. Cross Erie Street to the open grassy area opposite the parking lot. Staying right of the dirt road next to Fort Stanton Park's swimming pool, follow the thin dirt path diagonally across the field up into the woods. (Entrance into the woods is at the far right corner of the field.) Follow this trail into the woods no more than 20 feet before turning sharp left down a steep singletrack trail.

0.2 End of descent. Cross a wooden footbridge over the creek.

0.5 Cross Good Hope Road. Follow the Park Service's Hiker-Biker Trail sign across the street. This is a paved trail for the first 100 feet, then changes back to dirt and gravel.

0.9 Cross Naylor Avenue. The Hiker-Biker Trail is directly across the street, slightly to the right.

1.2 Cross 28th Street SE. The Hiker-Biker trail entrance is to the left.

1.6 Exit the trail on Park Drive SE and turn left. Follow this street for 1 block to Branch Avenue. Cross Branch Avenue. The Hiker-Biker Trail entrance is to the left.

2.1 Cross Pennsylvania Avenue. Reach the entrance to Fort Davis Park. Bear left at the entrance, continuing on the Hiker-Biker Trail down into the woods.

2.7 The trail turns into asphalt. Cross Fort Davis Road.

2.9 Cross Massachusetts Avenue. Continue straight on the Hiker-Biker Trail, which is surfaced with dirt and gravel. Enter Fort Dupont Park.

3.5 The trail forks. Turn left at the first fork, taking the lower trail (a right will take you up to Fort Dupont—0.5 miles.)

3.7 The trail comes to a T. Turn left, horseshoeing slightly downhill. Ridge Road should remain above you on your right.

4.4 The trail exits at the intersection of Fort Davis Road and Ridge Road. The Hiker-Biker Trail sign is catty-corner across this intersection. Cross the Fort Davis Road-Ridge Road intersection. The trail entrance at this point is somewhat overgrown. Keep your eyes peeled.

4.9 Cross C Street. The Hiker-Biker Trail entrance is to the right.

5.1 The trail splits. Bear left at this split.

5.2 The trail comes to a T. Turn right.

5.3 Cross East Capitol Street. Be careful of traffic. Take the crosswalk to the right. Then follow the Hiker-Biker Trail up the hill, back into the woods.

5.6 Exit the trail on 41st Street.

5.7 Cross Benning Street. Go straight up the unmarked embankment to the asphalt path and turn left. Follow this trail around as it does a full circle around Fort Mahan Park.

6.6 Arrive back at Benning Street and 41st Street. Follow the Hiker-Biker Trail signs back along the Fort Circle Trail to where you started at the Smithsonian's African-American History Museum.

Ride Information

Local Information

Fort Dupont Park
www.nps.gov/nace/ftdupont.htm
Washington Convention and Visitors Association, (202) 789-7069
www.washington.org

Local Events and Attractions

Washington, D.C., www.washington.org
Smithsonian Museums, (202) 357-2700
www.si.edu/start.htm
National Zoo, (202) 673-4717
www.si.edu/natzoo

39 Chesapeake & Ohio Canal

Here's a ride for those slow-twitch-muscle types who can ride on and on and on and on without so much as a need to stop and fill up the water bottle once or twice. With 185 miles of off-road riding in one fell swoop (and this is just one way), the C&O Canal Towpath is one ride sure to challenge those who thrive on endurance activities. But few (in fact, almost none) of the cyclists who take to the canal each year attempt to ride the entire distance at once. However, anyone looking for a great trip along the Potomac River (leaving right from Georgetown) with virtually no elevation gain in sight should love this ride. Try it in sections, camp overnight, stay at some of the inns along the way to Cumberland, Maryland, or just ride up and down the canal near the city. Either way, it's a jewel for cyclists looking for an endless trip off the beaten path that leaves right from town.

Start: C&O Canal visitor center
Length: 184.5 miles one way
Approximate riding time: Varies, depending on distance covered each day
Difficulty: Easy due to flat terrain
Trail surface: Crushed-stone and dirt towpath
Lay of the land: Flat canal towpath along the Potomac River
Land status: Maintained by the National Park Service
Nearest city: Washington, D.C.

Other trail users: Hikers, equestrians, and campers
Trail contacts: C&O Canal headquarters (301) 739-4200
Schedule: Open from dawn till dusk every day of the year
Fees and permits: No fees or permits needed
Map: National Park Service C&O Canal trail map

Getting There: From the White House: Take Pennsylvania Avenue NW toward Georgetown. Go 11 blocks to M Street, turn left into Georgetown, then go 2 blocks to Thomas Jefferson Street. Turn left on Thomas Jefferson Street. The Georgetown C&O Canal visitor center is here. *DeLorme: Maryland Atlas & Gazetteer:* Page C3
From the Metro: Take the Metro to the Foggy Bottom Metro station (Orange and Blue lines). Go north on 23rd Street 2 blocks to Washington Circle. Go counterclockwise on Washington Circle to Pennsylvania Avenue NW. Take Pennsylvania Avenue NW 5 blocks to Georgetown. From here, follow the directions above.

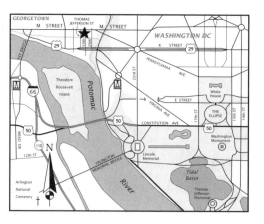

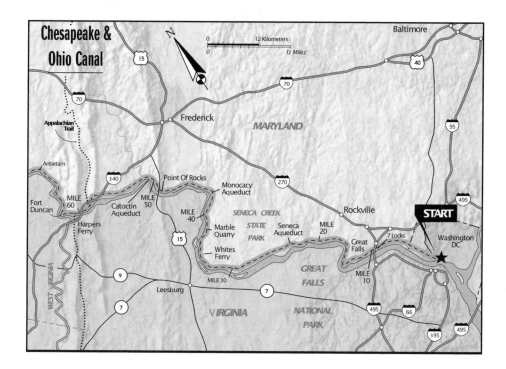

The Ride

In 1828, on a hot Fourth of July in Washington, D.C., ground was broken and the challenge to see who would reach the "western frontier" (Wheeling, West Virginia) first was underway. The competitors: the Chesapeake & Ohio Canal Company versus the Baltimore & Ohio Railroad. Both started digging the same day. Through high costs, floods, land-access problems, 185 miles of rugged earth along the Potomac River, and twenty-two years of backbreaking labor, the C&O Canal finally reached Cumberland, Maryland—eight years after the B&O. Nevertheless, eleven stone aqueducts, seventy-four lift locks, and 185 miles of canal were complete. (The remainder of the route to Wheeling, West Virginia, would be by road.) Unfortunately, not only did the railroad reach the west first, but it was also faster and more reliable, as floods, freezes, and drought often handicapped the canal. Losing money to the railroad and regularly repairing costly flood damage, the C&O Canal was forced to close its gates in 1924, less than one hundred years after its completion.

Today, however, it is one of the most successful and reliable resources in the nation. Its success comes not in profits, though, but in the pleasure it provides to the thousands who hike, bike, or horseback ride along the crushed-stone and dirt towpath each year. It is a reliable treasure chest of sights and wonders, delightful scenery, peace and solitude, and miles of serenity each day of the year. One of the best ways to enjoy the C&O Canal is to ride it in sections, beginning from different starting

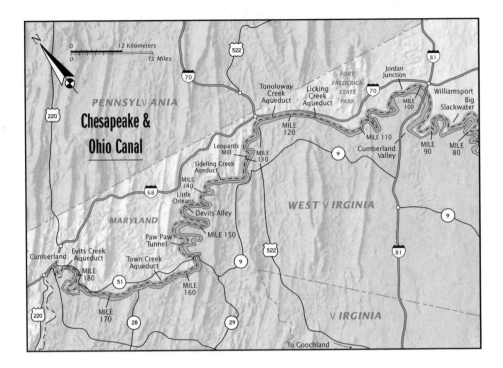

points. But there are plenty of campsites along the towpath to accommodate a one-shot effort from Washington, D.C., to Cumberland, Maryland.

The surface of the towpath is mostly dirt or crushed stone and remains in excellent condition. Due to floods, freezes, and tree roots, however, you should be prepared for some bumpy trails. Also be aware that after heavy rainfall and times of high water, some sections might be impassable. Keep this in mind before heading out on a long weekend of riding.

With regards to the maps, don't be fooled by this ride's profile. It looks like an uphill battle all the way to Cumberland. Over 185 miles, however, a 600-foot elevation gain is virtually unnoticeable, and the trail will feel absolutely flat.

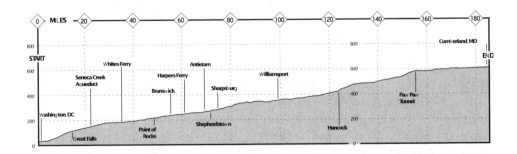

Miles and Directions

0.0 **START** at the C&O Canal visitor center at the corner of Thomas Jefferson Street and M Street in Georgetown.

3.1 Pass Fletcher's Boat House on the left through the tunnel. Bike rentals and repairs are available.

14.3 Great Falls Tavern visitor center.

22.8 Seneca Creek Aqueduct.

30.8 Edwards Ferry. Not in operation.

35.5 Whites Ferry. Last operating ferry on the Potomac.

42.2 Monocacy Aqueduct. The largest aqueduct along the canal.

44.6 Nolands Ferry.

48.2 Point of Rocks. Food available along Clay Street (State Highway 28).

55.0 Town of Brunswick. Phone, food, and groceries.

60.8 Harpers Ferry. C&O Canal Park headquarters. Phone, food, and grocery store. Cross Appalachian Trail.

69.3 Antietam Creek Aqueduct. Ranger station and camp.

72.7 Shepherdstown. Phone, food, and groceries.

99.8 Williamsport. Phone, food, and groceries.

124.0 Hancock. Visitor center. Phone, food, and groceries.

156.0 Paw Paw Tunnel.

184.5 Reach Cumberland. C&O Canal Towpath ends here. Phone, food, groceries.

Ride Information

Local Information

Washington Convention and Visitors Association, (202) 789-7069
www.washington.org

The Art of Mountain Biking

Everything you need to know about off-road bicycling in the Washington D.C./ Baltimore area can be found in this book. This section explores the fascinating history of the mountain bike itself and discusses everything from the health benefits of off-road cycling to tips and techniques for bicycling over logs and up hills. Also included are descriptions of the types of clothing that will keep you comfortable and riding in style; essential equipment ideas to keep your rides smooth and trouble-free; and explanations of off-road terrain, which will prepare you for the kinds of bumps and bounces you can expect to encounter.

The mountain bike, with its knobby tread and reinforced frame, takes cyclists to places once unheard of—down rugged mountain trails, through streams of rushing water, across the frozen Alaskan tundra, and even to work in the city. There are few limits on what this fat-tired beast can do and where it can take us. Few obstacles stand in its way, few boundaries slow its progress. Except for one—its own success. If trail closure means little to you now, read on and discover how a trail can be here today and gone tomorrow. With so many new off-road cyclists taking to the trails each year, it's no wonder trail access has become a contenious issue. A little education about the issue and some effort on your part can go a long way toward preserving trail access for future use. Nothing is more crucial to the survival of mountain biking itself than to read the examples set forth in this book and practice their message.

Without open trails, the maps in this book are virtually useless. Cyclists must learn to be responsible for the trails they use and to share these trails with others. This guidebook addresses why trail use has become so controversial and what can be done to improve the image of mountain biking. We also cover how to have fun and ride responsibly, how to do on-the-spot trail repair techniques. And we provide trail maintenance hot lines for each trail and the worldwide-standard rules of the trail.

Mountain Bike Beginnings

It seems the mountain bike, originally designed for lunatic adventurists bored with straight lines, clean clothes, and smooth tires, has become globally popular in the time it takes to race down a mountain trail.

Like many things of a revolutionary nature, the mountain bike was born on the West Coast. But unlike in-line skates, purple hair, and the peace sign, the concept of the off-road bike cannot be credited solely to imaginative Californians—they were just the first to make waves.

The design of the first off-road-specific bike was based on the geometry of the old Schwinn Excelsior, a one-speed, camel-back cruiser with balloon tires. Joe Breeze was the creator behind it, and in 1977 he built ten of these "Breezers" for himself and his Marin County, California, friends at $750 apiece—a bargain.

Breeze was a serious competitor in bicycle racing, placing thirteenth in the 1977 U.S. Road Racing National Championships. After races, he and friends would scour local bike shops, hoping to find old bikes they could then restore.

It was the 1941 Schwinn Excelsior, for which Breeze paid just $5.00, that began to shape and change bicycling history forever. After taking the bike home, removing the fenders, oiling the chain, and pumping up the tires, Breeze hit the dirt. He loved it.

His inspiration, though prescient, was not altogether unique. On the opposite end of the country, nearly 2,500 miles from Marin County, East Coast bike bums were also growing restless. More and more old beat-up clunkers were being restored and modified. These behemoths often weighed as much as eighty pounds and were so reinforced they seemed virtually indestructible. But rides that take just forty minutes on today's twenty-five-pound featherweights took the steel-toed-boot- and blue-jean-clad bikers of the late 1970s and early 1980s nearly four hours to complete.

Not until 1981 was it possible to purchase a production mountain bike, but local retailers found these ungainly bicycles difficult to sell and rarely kept them in stock. By 1983, however, mountain bikes were no longer such a fringe item, and large bike manufacturers quickly jumped into the action, producing their own versions of the off-road bike. By the 1990s, the mountain bike had firmly established its place with bicyclists of nearly all ages and abilities. Mountain bikes now command nearly 90 percent of the U.S. bike market.

There are many reasons for the mountain bike's success in becoming the hottest two-wheeled vehicle in the nation. They are much friendlier to the cyclist than traditional road bikes because of their comfortable upright position and shock-absorbing fat tires. And because of the health-conscious, environmentalist movement of the late 1980s and 1990s, people are more activity minded and seek nature on a closer front than paved roads can allow. The mountain bike gives you these things and takes you far away from the daily grind—even if you're only minutes from the city.

Mountain Biking into Shape

If your objective is to get in shape and lose weight, then you're on the right track, because mountain biking is one of the best ways to get started.

One way many of us have lost weight in this sport is the crash-and-burn-it-off method. Picture this: You're speeding uncontrollably down a vertical drop that you realize you shouldn't be on—only after it is too late. Your front wheel lodges into a rut and launches you through endless weeds, trees, and pointy rocks before you come to an abrupt halt in a puddle of thick mud. Surveying the damage, you discover, with the layers of skin, body parts, and lost confidence littering the trail above, that those unwanted pounds have been shed—permanently. Instant weight loss.

There is, of course, a more conventional (and quite a bit less painful) approach to losing weight and gaining fitness on a mountain bike. It's called the workout, and bicycles provide an ideal way to get physical. Take a look at some of the benefits associated with cycling.

Cycling helps you shed pounds without gimmicky diet fads or weight-loss programs. You can explore the countryside and burn nearly 10 to 16 calories per minute or close to 600 to 1,000 calories per hour. Moreover, it's a great way to spend an afternoon.

No less significant than the external and cosmetic changes of your body from riding are the internal changes taking place. Over time, cycling regularly will strengthen your heart as your body grows vast networks of new capillaries to carry blood to all those working muscles. This will, in turn, give your skin a healthier glow. The capacity of your lungs may increase up to 20 percent, and your resting heart rate will drop significantly. The Stanford University School of Medicine reports to the American Heart Association that people can reduce their risk of heart attack by nearly 64 percent if they burn up to 2,000 calories per week. This is only two to three hours of bike riding!

Recommended for insomnia, hypertension, indigestion, anxiety, and even recuperation from major heart attacks, bicycling can be an excellent cure-all as well as a great preventive. Cycling just a few hours per week can improve your figure and sleeping habits, give you greater resistance to illness, increase your energy levels, and provide feelings of accomplishment and heightened self-esteem.

Be Safe—Know the Law

Occasionally, even hard-core off-road cyclists will find they have no choice but to ride the pavement. When you are forced to hit the road, it's important for you to know and understand the rules.

Outlined below are a few of the common laws found in Virginia, Maryland, and D.C., as well as some common-sense ideas.

- In Virginia, Maryland, and D.C., you can pedal on any paved public road except urban freeways.

- Follow the same driving rules as motorists. Be sure to obey all road signs and traffic lights.
- Wear a helmet and bright clothing so that you are more visible to motorists. Bright colors such as orange and lime green are highly visible at night.
- Equip your bike with lights and wear reflective clothing at night. When riding at night, the bicycle or rider must be equipped with a white light visible at least 500 feet to the front and a red light or reflector visible at least 600 feet to the rear.
- Pass motorists on the left, not the right. Motorists are not expecting you to pass on the right, and they may not see you.
- Ride single file on busy roads so motorists can pass you safely.
- Use hand signals to show motorists what you plan on doing next.
- Ride with the traffic, not against it.
- Follow painted lane markings.
- Make eye contact with drivers. Assume they don't see you until you are sure they do.
- Ride in the middle of the lane at busy intersections and whenever you are moving the same speed as traffic.
- Slow down and announce your presence when passing pedestrians, cyclists, and horses.
- Turn left by looking back, signaling, getting into the left lane, and turning. In urban situations, walk your bike across the crosswalk when the pedestrian walk sign is illuminated.
- Never ride while under the influence of alcohol or drugs. Remember that DUI laws apply when you're riding a bicycle.
- Avoid riding in extremely foggy, rainy, or windy conditions.
- Watch out for parallel-slat sewer grates, slippery manhole covers, oily pavement, gravel, wet leaves, and ice.
- Cross railroad tracks at a right angle. Be especially careful when it's wet out. For better control as you move across bumps and other hazards, stand up on your pedals.
- Don't ride too close to parked cars—a person opening a car door may hit you.
- Avoid riding on sidewalks. Instead, walk your bike. Pedestrians have the right-of-way on walkways. By law, you must give pedestrians audible warning when you pass. Use a bike bell or announce clearly "On your left/right."
- Slow down at street crossings and driveways.

The Mountain Bike Controversy

Are off-road bicyclists environmental outlaws? Do we have the right to use public trails?

Mountain bikers have long endured the animosity of folks in the backcountry who complain about the consequences of off-road bicycling. Many people believe that fat tires and knobby treads do unacceptable environmental damage and that our uncontrollable riding habits are a danger to animals and other trail users. To the contrary, mountain bikes have no more environmental impact than hiking boots or horseshoes. This does not mean, however, that mountain bikes leave no imprint at all. Wherever people tread, there is an impact. By riding responsibly, though, it is possible to leave only a minimum impact—something we all must take care to achieve.

Unfortunately, it is often people of great influence who view the mountain bike as the environment's worst enemy. Consequently, we as mountain bike riders and environmentally concerned citizens must be educators, impressing upon others that we also deserve the right to use these trails. Our responsibilities as bicyclists are no more and no less than any other trail user. We must all take the soft-cycling approach and show that mountain bicyclists are not environmental outlaws.

Etiquette of Mountain Biking

When discussing mountain biking etiquette, we are in essence discussing the soft-cycling approach. This term refers to the art of minimum-impact bicycling and should apply to both the physical and social dimensions of the sport. But make no mistake—it is possible to ride fast and furiously while maintaining the balance of soft cycling. Here are a few ways to minimize the physical impact of mountain bike riding.

- **Stay on the trail.** Don't ride around fallen trees or mud holes that block your path. Stop and cross over them. When you come to a vista overlooking a deep valley, don't ride off the trail for a better vantage point. Instead, leave the bike and walk to see the view. Riding off the trail may seem inconsequential when done only once, but soon someone else will follow, then others, and the cumulative results can be catastrophic. Each time you wander from the trail you begin creating a new path, adding one more scar to the earth's surface.
- **Do not disturb the soil.** Follow a line within the trail that will not disturb or damage the soil.
- **Do not ride over soft or wet trails.** After a rain shower or during the thawing season, trails will often resemble muddy, oozing swampland. The best thing to do is stay off the trails altogether. Realistically, however, we're all going to come across some muddy trails we cannot anticipate. Instead of blasting through each

section of mud, which may seem both easier and more fun, lift the bike and walk past. Each time a cyclist rides through a soft or muddy section of trail, that part of the trail is permanently damaged. Regardless of the trail's conditions, though, remember always to go over the obstacles across the path, not around them. Stay on the trail.

- **Avoid trails that, for all but God, are considered impassable and impossible.** Don't take a leap of faith down a kamikaze descent on which you will be forced to lock your brakes and skid to the bottom, ripping the ground apart as you go.

The concept of soft-cycling should apply to the social dimensions of the sport as well, since mountain bikers are not the only folks who use the trails. Hikers, equestrians, cross-country skiers, and other outdoors people use many of the same trails and can be easily spooked by a marauding mountain biker tearing through the trees. Be friendly in the forest and give ample warning of your approach.

- **Take out what you bring in.** Don't leave broken bike pieces and banana peels scattered along the trail.
- **Be aware of your surroundings.** Don't use popular hiking trails for race training.
- **Slow down!** Rocketing around blind corners is a sure way to ruin an unsuspecting hiker's day. Consider this: If you fly down a quick singletrack descent at 20 miles per hour, then hit the brakes and slow down to only 6 miles per hour to pass someone, you're still moving twice as fast as the hiker!

Like the trails we ride on, the social dimension of mountain biking is very fragile and must be cared for responsibly. We should not want to destroy another person's enjoyment of the outdoors. By riding in the backcountry with caution, control, and responsibility, our presence should be felt positively by other trail users. By adhering to these rules, trail riding—a privilege that can quickly be taken away—will continue to be ours to share.

Trail Maintenance

Unfortunately, despite all of the preventive measures taken to avoid trail damage, we're still going to run into many trails requiring attention. Simply put, a lot of hikers, equestrians, and cyclists use the same trails—some wear and tear is unavoidable. But like your bike, if you want to use these trails for a long time to come, you must also maintain them.

Trail maintenance and restoration can be accomplished in a variety of ways. One way is for mountain bike clubs to combine efforts with other trail users (hikers and equestrians) and work closely with land managers to cut new trails or repair existing ones. This work not only reinforces to others the commitment cyclists have in caring for and maintaining the land, but it also breaks the ice that often separates cyclists from their fellow trail mates. Another good way to help out is to show up on a Saturday morning with a few riding buddies, ready to work at your favorite off-road domain. With a good attitude, thick gloves, and the local land manager's supervision, trail repair is fun and very rewarding. It's important, of course, that you arrange a trail-repair outing with the local land manager before you start pounding shovels into the dirt. Managers can lead you to the most needy sections of trail and instruct you on what repairs should be done and how best to accomplish the task. Perhaps the most effective trail maintenance, though, can be done by yourself and while you're riding. Read on.

On-The-Spot Quick Fix

Most of us, when we're riding, have at one time or another come upon muddy trails or fallen trees blocking our path. We notice that over time the mud gets deeper, and the trail gets wider as people go through or around the obstacles. We worry that the problem will become so severe and repairs so difficult that the trail's access may be threatened. We also know that our ambition to do anything about the problem is greatest at that moment, not after a hot shower and a plate of spaghetti. Here are a few on-the-spot quick fixes you can do that will hopefully correct a problem before it gets out of hand and get you back on your bike within minutes.

Muddy trails. What do you do when trails develop huge mud holes destined for EPA Superfund status? The technique is called corduroying, and it works much like building a pontoon over the mud to support bikes, horses, or hikers as they cross. *Corduroy* (not the pants) is the term for roads made of logs laid down crosswise. Use small and medium-sized sticks and lay them side by side across the trail until they cover the length of the muddy section (break the sticks to fit the width of the trail). Press them into the mud with your feet, then lay more on top if needed. Keep adding sticks until the trail is firm. Not only will you stay clean as you cross, but the sticks may soak up some of the water and help the puddle dry. This quick fix may last as long as one month before needing to be redone. And as time goes on, with new layers added to the trail, the soil will grow stronger, thicker, and more resistant to erosion. This whole process may take fewer than five minutes, and you can be on your way, knowing the trail behind you is in good repair.

Leaving the trail. What do you do to keep cyclists from cutting corners and leaving the designated trail? The solution is much simpler than you may think. (No, don't hire an off-road police force.) Notice where people are leaving the trail and throw a pile of thick branches or brush along the path, or place logs across the opening to block the way through. There are probably dozens of subtle tricks like these that will keep people on the designated trail. If this trick is executed well, no one will even notice know the thick branches scattered along the ground in the woods weren't always there. And most folks would probably rather take a moment to hop a log in the trail than get tangled in a web of branches.

Obstacles in the way. If there are large obstacles blocking the trail, try and remove them or push them aside. If you cannot do this by yourself, call the trail maintenance hot line to speak with the land manager of that particular trail and see what can be done.

We must be willing to sweat for our trails in order to sweat on them. Police yourself and point out to others the significance of trail maintenance. "Sweat equity," the rewards of continued land use won with a fair share of sweat, pays off when the trail is up for review by the land manager, and he or she remembers the efforts made by trail-conscious mountain bikers.

Rules of the Trail

The International Mountain Bicycling Association (IMBA) has developed these guidelines to trail riding. These "rules of the trail" are accepted worldwide and will go a long way in keeping trails open. Please respect and follow these rules for everyone's sake.

1. Ride only on open trails. Respect trail and road closures (if you're not sure, ask a park or state official first), do not trespass on private property, and obtain permits or authorization if required. Federal and state wilderness areas are off-limits to cycling. Parks and state forests may also have certain trails closed to cycling.

2. Leave no trace. Be sensitive to the dirt beneath you. Even on open trails, you should not ride under conditions by which you will leave evidence of your passing, such as on certain soils or shortly after a rainfall. Be sure to observe the different types of soils and trails you're riding on, practicing minimum-impact cycling. Never ride off the trail, don't skid your tires, and be sure to bring out at least as much as you bring in.

3. Control your bicycle! Inattention for even one second can cause disaster for yourself or for others. Excessive speed frightens and can injure people, gives mountain biking a bad name, and can result in trail closures.

4. Always yield. Let others know you're coming well in advance (a friendly greeting is always good and often appreciated). Show your respect when passing others by slowing to walking speed or stopping altogether, especially in the presence of horses. Horses can be unpredictable, so be very careful. Anticipate that other trail users may be around corners or in blind spots.

5. Never spook animals. All animals are spooked by sudden movements, unannounced approaches, or loud noises. Give the animals extra room and time so they can adjust to you. Move slowly or dismount around animals. Running cattle and disturbing wild animals are serious offenses. Leave gates as you find them, or as marked.

6. Plan ahead. Know your equipment, your ability, and the area in which you are riding, and plan your trip accordingly. Be self-sufficient at all times, keep your bike in good repair, and carry necessary supplies for changes in weather or other conditions. You can help keep trails open by setting an example of responsible, courteous, and controlled mountain bike riding.

7. Always wear a helmet when you ride. For your own safety and protection, a helmet should be worn whenever you are riding your bike. You never know when a tree root or small rock will throw you the wrong way and send you tumbling.

Thousands of miles of dirt trails have been closed to mountain bicycling because of the irresponsible riding habits of just a few riders. Don't follow the example of these offending riders. Don't take away trail privileges from thousands of others who work hard each year to keep backcountry avenues open to us all.

The Necessities of Cycling

When discussing the most important items to have on a bike ride, cyclists generally agree on the following four items.

Helmet. The reasons to wear a helmet should be obvious. Helmets are discussed in more detail in the "Be Safe—Wear Your Armor" section.

Water. Without it, cyclists may face dehydration, which may result in dizziness and fatigue. On a warm day, cyclists should drink at least one full bottle during every hour of riding. Remember, it's always good to drink before you feel thirsty—otherwise, it may be too late.

Cycling shorts. These are necessary if you plan to ride your bike more than thirty minutes. Padded cycling shorts may be the only thing keeping your derriere from serious saddle soreness by ride's end. There are two types of cycling shorts. Touring shorts are good for people who don't want to look like they're wearing anatomically correct cellophane. They look like regular athletic shorts with pockets, but have built-in padding in the crotch area for protection from chafing and saddle sores. The more popular, traditional cycling shorts are made of skintight material, also with a padded crotch. Whichever style you find most comfortable, cycling shorts are a necessity for long rides.

Food. This essential item will keep you rolling. Cycling burns up a lot of calories and is among the few sports in which no one is safe from the "bonk." Bonking feels like it sounds. Without food in your system, your blood sugar level collapses, and there is no longer any energy in your body. This instantly results in total fatigue and light-headedness. So when you're filling your water bottle, remember to bring along some food. Fruit, energy bars, or some other forms of high-energy food are highly recommended. Candy bars are not, however, because they will deliver a sudden burst of high energy, then let you down soon after, causing you to feel worse than before.

Energy bars are available at most bike stores and are similar to candy bars, but they provide complex carbohydrate energy and high nutrition rather than fast-burning simple sugars.

Be Prepared or Die

Essential equipment that will keep you from dying alone in the woods:

- Spare Tube
- Tire Irons
- Patch Kit
- Pump
- Money: spare change for emergency calls
- Spoke Wrench
- Spare Spokes: tape these to the chain stay
- Chain Tool
- Allen Keys: Bring appropriate sizes to fit your bike
- Compass/GPS
- Duct Tape
- First-Aid Kit
- Rain Gear: for quick changes in weather
- Matches
- Guidebook: In case all else fails and you must start a fire to survive, this guidebook will serve as an excellent fire starter.
- Food and Water
- Jacket

To carry these items, you may need a bike bag. A bag mounted in front of the handlebars provides quick access to your belongings, whereas a saddlebag fitted underneath the saddle keeps things out of your way. If you're carrying lots of equipment, you may want to consider a set of panniers. These large bags mount on either side of each wheel on a rack. Many cyclists, though, prefer not to use a bag at all. They just slip all they need into their jersey pockets and off they go.

Be Safe—Wear Your Armor

While on the subject of jerseys, it's crucial to discuss the clothing you must wear to be safe, practical, and—if you prefer—stylish. The following is a list of items that will save you from disaster, outfit you comfortably, and, most important, keep you looking cool.

Helmet. A helmet is an absolute necessity because it protects your head from complete annihilation. It is the only thing that will not disintegrate into a million pieces after a wicked crash on a descent you shouldn't have been on in the first place. A helmet with a solid exterior shell will also protect your head from sharp or protruding objects. And you can of course paste several stickers from your favorite bicycle manufacturers all over the helmet's outer shell, giving companies even more free advertising for your dollar.

Shorts. Padded cycle shorts provide cushioning between your body and the bicycle seat. Cycle shorts also wick moisture away from your body and prevent chafing. Form-fitting shorts are made from synthetic material and have smooth seams to prevent chafing. If you don't feel comfortable wearing form-fitted shorts, baggy padded shorts with pockets are available.

Gloves. You may find well-padded cycling gloves invaluable when traveling over rocky trails and gravelly roads for hours on end. When you fall off your bike and land on your palms, gloves are your best friend. Long-fingered gloves may also be useful, as branches, trees, assorted hard objects, and occasionally small animals will reach out and whack your knuckles. Insulated gloves are essential for winter riding.

Glasses. Not only do sunglasses give you an imposing presence and make you look cool (both are extremely important), they also protect your eyes from harmful ultraviolet rays, invisible branches, creepy bugs, and dirt. They also hide your glances at riders of the opposite sex wearing skintight, revealing Lycra.

Shoes. Mountain bike shoes have stiff soles that transfer more of the power from a pedal stroke to the drive train and provide a solid platform to stand on, thereby decreasing fatigue in your feet. You can use virtually any good light outdoor hiking footwear, but specific mountain bike shoes (especially those with inset cleats) are best. They are lighter and breathe well and are constructed to work with your pedal strokes instead of the narural walking cadence.

Other clothing. To prepare for Virginia's weather, it's best to dress in layers that can be added or removed as weather conditions change. In cold weather, wear a wicking layer made of a modern synthetic fiber next to your skin. Avoid wearing cotton of any type. It dries slowly and does not wick moisture away from your skin, thus chilling you directly as it evaporates. The next layer should be a wool or synthetic insulating layer that helps keep you warm but also is breathable. A fleece jacket or vest works well as an insulating layer. The outer layer should be a jacker and pants that are waterproof, windproof, and breathable. Your ears will also welcome a fleece headband when it's cold out.

Oh, Those Chilly Metropolitan Days

If the weather chooses not to cooperate on the day you've set aside for a bike ride, it's helpful to be prepared.

Tights or leg warmers. These are best in temperatures below fifty-five degrees. Knees are sensitive and can develop all kinds of problems if they get cold. Common problems include tendinitis, bursitis, and arthritis.

Plenty of layers on your upper body. When the air has a nip in it, layers of clothing will keep the chill away from your chest and help prevent bronchitis. If the air is cool, a polypropylene long-sleeved shirt is best to wear against the skin, beneath other layers of clothing. Polypropylene, like wool, wicks away moisture from your skin to keep your body dry. Try to avoid wearing cotton or baggy clothing when the temperature falls. Cotton holds moisture like a sponge, and baggy clothing catches cold air and swirls it around your body. Good cold-weather clothing should fit snugly against your body, but not be restrictive.

Wool socks. Don't pack too many layers under those shoes, though. You may restrict circulation, and your feet will get real cold, real fast.

Thinsulate or Gortex gloves. There is nothing worse than frozen feet—unless your hands are frozen. A good pair of Thinsulate or Gortex gloves should keep your hands toasty and warm.

Hat or helmet on cold days? Sometimes, when the weather gets really cold and you still want to hit the trails, it's tough to stay warm. We all know that 40 to 50 percent of the body's heat escapes through the head (overactive brains, I imagine), so it's important to keep the cranium warm. Ventilated helmets are designed to keep heads cool in the summer heat, but they do little to help keep heads warm during rides in subzero temperatures. Cyclists should consider wearing a hat on extremely cold days. Polypropylene skullcaps are great head and ear warmers that snugly fit over your head beneath the helmet. Head protection is not lost. Another option is a helmet cover that covers those ventilating gaps and helps keep body heat in. It does not, however, keep your ears warm. Some cyclists opt for a simple knit cycling cap sans the helmet, but these are not very good cranium protectors.

All of this clothing can be found at your local bike store, where the staff should be happy to help fit you into the seasons of the year.

To Have or Have Not—Other Very Useful Items

Though mountain biking is relatively new to the cycling scene, there is no shortage of items for you and your bike to make riding better, safer, and easier. We have rummaged through the unending lists and separated the gadgets from the good stuff, coming up with what we believe are items certain to make mountain bike riding easier and more enjoyable.

Tires. Buying a good pair of knobby tires is the quickest way to enhance the off-road handling capabilities of a bike. There are many types of mountain bike tires on the market. Some are made exclusively for very rugged off-road terrain. These big-knobbed, soft rubber tires virtually stick to the ground with magnetic-like traction, but they tend to deteriorate quickly on pavement. Other tires are made exclusively for the road. These are called "slicks," and they have no tread at all. For the average cyclist, though, a good tire somewhere in the middle of these two extremes should do the trick. Realize, however, that you get what you pay for. Do not skimp and buy cheap tires. As your primary point of contact with the trail, tires may be the most important piece of equipment on a bike. With inexpensive rubber, the tire's beads may unravel, or chunks of tread might actually rip off the tire. If you're lucky, all you'll suffer is a long walk back to the car. If you're unlucky, your tire could blow out in the middle of a rowdy downhill, causing a wicked crash.

Clipless pedals. Clipless pedals, like ski bindings, attach your shoe directly to the pedal. They allow you to exert pressure on the pedals during down- and upstrokes. They also help you maneuver the bike in the air or while climbing various obstacles. Toe clips may be less expensive, but they are also heavier and harder to use. Clipless pedals and toe clips both take a little getting used to, but they're definitely worth the trouble.

Bar ends. These clamp-on additions to your original straight handlebar will provide more leverage, an excellent grip for climbing, and a more natural position for your hands. Be aware, however, of the bar end's propensity for hooking trees on fast descents, sending you airborne. Opinions are divided on the general usefulness of bar ends these days. Over the last few years, bar ends have fallen out of favor with manufacturers and riders alike.

Backpack. These bags are ideal for carrying keys, extra food and water, guidebooks, foul-weather clothing, tools, spare tubes, and a cellular phone, in case you need to call for help.

Suspension forks. For off-roaders who want nothing to impede their speed on the trails, investing in a pair of suspension forks is a good idea. As with tires, there are plenty of brands to choose from, and they all do the same thing—absorb the brutal beatings of a rough trail. The cost of these forks, however, is sometimes more brutal than the trail itself.

Bike computers. These fun gadgets are much less expensive than they were in years past. They have such features as speedometers, odometers, clocks, altimeter, alarms, and global satellite positioning systems. Bike computers will come in handy when you're following these maps or just want to know how far you've ridden in the wrong direction.

Hydration pack. This is quickly becoming an essential item for cyclists pedaling for more than a few hours, especially in hot, dry conditions. The most popular brand is the Camelback, which can carry as much as one hundred ounces of water. Hydration packs strap on your back, with a handy hose running over your shoulder so you can drink water while still holding both bars on a rocky descent. These packs are a great way to carry a lot of extra liquid on hot rides in the middle of nowhere, plus keys, a camera, extra food, guidebooks, tools, spare tubes, and a cellular phone.

Types of Off-Road Terrain

Before roughing it off-road, you may first have to ride the pavement to get to your destination. Don't be dismayed. Some of the country's best rides are on the road. Once we get past these smooth-surfaced pathways, though, adventures in dirt await us.

Rails-to-Trails. Abandoned rail lines are converted into usable public resources for exercising, commuting, or just enjoying nature. Old rails and ties are torn up and a trail, paved or unpaved, is laid along the existing corridor. This completes the cycle, from ancient Indian trading routes to railroad corridors and back again to hiking and cycling trails.

Unpaved roads. These are typically found in rural areas and are most often public roads. Be careful when exploring, though, not to ride on someone's unpaved private drive.

Forest roads. These dirt and gravel roads are used primarily as access to forestland and are kept in good condition. They are almost always open to public use.

Singletrack. Singletrack can be the most fun on a mountain bike. These trails, with only one track to follow, are often narrow, challenging pathways through the woods. Remember to make sure these trails are open before zipping into the woods. (At the time of this printing, all trails and roads in this guidebook were open to mountain bikes.)

Open land. Unless there is a marked trail through a field or open space, you should not ride there. Once one person cuts his or her wheels through a field or meadow, many more are sure to follow, causing irreparable damage to the landscape.

Techniques to Sharpen Your Skills

Many of us see ourselves as pure athletes—blessed with power, strength, and endless endurance. However, it may be those with finesse, balance, agility, and grace that get around most quickly on a mountain bike. Although power, strength, and endurance do have their places in mountain biking, these elements don't necessarily form the framework for a champion mountain biker.

The bike should become an extension of your body. Slight shifts in your hips or knees can have remarkable results. Experienced bike handlers seem to flash down technical descents, dashing over obstacles in a smooth and graceful effort as if pirouetting in Swan Lake. Here are some tips and techniques to help you connect with your bike and float gracefully over the dirt.

Braking. Using your brakes requires using your head, especially when descending. This doesn't mean using your head as a stopping block, but rather to think intelligently. Use your best judgment in terms of how much or how little to squeeze those brake levers.

The more weight a tire is carrying, the more braking power it has. When you're going downhill, your front wheel carries more weight than the rear. Braking with the front brake will help keep you in control without going into a skid. Be careful, though, not to overdo it with the front brakes and accidentally toss yourself over the handlebars. And don't neglect your rear brake! When descending, shift your weight back over the rear wheel, thus increasing your rear braking power as well. This technique will balance the power of both brakes and give you maximum control.

Good riders learn just how much of their weight to shift over each wheel and how to apply just enough braking power to each brake so not to "endo" over the handlebars or skid down a trail.

Going Uphill—Climbing Those Treacherous Hills

Shift into a low gear (push the thumb shifter away from you). Before shifting, be sure to ease up on your pedaling to decrease pressure on the chain. Find the gear that best matches the terrain and steepness of each climb.

Stay seated. Standing out of the saddle is often helpful when climbing steep hills with a road bike, but you may find that on dirt, standing may cause your rear tire to lose its grip and spin out. Climbing requires traction. Stay seated as long as you can and keep the rear tire digging into the ground. Ascending skyward may prove to be much easier in the saddle.

Lean forward. On very steep hills, the front end may feel unweighted and suddenly pop up. Slide forward on the saddle and lean over the handlebars. This position will add more weight to the front wheel and should keep you grounded.

Keep pedaling. On rocky climbs, be sure to keep the pressure on, and don't let up on those pedals! The slower you go through rough trail sections, the harder you will work.

Going Downhill— The Real Reason We Get Up in the Morning

Shift into the big chain ring. Shifting into the big ring before a bumpy descent will help keep the chain from bouncing off. And should you crash or disengage your leg from the pedal, the chain will cover the teeth of the big ring so they don't bite into your leg.

Relax. Stay loose on the bike, and don't lock your elbows or clench your grip. Your elbows need to bend with the bumps and absorb the shock, while your hands should have a firm but controlled grip on the bars to keep things steady. Steer with your body, allowing your shoulders to guide you through each turn and around each obstacle.

Don't oversteer or lose control. Mountain biking is much like downhill skiing, since you must shift your weight from side to side down narrow, bumpy descents.

Your bike will have the tendency to track in the direction you look and follow the slight shifts and leans of your body. You should not think so much about steering but rather the direction you wish to go.

Rise above the saddle. When racing down bumpy, technical descents, you should not sit on the saddle but instead stand on the pedals, allowing your legs and knees to absorb the rocky trail.

Drop your saddle. For steep, technical descents, you may want to drop your saddle 3 or 4 inches. This lowers your center of gravity, giving you much more room to bounce around.

Keep your pedals parallel to the ground. The front pedal should be slightly higher so that it doesn't catch on small rocks or logs.

Stay focused. Many descents require your utmost concentration and focus just to reach the bottom. You must notice every groove, every root, every rock, every hole, every bump. You, the bike, and the trail should all become one as you seek singletrack nirvana on your way down the mountain. But if your thoughts wander, then so may your bike, and you may instead become one with the trees!

Watch Out!

Back-Road Obstacles

Logs. When you want to hop a log, throw your body back, yank up on the handlebars, and pedal forward in one swift motion. This technique clears the front end of the bike. Then quickly scoot forward and pedal the rear wheel up and over. Keep the forward momentum until you've cleared the log, and, by all means, don't hit the brakes, or you may do some interesting acrobatic maneuvers!

Rocks. Worse than highway potholes! Stay relaxed, let your elbows and knees absorb the shock, and always continue applying power to your pedals. Staying seated will keep the rear wheel weighted to prevent slipping, and a light front end will help you respond quickly to each new obstacle. The slower you go, the more time your tires will have to get caught between the grooves.

Water. Before crossing a stream or puddle, be sure to first check the depth and bottom surface. There may be an unseen hole or large rock hidden under the water that could wash you up if you're not careful. After you're sure all is safe, hit the water at a good speed, pedal steadily, and allow the bike to steer you through. Once you're across, tap the breaks to squeegee the water off the rims.

Leaves. Beware of wet leaves. These may look pretty, but a trail covered with leaves may cause your wheels to slip out from under you. Leaves are not nearly as unpredictable and dangerous as ice, but they do warrant your attention on a rainy day.

Mud. If you must ride through mud, hit it head on and keep pedaling. You want to part the ooze with your front wheel and get across before it swallows you up. Above all, don't leave the trail to go around the mud. This just widens the path even more and leads to increased trail erosion.

Urban Obstacles

Curbs are fun to jump, but as with logs, be careful.

Curbside drains are typically not a problem for bikes. Just be careful not to get a wheel caught in the grate.

Dogs make great pets but seem to have it in for bicyclists. If you think you can't outride a dog that's chasing you, stop and walk your bike out of its territory. A loud yell to "Get!" or "Go home!" often works, as does a sharp squirt from your water bottle right between the eyes.

Cars are tremendously convenient when we're in them, but irate motorists in big automobiles can be a real hazard when you're riding a bike. As a cyclist, you must realize that most drivers aren't expecting you to be there and often wish you weren't. Stay alert and ride carefully, clearly signaling all of your intentions.

Potholes, like grates and back-road canyons, should be avoided. Just because you're on an all-terrain bicycle doesn't mean you're indestructible. Potholes regularly damage rims, pop tires, and sometimes lift unsuspecting cyclists into spectacular swan dives over the handlebars.

Last-Minute Check

Before a ride, it's a good idea to give your bike a once-over to make sure everything is in working order. Begin by checking the air pressure in your tires to make sure they are properly inflated. Mountain bikes require about forty-five to fifty-five pounds of air pressure per square inch. If your tires are underinflated, there is greater likelihood that the tubes may get pinched on a bump or rock, causing the tire to flat.

Looking over your bike to make sure everything is secure and in its place is the next step. Go through the following checklist before each ride.

- **Pinch the tires to feel for proper inflation.** They should give just a little on the sides but feel very hard on the treads. If you have a pressure gauge, use it.
- **Check your brakes.** Squeeze the rear brake and roll your bike forward. The rear tire should skid. Next, squeeze the front brake and roll your bike forward. The rear wheel should lift into the air. If this doesn't happen, then your brakes are too loose. Make sure the brake levers don't touch the handlebars when squeezed with full force.
- **Check all quick releases on your bike.** Make sure they are all securely tightened.

- **Lube up.** If your chain squeaks, apply some lubricant.
- **Check your nuts and bolts.** Check the handlebars, saddle, cranks, and pedals to make sure that each is tight and securely fastened to your bike.
- **Check your wheels.** Spin each wheel to see that it spins through the frame and between brake pads freely.
- **Have you got everything?** Make sure you have your spare tube, tire irons, patch kit, frame pump, tools, food, water, and guidebook.

Repair and Maintenance

Fixing a Flat

TOOLS YOU WILL NEED

- Two tire irons
- Pump (either a floor pump or a frame pump)
- No screwdrivers!!! (They can puncture a tube.)

REMOVING THE WHEEL

The front wheel is easy. Simply disconnect the brake shoes, open the quick release mechanism or undo the bolts with the proper sized wrench, then remove the wheel from the bike.

The rear wheel is a little more tricky. Before you loosen the wheel from the frame, shift the chain into the smallest gear on the freewheel (the cluster of gears in the back). Once you've done this, removing and installing the wheel, like the front, is much easier.

REMOVING THE TIRE

Step one: Insert a tire iron under the bead of the tire and pry the tire over the lip of the rim. Be careful not to pinch the tube when you do this.

Step two: Hold the first tire iron in place. With the second tire iron, repeat step one, 3 or 4 inches down the rim. Alternate tire irons, pulling the bead of the tire over the rim, section by section, until one side of the tire bead is completely off the rim.

Step three: Remove the rest of the tire and tube from the rim. This can be done by hand. It's easiest to remove the valve stem last. Once the tire is off the rim, pull the tube out of the tire.

CLEAN AND SAFETY CHECK

Step four: Using a rag, wipe the inside of the tire to clean out any dirt, sand, glass, thorns, etc. These may cause the tube to puncture. The inside of a tire should feel smooth. Any pricks or bumps could mean that you have found the culprit responsible for your flat tire.

Step five: Wipe the rim clean, then check the rim strip, making sure it covers the spoke nipples properly on the inside of the rim. If a spoke is poking through the rim strip, it could cause a puncture.

Step six: At this point, you can do one of two things: replace the punctured tube with a new one, or patch the hole. It's easiest to just replace the tube with a new tube when you're out on the trails. Roll up the old tube and take it home to repair later that night in front of the TV. Directions on patching a tube are usually included with the patch kit itself.

INSTALLING THE TIRE AND TUBE
(This can be done entirely by hand.)

Step seven: Inflate the new or repaired tube with enough air to give it shape, then tuck it back into the tire.

Step eight: To put the tire and tube back on the rim, begin by putting the valve in the valve hole. The valve must be straight. Then use your hands to push the beaded edge of the tire onto the rim all the way around so that one side of your tire is on the rim.

Step nine: Let most of the air out of the tube to allow room for the rest of the tire.

Step ten: Beginning opposite the valve, use your thumbs to push the other side of the tire onto the rim. Be careful not to pinch the tube in between the tire and the rim. The last few inches may be difficult, and you may need the tire iron to pry the tire onto the rim. If so, just be careful not to puncture the tube.

BEFORE INFLATING COMPLETELY

Step eleven: Check to make sure the tire is seated properly and that the tube is not caught between the tire and the rim. Do this by adding about five to ten pounds of air, and watch closely that the tube does not bulge out of the tire.

Step twelve: Once you're sure the tire and tube are properly seated, put the wheel back on the bike, then fill the tire with air. It's easier squeezing the wheel through the brake shoes if the tire is still flat.

Step thirteen: Now fill the tire with the proper amount of air, and check constantly to make sure the tube doesn't bulge from the rim. If the tube does appear to bulge out, release all the air as quickly as possible, or you could be in for a big bang. Place the wheel back in the dropost and tighten the quick release lever Reconnect the brake shoes.

When installing the rear wheel, place the chain back onto the smallest cog (farthest gear on the right), and pull the derailleur out of the way. Your wheel should slide right on.

Lubrication Prevents Deterioration

Lubrication is crucial to maintaining your bike. Dry spots will be eliminated. Creaks, squeaks, grinding, and binding will be gone. The chain will run quietly, and the gears will shift smoothly. The brakes will grip quicker, and your bike may last longer with fewer repairs. Need I say more? Well, yes. Without knowing where to put the lubrication, what good is it?

THINGS YOU WILL NEED

- One can of bicycle lubricant, found at any bike store
- A clean rag (to wipe excess lubricant away)

WHAT GETS LUBRICATED

- Front derailleur
- Rear derailleur
- Shift levers
- Front brake
- Rear brake
- Both brake levers
- Chain

WHERE TO LUBRICATE

To make it easy, simply spray a little lubricant on all the pivot points of your bike. If you're using a squeeze bottle, use just a drop or two. Put a few drops on each point wherever metal moves against metal, for instance, at the center of the brake calipers. Then let the lube sink in.

Once you have applied the lubricant to the derailleurs, shift the gears a few times, working the derailleurs back and forth. This allows the lubricant to work itself into the tiny cracks and spaces it must occupy to do its job. Work the brakes a few times as well.

LUBING THE CHAIN

Lubricating the chain should be done after the chain has been wiped clean of most road grime. Do this by spinning the pedals counterclockwise while gripping the chain with a clean rag. As you add the lubricant, be sure to get some in between each link. With an aerosol spray, just spray the chain while pedaling backwards (counterclockwise) until the chain is fully lubricated. Let the lubricant soak in for a few seconds before wiping the excess away. Chains will collect dirt much faster if they're loaded with too much lubrication.

Appendix

Bicycle Clubs and Organizations

Local

MORE: Mid-Atlantic Off-Road Enthusiasts
Advocacy and riding club
P.O. Box 2662
Fairfax, VA 22031
(703) 502-0359
more@cycling.org, www.more-mtb.org

MAMBO: Maryland Association of Mountain Bike Operators
319 Dixie Drive
Towson, MD 21204
(410) 337-BIKE

St. Mary's Mountain Biking Club
St. Mary's College
St. Mary's City, MD 20686
(301) 862-0209, (301) 862-0308

Other Area Bicycle Clubs

Regional

Potomac Pedalers Touring Club (PPTC)
Potomac Pedalers Touring Club is a nonprofit educational, recreational, and social organization for bicycling enthusiasts. It was founded in 1967 and is registered in the District of Columbia with just under 4,000 members.
6729 Curren Street
McLean, VA 22101
(703) 442-8780, (202) 363-TOUR
http://blueridge.infomkt.ibm.com/bikes/PPTC.html

Washington Area Bicycle Association (WABA)
Bicycle advocacy group working on improving trails, education, and encouraging the use of bicycles for commuting.
733 15th Street NW, Suite 1030
Washington, DC 20005
(202) 628-2500, www.waba.org

Washington Women Outdoors
Offers day and overnight trips for women
P.O. Box 301
Garrett Park, MD 20896-0301
(301) 864-3070

Maryland

Annapolis Bicycle Club (ABC)
The Annapolis Bicycle Club's primary focus is in on-road recreational riding and touring. However, ABC hosts periodic off-road rides and is active in local cycling advocacy.
P.O. Box 224
Annapolis, MD 21404
(410) 295-5144, www.annapolis.net/abc

Baltimore Bicycling Club
(410) 792-8308
www.baltobikeclub.org

Chesapeake Mountain Bike Club
P.O. Box 3932
Crofton, MD 21114-3932
(301) 469-7481, www.annapolis.net/cmbc

Chesapeake Wheelmen
(410) 889-2502
www.chesapeakewheelmen.org

College Park Racing Team
4360 Knox Road
College Park, MD 20740
(301) 779-4848

College Park Bicycle Club
4360 Knox Road
College Park, MD 20740
(301) 779-4848
www.collegeparkracing.com

Lateral Stress Velo Club
A bicycle club and racing team from Baltimore, Maryland, including mountain bikers and road bikers who are members of both the National Off-Road Biking Association (NORBA) and the United States Cycling Federation (USCF).
(410) 685-7003, www.lateralstress.org

Oxon Hill Bicycle Club
Backcountry road rides
P.O. Box 81
Oxon Hill, MD 20750-0081
(301) 567-6760

Patuxent Area Cycling Enthusiasts (PACE)
(888) 425-PACE, www.bikepace.com

Virginia

Fredericksburg Cyclists Bicycle Touring Club
Encourages cycling for recreation, sport, fitness, and transportation in and around Fredericksburg
P.O. Box 7844
Fredericksburg, VA 22404
(540) 373-1451, www.bikefred.com

Potomac Velo Club/A-1 Cycling
A road and off-road racing club based in Dumfries
15611 Rhame Drive
Dumfries, VA 22026
(703) 670-2665
www.nv.cc.va.us/~nvportg/pvc2.htm

Prince William Elite Racing
12312 Mulberry Court
Lake Ridge, VA 22192
(703) 497-1671

Regulators Elite Cycling Team
A road racing club based in Clifton
12441 Popes Head Road
Clifton, VA 20124
(703) 803-2815

Reston Bicycle Club
P.O. Box 3389
Reston, VA 22090-1389
(703) 904-0900

Team Anarchy
A road racing club based in Warrenton
Steve Chalke
748 Cherry Tree Lane
Warrenton, VA 20186
(540) 349-8612

Winchester Wheelmen
Road and off-road club based in Winchester
P.O. Box 1695
Winchester, VA 22604

National

American Trails

The only national, nonprofit organization working on behalf of all trail interests. Members want to create and protect America's network of interconnected trailways.
P.O. Box 200787
Denver, CO 80220
(303) 321–6606
www.outdoorlink.com/amtrails

International Mountain Bicycling Association

Works to keep public lands accessible to bikers and provides information on trail design and maintenance.
P.O. Box 7578
Boulder, CO 80306
(303) 545–9011
www.greatoutdoors.com/imba

National Off-Road Bicycling Association

National governing body of U.S. mountain bike racing
1 Olympic Plaza
Colorado Springs, CO 80909
(719) 578–4717
www.usacycling.org/mtb

Outdoor Recreation Coalition of America

Oversees and examines issues related to outdoor recreation
(303) 444–3353
www.orca.org, info@orca.org

Rails-to-Trails Conservancy

Organized to promote conversion of abandoned rail corridors to trails for public use
1100 17th Street NW, 10th Floor
Washington, DC 20036-2222
(202) 331–9696
www.railtrails.org

League of American Wheelmen

190 West Ostend Street, #120
Baltimore, MD 21230-3731
(410) 539–3399

United States Cycling Federation

Governing body for amateur cycling
(719) 578–4581
www.usacycling.org

USA Cycling

1 Olympic Plaza
Colorado Springs, CO 80909
(719) 578–4581
www.usacycling.org

Ski Resorts

. . . for Mountain Biking?

Ski resorts offer a great alternative to local trail riding. During the spring, summer, and fall, many resorts open their trails for mountain biking and, just like during ski season, sell lift tickets to take you and your bike to the top of the mountain. Lodging is also available for weekend mountain bike junkies, and rates are often discounted from the normal ski-season prices. Some resorts even rent bikes and lead guided mountain bike tours. Call ahead to find out just what each resort offers in the way of mountain bike riding, and pick the one that best suits your fancy.

The following is a list of many of the ski resorts in the Washington, D.C./Baltimore area that say yes! to mountain biking when the weather turns too warm for skiing.

Massanutten
Harrisonburg, VA
(703) 289-9441

Wintergreen
Waynesboro, VA
(804) 325-2200

The Homestead
Hot Springs, VA
(703) 839-5500

Bryce
Basye, VA
(703) 856-2121

Wisp
McHenry, MD
(301) 387-4911

Timberline
Davis, WV
(800) 843-1751

Canaan Valley
Davis, WV
(304) 866-4121

Snowshoe
Marlinton, WV
(304) 572-1000

Whitetail
Mercersburg, PA
(717) 328-9400

Ski Liberty
Carroll Valley, PA
(717) 642-8282

Ski Roundtop
Lewisberry, PA
(717) 432-9631

Blue Knob
Claysburg, PA
(814) 239-5111

Hidden Valley
Somerset, PA
(814) 443-6454

Seven Springs
Somerset, PA
(800) 452-2223

Fat-Tire Vacations

Bicycle Touring Companies

There are literally dozens of off-road bicycling tour companies offering an incredible variety of guided tours for mountain bikers. On these pay-as-you-pedal, fat-tire vacations, you will have a chance to go places around the globe that only an expert can take you. Your experiences will be much different than those you can have sitting in a tour bus.

From hut to hut in the Colorado Rockies or inn to inn through Vermont's Green Mountains, there is a tour company for you. Whether you want hard-core singletrack during the day and camping at night or scenic trails followed by a bottle of wine at night and a mint on each pillow, someone out there offers what you're looking for. The tours are well organized and fully supported with expert guides, bike mechanics, and "sag wagons" that carry gear, food, and tired bodies. Prices range from $100 to $500 for a weekend to more than $2,000 for two-week-long trips to far-off lands such as New Zealand or Ireland. Each of these companies will gladly send you their free literature to whet your appetite with breathtaking photography and titillating stories of each tour.

Selected Touring Companies

Elk River Touring Center
Slatyfork, WV
(304) 572-3771

Vermont Bicycling Touring
Bristol, VT
(800) 245-3868

Backroads
Berkley, CA
(800) BIKE TRIP

Timberline Bicycle Tours
Denver, CO
(303) 759-3804

Roads Less Traveled
Longmont, CO
(303) 678-8750

Blackwater Bikes
Davis, WV
(304) 259-5286

Bicycle Adventures
Olympia, WA
(800) 443-6060

Trails Unlimited, Inc.
Nashville, IN
(812) 988-6232

About the Authors

Martín Fernández is a native of Lima, Perú, and now lives in Montgomery County, Maryland. When he's not riding his FAT in the backcountry trails of Maryland, Martín is hard at work designing publications and Web sites or trying to come up with an award-winning home-brew recipe. He is a graphic designer who enjoys the freedom of cycling more than anything and ponders the question of what his next book will be. A novel, perhaps?

When not conquering fiery new trails on his mountain bike or racing from town to town on his road bike, **Scott Adams** is hard at work on his next guidebook, cleaning up after his dogs, or exploring the backcountry and unique corners of this planet with his wife, Amy. Scott is a native of Virginia who lives his life to be outdoors but finds much of his time spent behind the monitor of a computer, preparing the next set of maps or arranging for the next book in the series. Few things reward him more than a long hike to the top of a mountain or an early-morning bike ride with no particular place to go.